Action and Interpretation

Action and Interpretation

Studies in
the Philosophy of the Social Sciences

Edited by
CHRISTOPHER HOOKWAY
Fellow of Peterhouse, Cambridge

and
PHILIP PETTIT
Professor of Philosophy, Bradford University

CAMBRIDGE UNIVERSITY PRESS

Cambridge
London   New York   Melbourne

Essay Index

Published by the Syndics of the Cambridge University Press
The Pitt Building, Trumpington Street, Cambridge CB2 1RP
Bentley House, 200 Euston Road, London NW1 2DB
32 East 57th Street, New York, NY 10022, USA
296 Beaconsfield Parade, Middle Park, Melbourne 3206, Australia

First published 1978

Printed in Great Britain at the
University Press, Cambridge

Library of Congress Cataloguing in Publication Data
Main entry under title:
Action and interpretation.
Includes index.
1. Social sciences – Addresses, essays, lectures.
2. Social sciences – Methodology – Addresses, essays,
lectures. 3. Science – Philosophy – Addresses, essays,
lectures. I. Hookway, Christopher. II. Pettit,
Philip, 1945–
H61.A39   300   77-7875
ISBN 0 521 21740 7

Contents

v

Notes on the Contributors

JOHN DUNN is Lecturer in Political Science at Cambridge University, and Fellow of King's College.

MARY HESSE is Professor of the Philosophy of Science at Cambridge University, and Fellow of Wolfson College.

CHRISTOPHER HOOKWAY is Research Fellow in Philosophy at Peterhouse, Cambridge.

NICK JARDINE is Lecturer in the History and Philosophy of Science at Cambridge University, and Fellow of Darwin College.

JOHN McDOWELL is Praelector in Philosophy at University College, Oxford.

PHILIP PETTIT is Professor of Philosophy at the University of Bradford.

ALAN RYAN is Fellow and Tutor in Politics at New College, Oxford.

JOHN SKORUPSKI is Lecturer in Moral Philosophy at the University of Glasgow.

Introduction

Problems in the philosophy of social science cluster around three issues. First, there is the question of whether forms of explanation to be found in social science conform to the pattern exhibited in the natural sciences. Many have denied that they do, arguing that at least the explanation of action by reference to mental states is distinct from ordinary explanation. A second issue has to do with the principles that we use in the selection of social-science theories. The question here is whether values intrude in such a way that theory choice has moral and political significance. And finally, the issue arises of whether there are forms of explanation in social science which do not depend on our explanations of people's actions. Individualists would say that there are not, while holists would argue that some social phenomena are to be explained by laws which do not obtain simply as the result of independently explicable human actions.

The problems discussed in this volume concern the first and second issues. Mostly they are raised against the background assumption that the way to explain people's sayings and doings, whether or not it is distinctive, is by reference to mental states. Such explanation involves the interpretative procedure of reading off states like beliefs and desires from the actions which they are invoked to explain. Hence the title which we have given to the volume: *Action and Interpretation.*

Although there are many varieties of interpretative explanation of behaviour, they all invoke states such as beliefs and desires. These states are 'intentional', in the sense that we identify them by reference to their objects but allow those objects to be taken only under certain descriptions. Suppose that we represent them so that their objects are propositions: we say that John believes or desires *that such-and-such*. Their intentionality means that we have no other way of picking them out than by reference to the propositional object and that if we try to redescribe that object, replacing 'such-and-such' by an equivalent sentence, we run the risk not only of picking out a different belief or desire, but of picking out a belief or desire which the agent does not actually have. To put the point by way of example: John may believe that the person who stole his wallet is anti-social, or he may desire that that person be punished, without believing or desiring these things of James, even though James is the thief in question.

The intentionality of beliefs and desires raises a problem. We cannot be sure of what a man believes or desires simply by seeing what 'object' is presented to his attention, for we do not know that we are describing the object appropriately. We cannot be certain of being helped by having him tell us what he believes or desires, for we rely on our assumptions about precisely such mental states of his when we translate what he says into our idiolect. And while an examination of his non-verbal behaviour will supplement those other sources of information, narrowing down the range of beliefs and desires which we can plausibly attribute to him, we cannot be sanguine that a considerable discretion in interpretation will not remain.

Perhaps this is a special case of a more general phenomenon: that attending to experience will not reduce the number of explanatory theories to one and that we must make use of principles of theory choice, and apply prior standards of plausibility and coherence, in selecting a theory from among those which are compatible with the same evidence. Quine describes this phenomenon as the underdetermination of theory by experience and argues that in good scientific practice theories are preferred to rivals which are equally compatible with the evidence on grounds such as that they are more simple and less novel.

Mary Hesse's paper in this volume is concerned with the consequences of the underdetermination of theory by data. She suggests that in the natural sciences theory choice is guided primarily by the pragmatic criterion of predictive success, but she does not think that the principle can always be applied in the social sciences. Thus she wonders whether we may not have to resort to more controversial principles in selecting our social theories. These principles would reflect freely adopted value goals and would make the choice of a social theory like the choice of a political stance.

Principles of theory choice are sometimes defended on the grounds that the theories which they select are more likely to be true: by using such principles, it is held, we are helped to grasp the unobservable mechanisms which explain phenomena. The suggestion that the social sciences are value-laden might be grounded in the view that principles used in the area cannot be justified in that kind of way. The idea would be that the principles serve only to express considerations of a practical nature. One way of motivating that idea is provided in Quine's argument for the indeterminacy of translation, which suggests that while theory choice in the natural sciences engages the issue of truth, it does not do so when we are dealing with the intentional. The argument is that with underdetermined theories as to someone's beliefs and desires, there is no language-independent realm of meanings in regard to which the theories differ. The realm of speech and behaviour on which the theories agree, being equally compatible with such data, is all that there is, and so the choice between the theories is one of practical significance only.

Christopher Hookway's paper is an attempt to construct a trouble-free version of Quine's argument and to draw out some of the implications of the argument for our understanding of interpretation, especially in social anthropology. He claims that a non-realist account of intentionality should be preferred because it provides the best explanation of how we normally understand each other so well and so easily, and because it can explain how public meanings inform our private intentional states.

Even if we have great leeway in making up our minds about how to interpret the behaviour of other people and other groups, it is arguable that certain general constraints must always be respected in any theory we espouse. Philip Pettit thinks that those constraints constitute an overall theory of human behaviour which he calls 'rational man theory'. His paper discusses the nature of that theory, its function, and the application that may be made of it in social science, particularly social psychology.

In his paper Alan Ryan concerns himself explicitly with social psychology, distinguishing between three sorts of rational explanation of action, in terms of maximising returns, meeting obligations and staging performances. He raises some of the familiar difficulties of both returns-maximising and obligation-meeting explanations and asks whether the dramaturgical option, particularly as exemplified in Erving Goffman's work, is really distinctive. The paper presents two readings of dramaturgical explanation: one depicts men as interested in cutting aesthetic figures, the other as concerned with negotiating definitions of their situations.

The contribution by John Skorupski shifts the emphasis from social psychology to social anthropology. He examines the way in which we understand the systems of thought and activity of another culture and tries to show how such interpretation is affected by our philosophical theory of meaning: that is, by our view of how language relates to the world. In the three main sections of his paper he investigates different conceptions of ritual, the plausibility of relativism, and the extent to which our interpretations can reveal incoherence in an alien belief system.

Nick Jardine is concerned with interpretation in the history of science, his aim being to defend the realist view according to which past investigators dealt, albeit not so successfully, with the same subject matter as their present-day counterparts. He criticises a principle of interpretation defended by Hilary Putnam – the principle of benefit of the doubt – and offers an alternative set of principles which he defends by appeal to a consensus theory of reference.

The question of realism is in the background of many of the papers in the volume, the realist assumption being generally made that we can conceive of the truth or falsity of a sentence even when we have no means of finally deciding the sentence's truth-value. In his paper John McDowell defends a moderate version of realism against the anti-realist arguments which Michael Dummett has put forward. Dummett's claim is that our grasp of a thought is constituted by our knowledge of how to determine whether it is true or false, rather than by a grasp of a possibly undetectable truth condition. Thus he questions the intelligibility of the suggestion that there might have been events in the distant past which, having left no trace, are now inaccessible. McDowell challenges such anti-realism, in respect of its implications both for our knowledge of the past and for our knowledge of other minds.

The final paper is by John Dunn, who seeks as a practising social scientist to confront the issues raised in the volume. He defends an interpretative or hermeneutic conception of the understanding of human behaviour but realises that the problems faced by a mentalist view of intentional states cast doubt on the possibility of a realist hermeneutic science. He argues that the difficulties are not such as to dissuade us from adopting a hermeneutic approach, and he suggests that the approach should not lead to any form of relativism.

This volume of essays is a by-product of some small meetings of philosophers and social scientists which were organised by the Thyssen Philosophy Group and financed through the generosity of the Fritz Thyssen Stiftung. The essays are reworked versions of some of the papers presented at those meetings. On behalf of the Thyssen Philosophy Group we would like to express our gratitude to the Fritz Thyssen Stiftung for its financial assistance and to the Director of the Stiftung, Dr Gerd Brand, for his advice and encouragement.

January 1977   CHRISTOPHER HOOKWAY
                                                            PHILIP PETTIT

Theory and Value in the Social Sciences

MARY HESSE

I

Many reasons have been given for supposing that the social sciences require different kinds of method and justification from the natural sciences, and conversely for supposing that these methods and justifications are or ought to be the same. I don't want to rehearse all these arguments here, but rather to concentrate on two features of the *natural* sciences which already suggest that the conventional arguments about similarities and differences are inadequate. These features can be roughly summed up in the by now fairly uncontroversial proposition that all scientific theories are *underdetermined* by facts, and the much more problematic propositions that, this being the case, there are further criteria for scientific theories that have to be rationally discussed, and that these may include considerations of value.

Whether the natural and the social sciences are seen as similar or different depends of course on the view we take of the natural sciences. The view I am going to presuppose, but not argue here, is that made familiar in recent post-deductivist discussions, with the addition of a crucial pragmatic dimension.[1] Let me summarise as follows:

(1) Theories are logically constrained by facts, but are underdetermined by them: i.e., while, to be acceptable, theories should be more or less plausibly coherent with facts, they can be neither conclusively refuted nor uniquely derived from statements of fact alone, and hence no theory in a given domain is uniquely acceptable.

(2) Theories are subject to revolutionary change, and this involves even the language presupposed in 'statements of fact', which are

[1] I have discussed these matters in *The Structure of Scientific Inference* (London, 1974), chaps. 1, 2 and 12, and in 'Truth and the Growth of Scientific Knowledge', in F. Suppe and P. D. Asquith (eds.), *PSA, 1976* (Philosophy of Science Assn, East Lansing, Mich., 1976). Since the notion of 'underdetermination' has been exploited particularly by Quine, I should say that I do not accept his distinction between 'normal scientific induction' and 'ontological indeterminism', according to which it seems to be implied that purely scientific theories can eventually be determined uniquely by inductive methods. Some of my reasons for this rejection will emerge below.

irreducibly theory-laden: i.e., they presuppose concepts whose meaning is at least partly given by the context of theory.

(3) There are further determining criteria for theories which attain the status of rational postulates or conventions or heuristic devices at different historical periods – these include general metaphysical and material assumptions, e.g. about substance and causality, atoms or mechanisms, and formal judgments of simplicity, probability, analogy, etc.

(4) In the history of natural science, these further criteria have sometimes included what are appropriately called value judgments, but these have tended to be filtered out as theories developed.

(5) The 'filtering-out' mechanism has been powered by universal adoption of one overriding value for natural science, namely the criterion of increasingly successful prediction and control of the environment. In what follows I shall call this the *pragmatic criterion*.

Points 4 and 5 need further explanation.

Value judgments related to science may be broadly of two kinds. They may be evaluations of the *uses* to which scientific results are put, such as the value of cancer research, or the disvalue of the nuclear bomb. But they may also be evaluations that enter more intimately into theory-construction as *assertions* that it is desirable that the universe be of such and such a kind *and* that it is or is not broadly as it is desired to be. Examples of positive evaluations of what is the case are: belief in the perfection of spherical symmetry, and consequent belief that the heavens are spherically symmetrical; belief that men ought to be and therefore are at the physical centre of the universe, and that they are biologically superior and unique among organisms; belief that mind is devalued by regarding it as a natural mechanism, and therefore that mind is in fact irreducible to matter. An example of negative evaluation of what is the case is the Marxist belief that in this pre-revolutionary stage of the class struggle various elements of social life that look like valuable supports of social stability are to be unmasked as in fact being obstacles to the desirable revolution. In the light of such a belief, for example, the immiseration of the proletariat becomes a positive value, and tends to become the essential category in terms of which complex social facts are described.

It is the second type of evaluation in science that I shall be concerned with. All examples of this type issue in assertions rather than imperatives, and hence involve a transition from *ought* judgments to *is* judgments. Are they not therefore immediately condemned as illicit

2

in any form of scientific argument? In reply to this objection two points can be made. First, there is no doubt that there are historical examples in which the genetic fallacy was not seen as a fallacy, so that in describing the thought processes involved in such examples the historian at least has to recognise forms of quasi-inference such as those just sketched. But the second and more important consideration depends on point 3 above, namely that since there is never *demonstrative* reasoning from evidence to theory, further determining criteria may well include factual judgments about the way the world is, and these are sometimes based persuasively on judgments of how it ought to be. There is no fallacy of logical inference, for logical inference is not appropriate here; there is rather the choice of some hypotheses for consideration among many other possible ones, in the hope that the world will be found to be good as the accepted value system describes the good.

In the case of the natural sciences, however, it may well be objected that the evaluative and teleological beliefs of past science either have been refuted, or have been eliminated by economy and simplicity criteria applied to theories. It would be a mistake to suppose that they could have been refuted by facts alone, because even if we do not accept the strong theory-ladenness thesis of point 2, it would generally be agreed that facts are susceptible of a multiplicity of theoretical interpretations, and that if such value judgments were regarded as of overriding importance (overriding, that is, all except logic), the facts could have been accommodated, though perhaps at a cost to economy. But the requirement of theoretical economy or simplicity is not an adequate general answer either, for at least two reasons. First, what have been held to be prima facie simple theories have often been abandoned for more complex ones. Examples are: field theories in place of action at a distance, atomic theories in place of phenomenal volume and weight relations in chemical reactions, and Copernicus's heliocentric universe, which in his theory required more parameters than the geocentric universe it replaced. In most such cases, what was of overriding importance was not facts plus prima facie simplicity, but facts plus interpretation in terms of some intelligible or desirable world-model. Secondly, no one has yet succeeded in presenting definitions of simplicity that are adequate for all the occasions on which appeal had been made to it. But it is at least clear that there is not one concept of simplicity but many, and the suspicion grows that simplicity is not in itself a final court of appeal but rather adapts itself to definition in terms of whatever other criteria of theory choice are taken to be overriding.

3

MARY HESSE

The most important of these other criteria in natural science is what I have called the *pragmatic criterion* of predictive success. In considering historical examples the question to be asked in philosophy of science is not so much what were the special local (social, biographical, psychological, etc.) factors at work in the immediate and short-term decisions of individuals, but rather whether there is any *general* criterion for the long-term acceptability of one theory rather than another, and for the replacement of old theories by new. This is to ask a question which presupposes that because all formal criteria such as verification, confirmation, and falsifiability seem to have broken down as criteria for theory choice in particular short-term scientific situations, therefore there are no general criteria of theory choice over the long term. But revolutionary accounts have not disposed of the objection that natural science, as well as being revolutionary in respect of *theories*, is also in some sense cumulative and progressive, and retains contact with the empirical world by means of long-term testing of theory complexes taken as wholes. If we press the question 'What is it that progresses?', the only possible long-term answer is the ability to use science to learn the environment, and to make predictions whose results we can rely on not to surprise us. It is this modification of the traditional empirical criteria of confirmation and falsifiability that I intend by the 'pragmatic criterion'.[2]

As successful prediction accumulates, the pragmatic criterion filters out both simplicity criteria and other value judgments. We can observe by hindsight that in the early stages of a science, value judgments (such as the centrality of man in the universe) provide some of the reasons for choice among competing underdetermined theories. As systematic theory and pragmatic success accumulate, however, such judgments may be overridden, and their proponents retire defeated from the scientific debate. Thus, the theological and metaphysical arguments against Copernicus, against Newton, and against Darwin became progressively more irrelevant to science. This is not to say, of course, that *our own* preferences in choices between underdetermined theories are not themselves influenced by our value judgments and by beliefs which we take for granted, or that these will not be visible to the hindsight of

[2] It was Duhem's holist account of theory-testing in *The Aim and Structure of Physical Theory* (Princeton, 1954; first published in 1906 as *La théorie physique*) which foreshadowed the demise of later and narrower criteria of empirical test. The work of I. Lakatos has more recently familiarised philosophers of science with the problem of theoretical acceptability in long-term historical perspective, although his criteria for 'progressive research programmes' do not include the predictive aspects of the pragmatic criterion adopted here. See particularly his 'Falsification and the Methodology of Scientific Research Programmes', in I. Lakatos and A. Musgrave (eds.), *Criticism and the Growth of Knowledge* (Cambridge, 1970).

4

future historians of science.[3] This is very likely to be so, but it does not conflict with the notion of accumulation of pragmatic success in science past, present, and future. There is also a sense in which value judgment enters into the very adoption of the pragmatic criterion itself – the judgment that the requirement of predictive success should override all other possible criteria of theory choice. This is the one value judgment that, of course, is *not* filtered out, but rather is presupposed in the pragmatic criterion. It is a judgment that has perhaps rarely been consciously adopted by any scientific society of the past, but it is one which, it is becoming increasingly apparent, may be consciously rejected in the future.

It is not my purpose here to discuss in detail the relation between what I have called the pragmatic criterion and more orthodox theories of objectivity and truth. But something more must be said to avoid misunderstanding. First, there is a difficulty about the notion of 'successful prediction'. If we were able to ignore the much-discussed difficulties referred to in point 2, and assume that there is a theory-neutral observation language for which there are clearly applicable truth criteria, we might be tempted to define 'increasingly successful prediction' in terms of an accumulating set of true observation statements deducible from the corpus of scientific theories. We cannot ignore these difficulties, however, or the consequent tendency to understand 'truth' not in a correspondence sense but as coherence within a given theory, and hence as theory-relative. Since theories of truth are themselves in considerable disarray, it is better to find some way of understanding 'successful prediction' independently of them. Here I suggest a pragmatic or ostensive appeal to the actual state of natural science since the seventeenth century, in which we can recognise an accumulation of successful prediction which overrides changing theories and is *independent* of particular conceptual schemes in which scientific successes are described in conflicting theories. The space-ship still goes, whether described in a basically Newtonian or relativistic framework. Pragmatic knowledge can be obtained without an absolutely theory-neutral descriptive language.

[3] Recent studies in the history and sociology of natural science indicate that there has been far more influence upon theories from evaluations and non-scientific standpoints than has generally been realised. See for example P. Forman, 'Weimar Culture, Causality, and Quantum Theory, 1918–1927: Adaptation by German Physicists and Mathematicians to a Hostile Intellectual Environment', in R. McCormmach (ed.), *Historical Studies in the Physical Sciences*, vol. 3 (Philadelphia, 1971); papers in M. Teich and R. M. Young (eds.), *Changing Perspectives in The History of Science* (London, 1973); and many references in Barry Barnes, *Scientific Knowledge and Sociological Theory* (London, 1974) and David Bloor, *Knowledge and Social Imagery* (London, 1976).

It may be illuminating to draw an analogy (only an analogy) between the method of natural science and the program of a computer designed to process environmental data and to learn to make successful predictions (for example, a character-recognition device). The criteria of success of such a device can be made independent of the actual 'language' system used in the computer to store and process data and to give the orders for testing theories on more data. Equal success in two or more computers is consistent with their having widely different internal language systems, although of course some language systems may be more convenient than others for given kinds of data, and indeed there may be feedback mechanisms in the program which permit change of language to a more convenient one when this is indicated by the success and failure rate.

A second possible misunderstanding of the pragmatic criterion arises from the fact that technological applications are the most striking examples of accumulating successful prediction. Philosophers of science should perhaps disengage themselves from the Popper-induced prejudice that pragmatic application has nothing to do with the logic of science. On the other hand, successful prediction does not necessarily issue in technical control. Many theories enlarge our pragmatic knowledge (for example, about fossils, or quasars), without necessarily forming the basis of technology.

A third difficulty is that the relation between the pragmatic criterion and any theory of truth is obscure and needs much more examination than can be given to it here. But in the particular case of some kind of correspondence theory, to which philosophers of truth seem now to be increasingly drawn, there does not seem to be any prima facie conflict between such a theory and the pragmatic criterion. Current correspondence theories of truth tend to be expressed in terms of some relation of 'satisfaction' which holds between the world and true statements, and are in themselves independent of the question how such satisfaction is identified in particular instances. There are notorious difficulties about such identifications – the same difficulties that underlie the notions of underdetermined theories and criticisms of the basic observation language. The pragmatic criterion trades these difficulties for others by bypassing the question of the reference of theoretical language, and resting on the non-linguistic concept of successful prediction.

In considering whether natural science as defined by points 1 to 5 is an adequate model for the social sciences, we can add two further points:

(6) There are not at present, and perhaps can never reasonably be expected to be, general theories in the social sciences that satisfy the pragmatic criterion of point 5 – namely, theories that provide increasingly successful prediction and control in the social domain.

(7) Moreover, since adoption of the pragmatic criterion itself implies a value judgment, it is possible to decide *against* it as an overriding goal for social science, and to adopt other value goals.

Point 7 does not presuppose the truth of point 6. I doubt if point 6 can be proved in any general way. On the actual present situation one can only observe what underlies complaints about the backwardness, theoretical triviality, and empirical rule-of-thumb character of most social science, in spite of limited success in establishing low-level laws in isolated areas. On the logical possibility, there have been attempts at general proof of the non-natural character of social science, attempts which derive from features of the social subject matter such as complexity, instability, indeterminacy, irreducible experimental interference with data, self-reference of social theorising as part of its own subject matter, etc. I do not believe such proofs can ever be conclusive, if only for the reason that most of these features are also found somewhere in the natural sciences. If we use as an analogy for the method of natural science the computer which learns to predict its environment, an immediate consequence is that there will be some environments and some types of data which do not permit learning by any computer of limited capacity, for any or all of the reasons just listed. The social environment *may*, wholly or partly, be such an environment. I doubt if anything stronger can be said, and I doubt whether any attempt to formalise the situation further at this general abstract level is worthwhile. Satisfaction of the pragmatic criterion by particular social-science theories needs to be argued case by case.

Point 7, however, remains. It is explicitly recognised in Marxist writings on the social sciences, and also in the older *Verstehen* tradition and in its more recent offshoot, hermeneutics (although the latter two traditions neglect the dimension of 'interest' that inevitably infects social theory according to Marxism). The rest of this paper will be devoted to exploring the consequences of point 7.

MARY HESSE

It is important to notice that point 7, together with points 1 to 5, imply a distinction between two sorts of 'value-ladenness' in social science. The first is analogous to theory-ladenness in natural science, and is the sense primarily in mind when empiricist philosophers have attempted to disentangle and exclude value judgments from scientific social theory. It is the sort of value judgment that I have mentioned in point 4, which becomes associated with theoretical interpretations by virtue either of the selective interest of the investigator (e.g. in preferring to investigate stable systems as norms), or of adoption of those hypotheses which assert the world actually to be in some respects as it is desired to be (e.g. acquired characteristics either are or are not inherited according to preferred ideology). I have suggested that the crucial point about the natural sciences is that though such judgments may function heuristically in hypotheses, operation of the pragmatic criterion frequently filters them out, and how the world 'ought to be' frequently fails in face of how the world is, or rather in face of the only plausible and coherent ways that can be found of interpreting facts and successful predictions. Where the pragmatic criterion works in social science we shall expect some value judgments to be filtered out in a similar way – for example, it seems not impossible that currently controversial questions about the relationship, if any, between intelligence quotient and racial origin might be sufficiently defined to be made rigorously testable, and laws might be derived which satisfy the criterion of successful prediction. (Whether it would be *desirable* to adopt and try to rigorously apply the pragmatic criterion here is entirely another question.)

But where the pragmatic criterion cannot be made to work in a convergent manner it is not possible to filter out value judgments in this way. A second type of value judgment may then be involved, which in varying degrees *takes the place of the pragmatic criterion* in selecting theories for attention. These judgments will be *value goals* for science that are alternatives to the pragmatic goal of predictive success. Such alternative goals have often been recognised in the literature, for example by Weber in his category of value-relevance, and by Myrdal in arguing for explicit adoption of a value standpoint, preferably one that corresponds to an actual power group in society.[4] But alternative value goals have usually been recognized in the negative sense of the

4 M. Weber, *The Methodology of the Social Sciences*, ed. E. A. Shils and H. A. Finch (New York, 1949), and *The Theory of Economic and Social Organization* (Oxford, 1947), chap. 1. The second part of *Methodology* and chap. 1 of *Theory* are reprinted in M. Brodbeck (ed.), *Readings in the Philosophy of the Social Sciences* (New York, 1968). G. Myrdal, *The Political Element in the Development of Economic Theory* (London, 1953), *Value in Social Theory* (London, 1958), and *Objectivity in Social Research* (London, 1970).

8

'unmasking' of so-called non-objective biases, rather than in the positive sense of being consciously adopted goals other than the pragmatic criterion. It is difficult to make such standpoints conscious and explicit while they are operative, but the literature is now full of studies in the critical sociology of sociology, where the standpoints of the past, and of other contemporary groups of sociologists, are 'unmasked'. It is a well-known Marxist ploy to uncover the non-intellectual interests even of self-styled positivists: those who argue most strongly for a value-free and objective social science are shown to be those whose social and economic interest is in the status quo, and in not having the boat rocked by encouragement to explicit criticism and value controversy. And such studies are not found only in Marxist writers. Robin Horton, for example, has given an interesting analysis of the styles in social anthropology during this century in terms of the changing attitudes of the West, in its imperialist and liberal phases, towards its former colonies as they become politically independent and aspire to cultural autonomy.[5]

Weber carefully distinguished value-relevance from the value-freedom of the social scientist with respect to political action. That is to say, he accepted that judgments of interest select the subject matter of the human sciences, but denied that the social scientist as such should use his theories to argue any particular political practice. Even with respect to value-relevance, he argued that theories must ultimately be shown to be causally adequate. Thus Weber's own value-interest in studying, for example, the interrelations of capitalism and the Protestant ethic was doubtless to refute Marx's contention that the ideological superstructure is unilaterally determined by the economic substructure. But Weber insists that his theory of such relationships must be shown to be a factual theory of cause and effect, confirmable by positive instances and refutable by negative. Without going into the detail of Weber's discussions of methodology, it can I think be fairly concluded that he sees the goal of knowledge and truth-assertion as essentially the same in the natural and social sciences, but that he has an over-simple view of the nature of causal laws in the natural sciences, which misleads him into extrapolating an almost naive Millean method into the social sciences. He does not doubt that judgments of value-relevance are separable from positive science, and can in this sense be 'filtered out' of cognitive conclusions. Thus he has

[5] R. Horton, 'Lévy-Bruhl, Durkheim and the Scientific Revolution', in R. Horton and R. Finnegan (eds.), *Modes of Thought* (London, 1973). For another unmasking of positivism, see A. Gouldner, *The Coming Crisis of Western Sociology* (London, 1970), especially chap 4.

9

not yet made the 'epistemological break' involved in recognising, questioning, and perhaps replacing the pragmatic criterion for social sciences, nor has he distinguished two sorts of judgments of value-relevance – those which can ultimately be eliminated by the pragmatic criterion and those which cannot because they depend on a view of causality that presupposes it.

There are others who have not understood the nature of this epistemological break. In a commentary on Myrdal's requirement of total explicitness of value standpoint and identification with some actual power-group, John Rex[6] finds an implied suggestion that objectivity inheres in the balance of power between such groups, and that this balance of power 'can be relatively objectively determined', as if what is is determined by the standpoint of the most powerful group. However, while it may be true that the most powerful group can to a greater or lesser extent impose its will upon the development of the social system, it does not at all follow that the theory informed by its value standpoint gives the true dynamical laws of that system on a pragmatic criterion, or the best theory on any other criterion except that truth resides in the barrel of a gun. Whether the unions or the sheikhs eventually gain control in Britain is irrelevant to the theoretical acceptability of either of their implied economic doctrines. And Christ and Socrates may have the best theories after all.

Myrdal himself is more careful, but he too leaves largely un-examined the exact relation between objectivity as sought in the natural sciences and the value criteria which are inevitably adopted in social science. Of science in general he writes:

Our steadily increasing stock of observations and inferences is not merely subjected to continuous cross-checking and critical discussion but is deliberately scrutinized to discover and correct hidden preconceptions and biases. Full objectivity, however, is an ideal toward which we are constantly striving, but which we can never reach. The social scientist, too, is part of the culture in which he lives, and he never succeeds in freeing himself entirely from dependence on the dominant preconceptions and biases of his environment.[7]

If 'objectivity' in this sense is the ideal which is unattainable, then valuations are a necessary evil. Seen in such negative light, it is unlikely that the choice between valuations will be subjected to logical or philosophical scrutiny, and the vacuum is likely to be filled by power criteria or worse, in the manner of Rex. But if it is true that the ideal objectivity is unattainable and that valuations are necessary, the philosopher will surely be better advised to present this necessity in

---

[6] J. Rex, *Key Problems of Sociological Theory* (London, 1970), pp. 164–6.
[7] *Value in Social Theory*, p. 119.

a positive light, and to critically examine the value choices that are then open. In points 4 to 7 I have attempted to articulate such a positive view by distinguishing value-laden theories, subject to the pragmatic criterion, from the value goals adopted for the total scientific enterprise.

Mannheim is another exponent of the sociology of sociology who has been misled by neglect of this distinction. As is well known, he adopts a relationism of total ideology according to which all knowledge (except logic, mathematics and natural science) is knowledge only in relation to some observer standpoint.[8] In our terms, this may be interpreted as a recognition of the value-ladenness of the social sciences, and the suggestion that some observer standpoint determines the criterion of evaluation. He then asks: Which standpoint is optimum for establishing truth? and goes on to reject the two classical Marxist answers – the proletariat, and the class-self-conscious Party subsection of the proletariat – and to put forward the intelligentsia, who, he claims, are powerless and interest-free, and understand the sociology of knowledge. Whatever be the merits of this particular choice, it is clear that Mannheim has now retreated from his fleeting glimpse of irreducible commitment to value goals and is asking for an ideal standpoint from which truth is seen in the same sense of truth as that appropriate to natural science. Apart from the falsity of the claim that the intelligentsia are disinterested, this leads Mannheim into the logical circle of sociology of knowledge that has often been discussed, namely: In relation to what observer standpoint is it *true* that the intelligentsia are disinterested? Whatever the answer, truth as thus defined is clearly still relational and not objective in the sense of the pragmatic or whatever other criterion is adopted for the natural sciences.

Of all writers on the sociology of knowledge, Alvin Gouldner perhaps comes closest to embracing point 7 explicitly. After a careful and devastating analysis of the sociological origins and determinants of American functional sociology, and a more brief analysis of Soviet sociology, he comes in his Epilogue ('The Theorist Pulls Himself Together, Partially') to the crucial question: What then are the sociological origins and determinants of Gouldner's unmasking exercise in respect of the American sociologists? He goes on explicitly to reject the approach of those methodologists 'who stress the interaction of

---

[8] K. Mannheim, *Ideology and Utopia* (London, 1936), especially chaps. 2 and 5. It is of course ironic that it is the introduction of ideological and social criteria into the interpretation of *natural* scientific theories, by Kuhn, Feyerabend, and others, that has played a large part in the revival of contemporary debate about sociology of knowledge.

MARY HESSE

theory and research...the role of rational and cognitive forces',[9] that is, the orthodox philosophers of science who reject value commitments. Rather, the sociologist must be *reflexive* – self-aware of his own place in his own standpoint – and must accept his involvement in it in a manner that requires a new *praxis* – a new lifestyle in which there is no ultimate division of himself as sociologist from himself as man. But more significant than this note of introspective moralising is Gouldner's description of the sociologist's task in the following terms:

Commonly, the social theorist is trying to reduce the tension between a social event or process that he takes to be real and some value which this has violated. Much of theory-work is initiated by a dissonance between an imputed reality and certain values, or by the indeterminate value of an imputed reality. Theory-making, then, is often an effort to cope with threat; it is an effort to cope with a threat to something in which the theorist himself is deeply and personally implicated and which he holds dear.[10]

Thus, 'the French Revolution, the rise of Socialism, the Great Depression of 1929, or a new world of advertising and salesmanship' are facts-as-personally-experienced, requiring not so much explanation in the sense of the natural sciences (which perhaps we can never have), as redescription (interpretation, understanding) in terms which make them cohere with a chosen order of values. One might compare with Weber's desire to rescue human ideals from dominance by substructures, whether economic or bureaucratic; Durkheim's sense of the need for social cohesion and stability in face of man's inordinate and irrational desires; the note of protest inseparably bound into Marx's 'scientific' concept of exploitation of man's labour power; and Gouldner's own quite unconcealed negative evaluation of the sociologies of Goffman and Garfinkel, whose origins he 'unmasks' and whose adequacy he judges not on grounds of a spurious 'objectivity' but on grounds of his own sense of the moral degradation of their pictures of the social world ('anything goes', 'espionage agents', 'demonic', 'camp', 'kicks', 'the cry of pain...is Garfinkel's triumphal moment', 'sadism').[11] In the light of Gouldner's rather clear-sighted adoption of criteria other than the pragmatic, we may accept the challenge implicit in his statement early in the book that 'whether social theories *unavoidably* require and must rest *logically* on some background concepts [valuations] is a question that simply does not concern me here ...this is a problem for philosophers of science'.[12] Though he appears here to remain agnostic, if his own analysis is acceptable it provides strong grounds for the methodological adoption of point 7, that is for

[9] *The Coming Crisis*, p. 483.
[10] *Ibid.* p. 484.
[11] *Ibid.* pp. 378–95.
[12] *Ibid.* pp. 31–2.

12

the recognition that where the pragmatic criterion is inoperative, other value goals for social science should be self-consciously' adopted.[13]

III

By way of conclusion let me rebut some possible empiricist misunderstandings, draw a consequence for the sociology of knowledge, and suggest an analogy for the choice of value goals.

It may be objected that, in emphasising the need to make explicit choice of value goals for science as well as theoretical value assumptions, I have neglected the role that the pragmatic criterion (or indeed any realist criterion of truth that might be proposed) actually plays in the social sciences. To this objection I would reply that nothing I have said about the inapplicability of the pragmatic criterion or about the choice of value goals is intended to exclude the possibility that there are areas in the social sciences where the methods and criteria of the natural sciences are both workable and desirable. There are general laws of human behaviour (though I suspect only low-level laws rather closely circumscribed in domain), there are models and ideal types whose consequences can be explored deductively and tested, and there are limited predictions which are sometimes successful. Where these things are the case, we may speak of 'objectivity' in the social realm in whatever sense we wish to speak of it in the natural realm, and we *may* (not *must*) make the same choice of value goals for the social as for the natural sciences. What I am arguing is that it would be wilfully blind and neglectful of the responsibility of social science as a cognitive discipline to ignore the fact that much social science which is currently acceptable is not and probably never can be of this kind. I have been primarily concerned with the consequence that non-pragmatic value choices have to be made. There will of course be difficulties in demarcating one type of value choice from others, both where there are doubts about how far the pragmatic criterion can be taken and also about how far it should be taken, as in recent disputes, for example, about the racial inheritance of characteristics, or about whether Garfinkel should collect data that involve severe mental disorientation

---

[13] Another writer who makes explicit the choice of value goals for knowledge is J. Habermas, especially in his Appendix to *Knowledge and Human Interests* (London, 1972). Habermas there makes a threefold distinction: the *technical* interest of the empirical sciences; the *practical* interest of the historical sciences, defined as 'the intersubjectivity of possible action-orienting mutual understanding' (p. 310), somewhat in the *Verstehen* tradition; and the *emancipatory* interest of the social sciences, whose function is *critique* of the established social order. In the light of examples such as are quoted in note 17 below, this is to put matters into a rather too restricted straitjacket.

13

of people in their ordinary social relationships. No general rules can be given about such disputes, because they are themselves essentially value disputes about the goals of particular social researches. But all of this does not entail that there are no facts or laws in the social sciences, nor that where there are such, social theory should not be consistent with them. As in the natural sciences, social theories are *constrained* but not *determined* by facts. Whether we wish to extend the use of the concept of 'objectivity' beyond the domain of such facts to the recognition of value choice, as Myrdal does,[14] is partly a verbal matter.

A more fundamental empiricist objection, however, is the following.[15] It may be suggested, first, that there is great difficulty in actually articulating viable goals for social science which are alternatives to the pragmatic criterion, and second, that where such goals are apparently identified and described, their operation always in fact involves the pragmatic criterion. Traditionally various versions of the *Verstehen* thesis have been appealed to to provide alternative goals, but it seems that in any attempt to *understand* a person's behaviour, one is seeking to fulfil one's expectations about his future behaviour. Indeed, all human interaction depends on the success of some such predictions about mutual responsiveness, and this seems not unlike an application of the pragmatic criterion. This is surely correct, and it is not surprising to find successful fulfilment of expectations as a criterion in all reasoning about the world, including all lowest-level inductive generalisations, whether about objects or persons. But this argument must not be made to prove too much. It certainly does not show that the pragmatic criterion as described in point 5 is sufficient to determine uniquely the theoretical interpretation of people's behaviour, for in this context we lack the wide-ranging and systematic generality characteristic of natural science, and consequently we lack what I have called the filtering-out mechanism that eventually eliminates value judgments as criteria of theory choice.

Secondly, a remark about consequences for the programme of the sociology of knowledge. Whether or not we wish to use epistemologically loaded terms like 'cognition', 'knowledge', 'objectivity', and 'truth' for acceptable theories in social science, a consequence of my

---

[14] Primarily in his later *Objectivity*, pp. 55–6, where he supplements the positivist view of objectivity implied in *Value*, p. 119 (quoted above) in the following terms: 'The only way in which we can strive for "objectivity" in theoretical analysis is to expose the valuations to full light, make them conscious, specific, and explicit, and permit them to determine the theoretical research.'

[15] This objection was raised by participants in the Ross-on-Wye Conference, 26–8 September 1975.

arguments is that criteria of acceptability are *pluralist* – as pluralist as our choices of value goals. And if we wish to talk of *choice* of values it also follows that we presuppose a certain area of freedom in the activity of theorising – we are not wholly constrained to adopt particular theories either by the facts, or by adoption of particular value goals, or by social and economic environment. Thus it would be inconsistent with the present thesis to hold a form of the sociology of knowledge according to which socio-economic substructure determines all forms of knowledge, including presumably adoption or non-adoption of the sociology of knowledge itself. As has often been pointed out, such a determinist view, while not actually self-contradictory, is somewhat self-defeating.[16]

But a weaker form of sociology of knowledge has been implicit in my presentation of the value basis of social science, because one of the grounds for holding that value choices are inseparable from social theories is precisely that other people's theories, and sometimes one's own, can be shown to be partially determined by social environment and interests. And yet if this 'can be shown' is taken in the sense of objective empirical knowledge, we are on the horns of the same dilemma: *either* here at least (and in the least likely place) we have got to accept a kind of sociology that is objectively empirical and interest-free, *or* it 'can be shown' only on the basis of yet another, and probably interest-influenced, value choice. The first horn of the dilemma is lethal, but the second is graspable just in virtue of the pluralist conception of value choice that has been generally adopted here. The question now becomes: Given that we are not *compelled* to adopt it, does the weaker sociology-of-knowledge thesis nevertheless commend itself to our value system as desirable – illuminative of dark areas in social interaction, and conducive to understanding of others and of ourselves? The question can only be answered by consideration of particular examples, and in terms of one's personal reaction to them. I would answer for myself that many examples in the work of Marx, Mannheim, Myrdal, Gouldner, and some current 'critical sociology'[17] do seem to be thus illuminating.

[16] For a discussion of this see my 'Models of Method in Natural and Social Sciences', *Methodology and Science*, 8 (1975), 163.

[17] There are some good (and some bad) examples in R. Blackburn (ed.), *Ideology in Social Science* (London, 1972). C. B. Macpherson describes the function of social theory as *justification* of a social system (*ibid.* pp. 19, 23 – cf. Gouldner's 'reduction of tension' quoted above); M. Shaw, on the other hand, in a critique of Gouldner, takes the goal to be the overcoming of academic sociology 'in the development of the revolutionary self-consciousness of the working class' (*ibid.* p. 44). In more moderate vein, in I. L. Horowitz (ed.), *The New Sociology: Essays in Social Science and Social Theory in Honour of C. Wright Mills* (Oxford, 1964), S. W. Rousseas and J. Farganis assert that

Finally, a convenient analogy. I suggest that the proposal of a social theory is more like the arguing of a political case than like a natural-science explanation. It should seek for and respect the facts when these are to be had, but it cannot await a possibly unattainable total explanation. It must appeal explicitly to value judgments and may properly use persuasive rhetoric. No doubt it should differ from most political argument in seeking and accounting for facts more conscientiously, and in constraining its rhetoric this side of gross special pleading and rabble-rousing propaganda. Here the inheritance of virtues from the natural sciences comes to the social scientist's aid, and I hope nothing I have said will be taken to undermine these virtues. The fact that the view of the social sciences presented here is more often associated with the particular choice of value goals of the revolutionary left[18] does not in the least invalidate the general argument, nor reduce – rather, it increases – the need for the moderate centre and right to look to its own value choices. Neither liberal denial that there are such value choices nor cynical right-wing suppression of them from consciousness will meet the case.

Hume attempted to divorce the question of truth from that of value, while certain scientific humanists have attempted to derive value from truth. A consequence of my argument on the other hand has been that, at least in the sciences of man, a sense of 'truth' that is not merely pragmatic may be derivable from prior commitment to values and goals.[19]

ideology (inseparable from social theory) 'must be concerned with the human condition and its betterment in an always imperfect world. Its justification for being is, in a word, progress' (p. 274).

[18] It is significant that G. S. Jones, in an Althusserian piece in Blackburn's *Ideology*, denies that it is values or interpretations that are involved in theory choice, and holds that what is required is new concepts of structure (p. 114). In other words, the hard Marxist reverts to a view of the social sciences as theory-laden only, but of course the theory (and the values) are those of Marx.

[19] I should like to express my thanks to those who commented on a first draft of this paper at the meeting of the Thyssen Philosophy Group at Ross-on-Wye in September 1975, and also to David Thomas for discussions on the general problem of values in social science.

Indeterminacy and Interpretation

CHRISTOPHER HOOKWAY

I

Anthropologists often attempt to ascribe beliefs and desires to the members of alien tribes that they are studying: they hope to secure an understanding of the aliens' behaviour by attributing various cognitive attitudes to them and providing interpretations for the language they use. The evidence available to them is apparently strictly limited: they can observe the actions the aliens perform, although they cannot observe the intentional descriptions which characterise those actions; they can observe what linguistic performances the aliens volunteer or approve of; and they can observe in what circumstances these actions and utterances are forthcoming. It is not clear that there is much more evidence than this. They are given a non-intentional characterisation of the subject's behaviour and certain relations of the subject's to his environment: on this basis they have to provide theories of interpretation that move beyond the non-intentional. There is a problem about how they can do this. It appears that the theory of interpretation is underdetermined by the non-intentional evidence available – this can give rise to scepticism about the possibility of the kind of knowledge of other cultures promised by the anthropologist. The obstacles to understanding the behaviour of aliens remain when we have solved the general problem of other minds: we have to allow that the subjects may employ standards of reasonableness different from our own; or if we hold the view that intentionality is to be explained in terms of functional role in a structured practice constituted by rules, we may have to admit that the functional roles expressed by certain native sentences cannot be expressed in our own language at all. It is assumed that the cognitive states and attitudes of the natives are there to be investigated, an objective subject matter whose investigation poses trying methodological problems: a realist attitude to the subject matter is held. Thus Martin Hollis argues that we must assume that the natives share our standards of rationality, and he regards this as a substantive *a priori* principle about what people are like.[1] Peter Winch appears to think that the inquirer must attempt to infiltrate the rule-governed practices constitutive of the native form of life.[2] Both seem to regard the difficulties facing the anthropologist as largely methodological. Hollis recognises that the methodological difficulties involved in understanding alien cultures may also arise in attempting to understand members of one's own culture, but he does not appear to regard this as a threat to the objectivity of the questions posed – presumably he thinks that no such difficulties attend my own understanding of my own psychological states. I suspect that Winch would draw the line between the understanding of members of one's own and other cultures.

In this paper, I wish to consider an argument that moves from the methodological problems facing the anthropologist to the view that actions, linguistic performances and cognitive attitudes do not have intentional characterisations as intrinsic properties. In other words, the translator cannot ask the question: What is the meaning of the native sentence S? Rather, he must ask for the meaning assigned to S by translation schema T, where there are alternatives to T which are empirically entirely satisfactory but which yield non-equivalent translations to S. Quine's thesis of the indeterminacy of translation attempts to justify a non-realist attitude to psychological states by arguing from the problems of the translator. In turn, it imposes constraints upon adequate theories of mind which have implications for those attempting to understand other cultures. It provides a foundation for some arguments that urge a radical discontinuity between the social and physical sciences; and, perhaps most important, if it is valid, it provides an abstract formulation of a problem in terms of which we can perspicuously formulate a range of responses to problems about understanding other cultures and other members of this culture.

Quine has made a number of attempts to formulate his thesis and the arguments for it. Unfortunately, none of these attempts is particularly clear, so I have felt it worth while to devote a considerable proportion of this paper to an attempt to state both the thesis and the arguments. A number of refutations have been offered, but most seem to miss the point. There are a number of reasons for this, two of which can be mentioned here. It is perhaps useful to distinguish three questions that arise:

[1] M. Hollis, 'The Limits of Irrationality', in B. Wilson (ed.), *Rationality* (Oxford, 1970).
[2] P. Winch, *The Idea of a Social Science* (London, 1958), and 'Understanding a Primitive Society', in Wilson (ed.), *op. cit.*

(1) Is translation indeterminate?

(2) How much translational indeterminacy is there?

(3) How should we react to the indeterminacy in our theory of nature, and in our conception of psychological inquiry?

While an affirmative answer to question 1 is presupposed by the other two, it is possible that a variety of responses to the later questions may be compatible with translational indeterminacy. Quine discusses all of these questions and takes up a distinctive stand on each of them; so we may be able to disagree with a substantial proportion of Quine's discussion without disputing the indeterminacy of translation. Much of the argumentation in Quine's *Word and Object* is concerned to show that indeterminacy infects the apparatus of quantification and identity which makes explicit the ontological commitments of a theory: even the ontological commitment of an observation sentence is said to be indeterminate. We may be disposed to reject this view – denying that the translation of 'Gavagai' is indeterminate – without denying that some translation is indeterminate. The indeterminacy thesis is justified by the use of a highly abstract argument based on methodological features of the translation situation: it can only be refuted by a demonstration that the abstract argument is ineffective. Furthermore, a circularity is present in the discussion which is innocuous and is inevitable on Quine's views of the nature of philosophy, but which makes the views expressed curiously impenetrable to the outsider. Clearly one way to respond to question 3 is to show that the indeterminacy thesis is a consequence of the preferred theory of nature and is compatible with the favoured conception of the social sciences, so Quine is often at pains to show that the indeterminacy of translation follows from his favoured physicalism. This has led one critic to object that the thesis fatally depends upon dubious physicalist premises. However, Quine appears also to use the indeterminacy thesis to support his physicalism – rather as Davidson argues from the related anomalism of the mental to a physicalist monist theory of nature.[3] Part of the difficulty here is that it is not easy to distinguish passages where Quine is concerned with our first question from passages where he is concerned with the third. But it is worse than that, because Quine's naturalist mistrust of First Philosophy compels him to regard his methodological and ontological inquiries as *part of* the theory of nature: his inquiry cannot but reflect his views about the limits of respectable inquiry. Fortunately, I hope we can distinguish an abstract

---

[3] D. Davidson, 'Mental Events', in L. Foster and J. W. Swanson (eds.), *Experience and Theory* (London, 1970).

structure of argument which is explicit in many of Quine's writings which does not obviously rest on unpalatable assumptions. It is with this structure of argument that we shall be concerned.

II

First then, what is the content of the indeterminacy thesis? In *Word and Object*, Quine offers three formulations of the thesis he is concerned to establish; only one makes use of the idiom of translation. A speaker's linguistic knowledge – the meanings he attaches to his words – is manifested primarily in his dispositions to assent to or dissent from sentences. If we wish to penetrate his linguistic knowledge we must attach meanings to his words in such a way that his verbal dispositions – in particular his dispositions to assent to or dissent from sentences – are explained. The idea is that we interpret his words so that they are expressive of an intelligible belief set. We may later wish to extend the range of verbal behaviour to be considered, although that would require us to make assumptions about desires. Given this picture of verbal behaviour, Quine's first formulation is:

> two men could be just alike in all their dispositions to verbal behaviour under all possible sensory stimulations, and yet the meanings or ideas expressed in their identically triggered and identically sounded utterances could diverge radically, for the two men, in a wide range of cases.[4]

This formulation still employs a mentalistic idiom and suggests a sceptical position familiar from the writings of C. I. Lewis and Russell: there is no reason to think we do not each inhabit a private world of private meanings, the differences in our meanings being undetectable in principle. This picture is certainly lurking in the background of much of Quine's discussion: if we refuse to draw the ontological conclusions Quine recommends from this argument, it may be the position to which we are condemned. However, Quine is forced to attempt a reformulation which abstains from talk of meaning:

> the infinite totality of sentences of a given language can be so permuted, or mapped onto itself, that (*a*) the totality of the speaker's dispositions to verbal behaviour remains invariant, and yet (*b*) the mappings are no mere correlation of sentences with equivalent sentences, in any plausible sense of equivalence however loose.[5]

A less abstract paraphrase is immediately forthcoming:

[4] W. V. O. Quine, *Word and Object* (Cambridge, Mass., 1960), p. 26.
[5] *Ibid.* p. 27.

manuals for translating one language into another can be set up in divergent ways, all compatible with the totality of speech dispositions, yet incompatible with one another.[6]

So, if I wish to translate from L_1 into L_2, there are alternative manuals I may use. Observations of speech behaviour of users does not provide grounds for discriminating between them: the second and third formulations make this point for the case where L_1 is L_2, and where it is not, respectively. (It is not really satisfactory to put it like that, unless one has an appropriate criterion of identity for languages. However, I think the thought being expressed is intuitively apparent.)

Exegetical problems arise at once. For instance: In what sense can the alternative manuals of translation be said to be incompatible? We must consider this below. First, we should note that the formulations so far considered only declare that all possible observations of verbal behaviour do not determine a unique interpretation of the sentences of a language. Quine clearly wants a further conclusion: not only is translation not determined by the relevant evidence; rather, in the case of translation there is no question of one of the theories (translation manuals) being true and the rest false. The translator is not forced to guess which of the permissible theories is correct – as he would be on the C. I. Lewis picture.

Where Indeterminacy of translation applies, there is no real question of right choice: there is no fact of the matter even to *within* the acknowledged underdetermination at a theory of nature.[7]

The most puzzling aspects of the argument concern this additional stage.

Quine adopts the idiom of *radical* translation. We are to consider the plight of an interpreter faced with speakers of a wholly alien language. This problem is taken as a model for the interpretative endeavours of the translator concerned with understanding other speakers of a language with which he or his fellows are familiar. The apparent additional aids which seem to render his problem more tractable are in fact misleading distractions. We are all skilled at living with the indeterminacy: there are principles of choice which we use to cut down the number of competing translation manuals; some are easy of application and achieve almost universal adoption. Thus in interpreting the words of fellow English-speakers I try to allow that they use words as I do: in understanding French-speakers it pays to conform to the established practices of translation. Some have attempted to

---

[6] *Ibid.*
[7] W. V. O. Quine, 'Reply to Chomsky', in D. Davidson and J. Hintikka (eds.), *Words and Objections: Essays in the Work of W. V. Quine* (Dordrecht, 1969), p. 303.

confute Quine by commending principles of translation which restrict choice. Quine's response is that these are 'regulative maxims'. Although their adoption is not wholly arbitrary, they are not to be classified as methodological principles of *evidence* which aid inquiry – they help to settle the question which to use, not to settle the question which captures the real meanings. So, from the point of view of problems of inquiry, the radical translator is no worse off than the fellow speaker of English: and we concentrate on the plight of the former to avoid misleading appearances to the contrary.

III

The most interesting argument produced by Quine (referred to as 'the argument from above')[8] appears to have a very simple structure. (*a*) Assume as premise that the theory of nature is underdetermined by all possible observation – perhaps by all possible observation and the principles of scientific method. (*b*) It follows that translation is underdetermined by all possible observation – in other words, if there can be no pragmatist definition of physical truth, there can be no pragmatist definition of synonymy. (*c*) The final conclusion from this is that if we lack a pragmatist definition of synonymy we should not adopt a realist attitude to the theory of meaning – sentences lack determinate meanings and actions do not have determinate intentional descriptions, except relativised to particular theories of interpretation. It is the final stage which is least clear, and Quine does not appear to have explicitly discussed it in print.

There will probably be little dispute over Quine's initial premise: the underdetermination of theory by possible observation has become generally accepted. However, it will be useful to consider some features of the model of inquiry Quine assumes. Like most pragmatists he is interested in the position of an investigator already possessed of a theory, or corpus of beliefs, considering how to change it. His motivation may be that the causal process of perception has produced an anomaly in the set of beliefs – Quine's account of the role of perception can be found in chapter 1 of *The Web of Belief* ('Belief and Change of Belief') or in the first section of *The Roots of Reference* ('Reception and Perception').[9] Or else he may desire a simpler or more coherent corpus – perhaps he wishes to form an opinion on a question con-

---

[8] W. V. O. Quine, 'On the Reasons for the Indeterminacy of Translation', *Journal of Philosophy*, 67 (1970).

[9] W. V. O. Quine and J. S. Ullian, *The Web of Belief* (New York, 1970); W. V. O. Quine, *The Roots of Reference* (La Salle, Illinois, 1974).

cerning which he has hitherto remained agnostic. There are general methodological principles that are used in comparing possible successors to the present corpus of beliefs – Quine is insistent that philosophers discover these only by observing the practices of skilled investigators. In *The Web of Belief* a list of five 'virtues of hypotheses' is presented – each a principle to be adhered to where possible in revising one's theory. However, it is simpler to consider just two general principles which are prominent in *The Roots of Reference*, not least because they show the two distinct ways in which the principles function. These are the principles of simplicity and conservatism, familiar from *Word and Object*. Suppose our investigator has corpus T_1 and he is considering whether to abandon it in favour of T_2 or T_3. Insofar as T_2 is simpler than T_3 according to our intuitive sense of simplicity, then T_2 is to be preferred: that T_2 is simpler than T_1 (or not anomalous as T_1 is) and is simpler than T_3 provides a prima facie reason for adopting T_2. This sense of simplicity is extremely complex: it reflects our entrenched views on similarity and analogy and our unthinking inductive habits. Quine now calls it the principle of *induction*. The second principle applies to certain relations between theories: thus if the gap from T_1 to T_2 is 'smaller' than that between T_1 and T_3 then there is prima facie reason to accept T_2. It is arguable that Quine has *one* principle of simplicity to be applied both to theories and to transitions between theories. Quine now calls the conservative principle a principle of *empiricism*. 'Short leaps' are governed by the maxim of *relative empiricism*. Don't venture further from sensory evidence than you need to.[10] As the principles are not ordered, they may conflict in practice: we must arbitrate between them. 'They are related dialectically.'[11]

Thus, for Quine, not only may alternative theories agree with all possible observation, but also it is unlikely that scientific method will determine one of those theories as best. The kind of pragmatist or methodological definition of truth popularly ascribed to Peirce is not forthcoming. Several claims are entangled here. Quine clearly thinks that we may be forced to make an arbitrary choice between theories not discriminated between by methodological principles. It is also clear that the theory one ends up with may depend upon individual standards of simplicity – Quine admits that these may vary. It will also depend upon historical features of the process of investigation: conservatism may counsel that one who adheres to T_1 should adopt T_2, while one who adheres to T_0 should adopt T_3. Popper disputes methodological definitions of truth from another angle: where Quine

[10] *The Roots of Reference*, p. 138. [11] *Ibid.* p. 137.

fears too many successful theories, Popper suspects that there may be too few.[12] There is no reason to think that one must side with Quine on this for the argument to get going. The notion of all possible observations may already arouse suspicions. A weaker formulation is available. There is no reason to think we could ever be forced by the observations we have made to adopt just one theory; there will always be alternatives.

IV

What is the methodological situation of the translator? According to Quine, he must attempt to define a function which maps each sentence of the alien language onto a sentence of the translator's language. The function must meet certain constraints. An observation sentence of the alien language – a sentence which is assented to only in certain observation conditions, but is responded to in the same way by all native speakers – must be mapped onto a sentence of the home language generally assented to in the same circumstances. A stimulus-analytic sentence of the alien language – where all speakers agree in assenting to the sentence at all times – should be translated into a stimulus-analytic sentence of the home language. Finally, truth-functional logic should be read into the alien language. This function can be called an *analytical hypothesis*. The conditions Quine imposes are probably intended to remind us of the idea found in the work of Carnap that a conceptual scheme can be characterised by specifying the empirical meanings of the basic sentences and the analytic connections obtaining. He wishes to show that insofar as those notions (empirical meaning and analyticity) can be made empirically respectable, they do not suffice to uniquely specify a conceptual framework. Two problems may be distinguished. We may ask whether analytical hypotheses are underdetermined by observation, but we may also wonder whether Quine has chosen the correct constraints on translation. He requires that generally accepted truisms be translated into generally accepted truisms (for such sentences are stimulus-analytic), yet it seems clear that such claims often become rejected with time. 'The sun circles the earth' may have been stimulus-analytic in the middle ages: I suspect that there are now speech communities in which it is stimulus-contradictory. We may thus question his second constraint; others may feel that there are constraints that he has ignored. (For instance, Davidson requires that we replace Quine's theory of translation with a theory of *interpretation* formally analogous

[12] K. R. Popper, 'Of Clouds and Clocks', in *Objective Knowledge* (Oxford, 1972).

24

to the Tarskian truth definition constructed with the aid of a very generous principle of charity.[13] We are constrained to regard the aliens as truthful as far as possible. If such a theory is possible, we may prefer a truth theory which provides a genuine interpretation because the interpretative expression is used, rather than mentioned. This may reduce the amount of underdetermination but is unlikely to eliminate it. The principle of charity is less obviously justified.)

We shall examine the argument for stage *b*, considering the status of the principles of translation, in passing, in the next section. In order to establish what sentences of the alien language mean we must determine what beliefs they express. This does not mean that we must be able to specify the full corpus of beliefs without using linguistic evidence: we guess at a few beliefs, this gets us started on a few observation sentences, the preliminary translations determine further translations suggesting further beliefs, etc. Our translations of the initial bridgehead may have to be revised. The problem is that we may be able to reinterpret the sentences consistently if we are prepared to change our view of the native's beliefs. If we cannot predict what theory an alien holds from what observations he has made, then, if we are sufficiently ingenious, we should be able to reinterpret his sentences so that he can be regarded as having any theory compatible with his observations. We may be forced to adopt some very complex translations: requiring the alien to use intricate locutions to express what we regard as simple propositions. We may be forced to credit the alien with very bizarre opinions; but it appears *a priori* that we are not constrained by the kind of evidence we have considered to ascribing just one corpus of beliefs to him. Translation is underdetermined because we cannot tell which theory the aliens have, and also because when that question is answered there may be open questions about which sentences of the language express which parts of the theory. So translation is not settled when we know what theory the alien has, and what theory he has is not determined by what observations he would regard as compatible with it. We cannot regard him as rational in the hope of reducing the amount of underdetermination to those theories compatible with scientific method. Quine would be reluctant to attribute the same simplicity intuitions to the aliens. Moreover, the operation of the conservatism principle is determined by antecedent cognitive states: theories that are too different from our own to count as real options for us may be real options for the aliens.

[13] D. Davidson, 'Radical Interpretation', *Dialectica*, 27 (1973).

CHRISTOPHER HOOKWAY

V

Three criticisms of this stage of the argument may be envisaged. First of all, it may be remarked that beliefs also interact with desires to determine actions. If it proved impossible to understand the *behaviour* of the agent, given the set of beliefs we have ascribed to him, then the belief ascriptions must be in error. If we make no *a priori* restrictions on the plausibility and complexity of desire ascribable, then it seems that the need to construct a theory of action imposes no further restrictions. And to do so would be to make substantive *a priori* assumptions about psychological matters. If any desire is the desire to bring it about that P (for some P), then the constraints imposed by Quine are sufficient to ensure that the desire will be appropriately formulated on any of the available translation manuals. This might entail that many of the agents' avowals of desire prove to be false: the complaint that reports of desires would restrict the available alternatives leads us to the second criticism which has been made by Kirk and endorsed by Blackburn.[14] The semantical and intentional discourse of the subjects provides an additional control: if we ask them what entails what, and what different words mean, we might restrict the range of alternatives to one. Unfortunately, this is not satisfactory. The problem we face is how to understand the nature of semantical discourse: this proposal is that we ground the study in the semantical claims of others. To appeal to testimony is to adopt a secondary means of inquiry which depends upon a more direct mode of investigation of the subject matter being available: what is at issue is the nature of that more direct inquiry. We wish to know how one alien knows what other aliens mean – and, of course, that is relevant to his own usage – as well as how *we* can know what an alien means. At first sight, any impediments that prevent *our* discovering a unique theory of interpretation would also affect other aliens.

Thirdly, critics may claim that Quine has not attended sufficiently to the inferences that aliens make and find plausible. It is suggested that some of the translation schemes will result in our having to ascribe very odd patterns of inference to aliens;[15] or that inference patterns which are relevant to specifying sentence–sentence connections which constitute the fabric of the theory are not reflected in the

[14] R. Kirk, 'Underdetermination of Theory and Indeterminacy of Translation', *Analysis*, 33 (1972–3); S. Blackburn, 'The Identity of Propositions', in Blackburn (ed.), *Meaning, Reference and Necessity* (Cambridge, 1975).
[15] H. Putnam, 'The Refutation of Conventionalism', *Noûs*, 8 (1974), 35.

evidence Quine considers.[16] However, in most cases, if an agent would infer R from P and Q he would also believe that if P and Q then (it is likely that) R. Most of the inferential connections will be reflected in stimulus-analytic sentences, for part of their role is to indicate sentence–sentence connections. Bizarre inference patterns are likely to show up in counter-intuitive translations of stimulus-analytic sentences. Dummett suggests that there must be rules of inference as well as beliefs. However, there is no reason to think that the agent would not assent to sentences expressing applications of that rule – even if that involves an indefinite regress of rules and rule-expressions. For instance, if *modus ponens* is the rule in question, he may assent to 'If it is raining, and it is raining only if there are clouds in the sky, then there are clouds in the sky'. Finally, it is important that rules require metalinguistic formulation: they can be regarded as norms concerning how words should be used. Thus to appeal to rules is once again question-beggingly to appeal to semantical discourse in order to understand how semantical discourse is to be understood. For if indeterminacy obtains it is likely to infect the translation of the object language into a metalanguage involved in the rule-formulation. Furthermore, for rules to provide us with assistance, it is necessary that we be able to determinately translate the metalanguage – which is unlikely.

So, it seems that translation is underdetermined by all possible data available to a radical translator. In that case such social science as depends upon intentional characterisation of subjects' states is similarly underdetermined, so that we must be wary of appealing to psychological generalisations to reduce the extent of the underdetermination.[17] This has a role in interpretation; but, once again, the nature of this role is part of the problem, so cannot be introduced to effect a solution. If psychological generalisations are grounded in observations of the behaviour of those whose behaviour we understand, they cannot provide an essential *empirical* constraint rendering interpretation determinate.

VI

The final stage of Quine's arguments is the most difficult. Given the underdetermination of translation theory by possible observations, we are invited to conclude that in the field of translation, there is

[16] M. Dummett, *Frege: Philosophy of Language* (London, 1973), and 'The Significance of Quine's Indeterminacy Thesis', *Synthèse*, 27 (1974).
[17] D. K. Lewis, 'Radical Interpretation', *Synthèse*, 27 (1974); Putnam, *op. cit.*

CHRISTOPHER HOOKWAY

no objective fact of the matter. A number of critics of Quine's views[18] have protested that Quine has done nothing to justify his view that underdetermination by evidence impugns the objectivity of translation but not of (say) physics. Both are empirically underdetermined, yet only translation displays indeterminacy. Quine clearly believes that the criticism is unwarranted, and he tried to pre-empt it in an obscure passage in *Word and Object*. An examination of this discussion may enable us to see the force of this stage of the argument; although I should add that the passage is very unclear, and I am unsure how true the reconstruction that I shall provide is to it.

The problem is this. Neither 'true' nor 'means the same as' can be methodologically defined; we have a criterion for neither. Because of this, 'means the same as' is discredited; in spite of it, 'true' remains a respectable notion. How can that be? One response could be that although there can be no *criterion* of truth, the notion can be *defined* in unproblematic terms: Tarski has shown us how to do that. For an account of how another philosopher who shares Quine's pragmatist sympathies saw Tarski's definition as making it possible to hold to realism in the absence of a methodological definition of truth, see Popper's paper on the Semantic Theory of Truth in his book *Objective Knowledge*.[19] The early sections of Quine's 'Two Dogmas of Empiricism' are an attempt to show that there is no readily available definition of synonymy that is equally unproblematic.[20] Perhaps, then, the crucial asymmetry is that 'true', unlike 'means the same as', can be defined in unproblematic ('limpidly extensional') terms. In just one of the two cases can the failure of a methodological definition be mitigated.[21]

There is much that can be questioned in this argument. The requirement that respectable notions be definable and Quine's conception of what is unproblematic can both be challenged. However we shall pursue another line of objection. Tarski's work shows us how to define 'true-in-L' for particular L; it does not provide an account of the non-relativised notion of truth. The definition is merely an immanent one. The objector could point out that we can do that for 'means the same as'. We can easily define what it is for two expressions to mean the same-by-analytical-hypothesis-F, so no genuine asymmetry has

[18] E.g. N. Chomsky, 'Quine's Empirical Assumption', in Davidson and Hintikka (eds.), *Words and Objections*; R. Rorty, 'Indeterminacy of Translation and of Truth', *Synthèse*, 23 (1972); Blackburn, 'The Identity of Propositions', *loc. cit.*; and Dummett, *op. cit.*
[19] K. R. Popper, 'Philosophical Comments on Tarski's Theory of Truth', in *Objective Knowledge*.
[20] W. V. O. Quine, 'Two Dogmas of Empiricism', in *From a Logical Point of View* (Cambridge, Mass., 1953).
[21] Quine, 'Notes on the Theory of Reference', in *From a Logical Point of View*.

28

been provided. Is there a way to reinstate the asymmetry? This question takes us to the heart of the matter. Consider Quine's argument against relativism:

> Have we now so lowered our sights as to settle for a relativistic notion of truth – rating statements of a theory as true for that theory and brooking no higher criticism? Not so. The saving consideration is that we continue to take seriously our own aggregate science, our own particular world theory or loose fabric of quasi theories whatever it may be.[22]

To 'take a theory seriously' is, presumably, to regard its sentences as true, rather than just 'true for that theory'. To understand this we must examine both what it means to regard sentences as simply *true*, and also why Quine thinks that we are rational to do this.

Tarski's definition makes contact with the non-relativised notion of truth by its criterion of adequacy for putative truth definitions. A predicate T is a truth predicate if it is defined in such a way that for any sentence of the object language s, the defining theory entails a sentence of the form

Ts if and only if p

where 'p' is the translation of s in the metalanguage. It is clearly a feature of our understanding of the notion of truth that we assent to biconditionals such as

'Cambridge is a city' is true if and only if Cambridge is a city.

This feature is behind Ramsey's claim that the two propositions '"Cambridge is a city" is true' and 'Cambridge is a city' have the same content; and it is implicit in Quine's view that the expression 'is true' is primarily a 'device of disquotation'. The important point is that by uttering a sentence *assertively* one commits onself to its truth: there is an intimate link between truth and assertion. Indeed, if one holds that relativism is intelligible only if the relativist can make the relativity of his assertions explicit by utterances of the form

s is true in L

then relativism may not be a coherent option at all. For by asserting that s is true-in-L, the speaker commits himself to the truth of the claim that s is true in L; yet this commitment is not itself explicitly relativised. If total relativism is to be explicit, then there must be no sentences that we use rather than mention: yet assertion involves the use of a sentence. So total explicit relativism is inconsistent with the making of any assertions at all. This only shows that relativism cannot be total: it may be justified over a restricted area such as theoretical science.

[22] Quine, *Word and Object*, p. 24.

But even this may be untenable if we insist that a speaker's grasp of the notion of truth should be expressed in a willingness to assent to the kind of biconditional we drew attention to on the previous page in every case. For, if our relativist must assent to

s is true in L if and only if p

if he assents to

s is true in L

then he must be able to infer, and assert, that p.

This argument would show that relativism is not a genuine option at all; but it rests on two questionable assumptions. The first of these is that relativism cannot be coherently espoused if the relativist cannot make his commitment wholly explicit in the way indicated. An objector might complain that relativism could be manifested in some other feature of the relativist's linguistic practice, although it is difficult to see what this could be. The second is the rather less plausible claim that a speaker with a grasp of the concept of truth must be able to manifest this by assenting to a biconditional of the appropriate kind involving any ascription of truth he is prepared to make. We shall not discuss these assumptions further here; they would take us too far afield. Fortunately, there is another argument suggested by Quine's discussion which would equally show relativism to be an unreasonable position in the Theory of Nature. We can articulate it by considering another interpretation of 'taking a theory seriously'. We take our commonsense beliefs seriously by using them as a basis for action. Our commonsense view of the world provides a background against which we conduct our projects and activities. Now, Quine seems to hold a view of theoretical science and its relation to common sense similar to Peirce's Critical Commonsensism, or Popper's Commonsense Realism. Our theory of nature is the result of successive attempts to correct and refine our commonsense view of the world: there is no basis for drawing a distinction between common sense and theoretical science that warrants a distinct attitude to each. For so long as we operate with a general view of the world there is no reason to distance ourselves from it in a relativist fashion. Thus:

May we conclude that translational synonymy is no worse off than truth in physics? To be thus reassured is to misjudge the parallel. In being able to speak of the truth of a sentence only within a more inclusive theory, one is not much hampered; for one is always working within some comfortably inclusive theory, however tentative...the parameters of truth stay conveniently fixed most of the time. Not so the analytical hypotheses that constitute the parameter of translation. We are always ready to wonder about the meaning of a foreigner's remark without reference to any one set of analytical hypotheses, indeed even in the absence of any.[23]

The point seems to be that we now hold a non-relativist attitude towards theories, and there is no reason to abandon it. The evolutionary picture of the growth of knowledge that Quine provides seems to presuppose it: to abandon it neither removes anomalies nor simplifies our conception of inquiry. This involves seeing relativism as an alternative conception of the world which is to be discarded according to our normal methodological canons, which is of course how it should be according to Quine's conception of philosophy, if relativism is indeed coherent. Neither of these lines of argument would rule out relativism about synonymy. There is no analogue of assertion to provide a transcendent basis for our notion of synonymy, no act by which we commit ourselves to absolute synonymy relations. Consequently there is no obstacle to relativising reports of translations or synonymy relations explicitly to a particular translation theory, or, demonstratively, to the analytical hypothesis the speaker's community uses. (It may even be possible that our ordinary use of translational notions somehow involves a covert demonstrative reference of this kind. In that case we may be able to reconcile our normal idioms of propositional attitude with a recognition of the indeterminacy of translation by construing them as Davidson does in his paper 'On Saying That',[24] and thus avoid treating the indeterminacy thesis as a proposal to revise our current linguistic practice.)

Once we recognise that relativism of this kind is at least an option in translation theory, we can see how to construct a Quinean response to the charge that the argument involves arbitrary discrimination in favour of the theory of nature and against translation theory. Consider a translator attempting to translate from one language into another. He works out three translational hypotheses that fit all the evidence considered by Quine. Our translator then has *four* theories about the meanings of the words of the other language to choose between, and the evidence available equally supports all four. Three of the theories assert that one of the three hypotheses he has constructed correctly yields the true meanings of the expression of the other language. If we call the three hypotheses F_1, F_2 and F_3, then these three theories assert:

(1) S means T if and only if S means-by-F_1 T

[23] Quine, *Word and Object*, p. 76.
[24] D. Davidson, 'On Saying That', in Davidson and Hintikka (eds.), *Words and Objections*.

(2) S means T if and only if S means-by-F_2 T

(3) S means T if and only if S means-by-F_3 T

The fourth theory asserts that whereas there are objective truths about what expressions mean-by-F_1, mean-by-F_2, etc., there are no objective truths about what expressions mean *tout court*. There is no absolute notion of meaning to which these relativised notions approximate. This fourth hypothesis makes the claim that translation is indeterminate. So the indeterminacy thesis itself is underdetermined by the empirical data. We can see why the underdetermination of choice of translation theory by observation is necessary for the indeterminacy thesis: if only one translation theory was ever empirically adequate, then there is no reason not to treat that as capturing the absolute notion of meaning. It is the only meaning notion available, after all. This reconstruction shows that Quine is as much a scientific realist with respect to translation as with respect to physics. In settling for the indeterminacy thesis, he is opting for just one among a number of empirically equivalent theories which he regards as true. Translational determinacy is abandoned as a *bad theory*, but why is it bad? We shall take up this question in the final section.

We close this section with two comments on the argument so far. Some might object that the terms in which the argument have been posed presuppose intentional or translational notions which are not relativised to particular translational hypotheses, so that it is incoherent. For instance, the identification of alien assent and dissent or alien assertion proceeds unrelativised to any particular translation theory, and it is used in collecting the data against which we test theories for empirical adequacy. If that much intentional data is permitted, surely it is arbitrary to exclude more; for instance, we may at least identify what an agent finds silly or absurd. A related difficulty was pointed out by John Wallace.[25] The evidence takes the form of claims about the conditions under which tokens of particular utterance types are volunteered or endorsed. But the notion of utterance type is itself translational, as Wallace puts it: which utterances are tokens of the same type is not determined by a purely physical characterisation of the events in question. Neither difficulty need embarrass a defender of indeterminacy. There is no real alternative to treating most utterances as assertions, and we can identify a sign of assent because of its connection with assertion: speakers will assent to what they will assert. The problem with relying on absurdity reactions is that we cannot expect the aliens to share our standards of absurdity, and they

[25] J. Wallace, 'A Query on Radical Translation', *Journal of Philosophy*, 64 (1967).

cannot be keyed to specific semantic features of sentences of the language. The correct response to Wallace is that Quine does not provide us with a general argument against the use of *all* 'translational' notions, as Wallace uses that term. An acknowledgement of indeterminacy may be warranted in the semantic case, but not in the syntactic case.

Finally, a remark about theory identity. It seems that to accept indeterminacy in translation is to devalue Quine's resolute anti-relativism in the theory of nature. Suppose that we hold theory T_1, and we are wondering whether to replace it with T_2 or T_3. T_2 and T_3 are empirically equivalent, but they are different theories and are not logically equivalent. Thus for some sentence S the sentence itself is a part of T_2, while its negation is a part of T_3. Quine holds that it is a genuine question whether T_2 or T_3 is true, and which should be adopted. Suppose, then, that we decided that the best way to revise our corpus of beliefs is to assent to the set of sentences that makes up T_2, rather than to that that comprises T_3. Then there will be an adequate manual of translation from our language into itself that fits all our verbal dispositions according to which we have adopted T_3 rather than T_2. If the indeterminacy thesis is true, then there is no fact of the matter which of the two empirically equivalent theories we have adopted. Once we attempt to construct a semantic criterion of theory identity, it seems to be impossible to distinguish empirically equivalent theories. From the point of view of the inquirer now holding to T, the difference between T_2 and T_3 is perfectly clear, of course, as they represent distinct incompatible reformations of his set of beliefs. This is presumably to be expected according to any theory which allows linguistic expression an essential role in the settling of questions about belief identity.

VII

Nothing we have presented so far compels the abandonment of a realist attitude towards meanings and propositions. Why should we treat the thesis of the indeterminacy of translation relations as the most plausible account of these areas of our experience? The problem can be approached via an analogy with our practices of measurement. The principles we use in choosing between alternative physical theories are supposed to be principles of evidence; they are adopted because they are expected to lead to truth. In constructing a physical theory, we may have to choose whether to cast our measurements in terms of feet and inches or in terms of metres. The principles that guide this choice are not principles of evidence – we do not consider the question of which standard of measurement reveals the *truth* about length. We have to rely on maxims which are concerned with which scale will be easiest to use, with which fits our practical needs best – they can be called *regulative principles*. It is not an arbitrary matter which scale we use – for many purposes, for instance, a decimal scale will have obvious advantages. Now, we have principles for choosing between alternative translational theories, and usually they can be expected to show one translational theory to be far superior to its rivals. The question is: Is choice between translational theories governed by principles of evidence or regulative principles? Is the choice whether to use 'means-by-F_1' or 'means-by-F_2' like the choice whether to record measurements in centimetres or inches? To adopt the option of recognising indeterminacy in translation is to regard choice between translational theories as analogous to choice between systems of measurement.

There are at least two ways of arguing for this position. First, one might argue that if the relativist theory can make reasonable sense of our translational practice, then it is likely to be simpler than any alternative because it is not committed to the existence of entities like propositions which are required to render translation relations determinate. Given that the notion of synonymy cannot be operationally defined, then presumably we have to invoke propositions which sentences express and which fix the meanings of the sentences in question. If we can avoid commitment to these and still do some justice to the facts of translational practice, we should surely do so. Some passages suggest that Quine would argue in this fashion. The second line of defence is to provide an argument which shows that the relativist position provides a better account of our translational practice than the alternatives – that problems arise on the rival views which we do not face if we acknowledge indeterminacy. Perhaps denying indeterminacy leads to insuperable difficulties in understanding the epistemology of interpretation and translation. This is not to advocate a reform of our interpretational practice on the basis of sceptical arguments: it is rather to offer a view of our interpretational practice according to which the sceptical arguments are unfounded.

This second form of argument is more attractive because it does not rely on assumptions about the merits of ontological parsimony which not all would share. It is of particular interest to us because it relates directly to those epistemological problems about interpretation that were introduced in the first section. It appears that the principles of translation we use impute to those whose behaviour we attempt to interpret standards of rational inference and reasonable behaviour which are substantially our own. If we do not assume such principles, then, as Hollis remarks, it is hard to see how translation gets started at all. The question of which principles should be used and how they can be justified is a subject of much controversy among philosophers interested in anthropology and among methodologically sensitive anthropologists, for it is difficult to reconcile standards of scientific objectivity with this imposition of our own criteria of reasonableness on to the subjects of study. In the remainder of this paper, I wish to sketch an attitude to these problems consonant with recognising indeterminacy and relate this to some other discussions.

Suppose we allow the translator a maxim – Use the best translation theory. Now, which is best may well turn upon what it is to be used for, which in turn may depend upon what kinds of social interactions between translator and native the translation is to be used to facilitate. Consider, then, an investigator who, wishing to be able to converse with a native in his own language, constructs an analytical hypothesis or theory of interpretation which meets certain empirical constraints. He may adopt the simplest possible translation function, although that involves attributing many false beliefs and unintelligible desires to the native and also, perhaps, a very complex structure of theory. Simplicity of translation function is a virtue of translation theories because it facilitates quick, easy translation in a conversational context. Another investigator may be prepared to forgo simplicity of translation function for the sake of crediting the native with beliefs or inferential strategies that are intelligible to him. This makes it possible to anticipate native reactions to novel situations, to treat the native as a person: it is because we often wish to be able to do this that it is a virtue of translation theories that they show the natives to be reasonable by our standards. A third investigator may wish to maximise truthfulness among the natives' beliefs, to find that their desires resemble his own: this would be a virtue in a translation theory if it was to be used to facilitate common projects involving both native and investigator. It is feasible that different translation theories could answer to those needs; one theory would have one virtue, another the others. Then which theory one should adopt would depend upon the practical needs to which the theory is to respond.

This picture is very crude. It does not provide a plausible account of how translation proceeds: for instance, in normal cases one translational theory will satisfy all needs. There are particular advantages, moreover, in having just one theory. However, the sketch can be used to articulate some truths about translation. The first point is about interpreting the behaviour of other members of one's own society: we normally understand each other by adopting a homophonic system of translation, assuming that others use words as we do. There is good reason to expect this system to prove to be the best on all counts. It offers a very simple system of translation, and does not burden us with distinct systems of translation for interpreting the speech of ourselves and others. Furthermore, by virtue of our belonging to the same society, it will show a substantial amount of agreement about the nature of the world between ourselves and others. This is especially the case because that translation system will have been involved in the development of theoretical knowledge by communal inquiry. It will also ascribe to the others a framework of theory that is very simple by our standards – because we probably share most of it, and do not find it implausible. Finally, the theory of translation I find best to interpret the verbal behaviour of other members of my society will coincide with the system they find best to interpret my verbal behaviour. These considerations alone (there are certainly more) show that the translation theory I use makes it easy to converse, learn from and engage in co-operative inquiry with other members of my society.

The principles which are in tension in translating alien languages tend to pull in the same direction when I am translating other speakers of my own language. This still obtains when I am translating the language of a society similar to my own, although to a lesser extent: that is presumably why the societies are similar. So the intuitive idea of understanding derived from experiences with other speakers of the same language does not carry us very far when the problem concerns understanding the verbal behaviour of aliens. In one sense I can understand aliens as I understand my peers: by constructing an empirically adequate theory of translation. At the same time, I cannot understand them in the same way, if that involves having a theory which satisfies all these constraints. If the societies are dissimilar, that is impossible. A response to this consonant with Quine's indeterminacy thesis would be that the difficulties are not epistemological impediments to resolving a particular question, but arise because we have not specified adequately what the problem is. In the homophonic case, this is not necessary because the different desiderata are found in one theory. Quine believes that the one dominant objective of the physical scientist is an efficient means of prediction, and hence explanation. For the anthropologist there is not one dominant objective; this is partly because the kind of understanding sought is not determined by the familiar case of understanding a fellow speaker of the same language.

One way to recognise it would be to use different theories of translation for different inquiries.

The interesting problems about anthropological interpretation then come to involve what virtues in translational theories we should recognise. What kinds of intelligibility should be imputed to an alien corpus? Quine claims that translation theories should at least approximate to preserving stimulus meaning: David Lewis has sketched a variety of constraints to be met by adequate translational theories. The puzzles concern just how one should argue for those positions, and here, it seems, the abstract argument we have investigated offers little assistance. I suspect that we can come to an understanding of those difficulties only via a detailed examination of the kinds of principles invoked in anthropological practice, and a consideration of the motives behind exercises in translation. Philosophical argument is also relevant: we may be able to show that certain conditions must be met by any translational theory that allows us to treat the alien as a *person*. Rorty and Davidson have both argued that we must attribute most of our own beliefs and standards to him if we are to regard him as an inhabitant of the *same world* as ourselves.[26] Considerable charity is obligatory on the translator. But considerations of that kind would take us beyond the scope of this paper.

It does not follow from this that the argument we have examined has no consequences for our understanding of anthropological interpretation. For, if we accept the argument, we must at least acknowledge that the rules we apply in choosing between translations are dependent upon our conception of the point or nature of anthropological understanding. There is no notion of synonymy to provide a rationale for an account of correct translation which will provide a source of data for an anthropological investigation. Consideration of *meaning* does not help. Winch defends a distinctive approach to these problems on the basis of some philosophical considerations about the theory of meaning – considerations about the nature of rules the mastery of which constitutes knowledge of a language. Consequently, it will be helpful to cast our discussion of whether the indeterminacy thesis is true in the form of a discussion of the notion of a semantic rule. However, we must approach this by considering an alternative, somewhat implausible mentalist theory. Suppose that there is a 'language of thought' in which an individual formulates his thoughts, surmises and conjectures: for communicative purposes he must

[26] R. Rorty, 'A World Well Lost', *Journal of Philosophy*, 69 (1972); D. Davidson, 'The Very Idea of a Conceptual Scheme', *Proceedings of the American Philosophical Association*, 47 (1973–4), 5–20.

translate his thoughts into the public language. The important point
is that the intentionality of thoughts is determinate and *sui generis*;
an example of such a view is Chisholm's theory of intentionality, as
presented in his paper 'Sentences about Believing'.[27] Each native has
a translational scheme which he uses to transform thoughts into words:
he can justify the use of his scheme by observing the verbal behaviour
of his fellows. Each uses the scheme which seems simplest to him; each
scheme meets the kinds of empirical constraints we have considered.
However, owing to differences in the structures of their thought
patterns and standards of simplicity, and to differing dialectical
weightings of the varied principles of interpretation, each uses a different translational hypothesis. This might impede the construction of an
empirical science of psychology: it might lead to squabbles about the
revisions most appropriate in case of anomaly, otherwise it would not
show. The position is a crude version of the view found in some
writings of C. I. Lewis and Russell – that meanings are private and
irrelevant to communication. As each uses a different system of translation, there is no answer to the question of which is correct – for each
strives to make his practice conform to that of the others.

A sceptical problem is thus raised. We may be able to use intuition
to render meaning determinate at the individual level, but this is
insufficient to fix meanings in a social context: a public intuition is
presumably required to resolve that. It is, perhaps, more natural to
respond by regarding the public language as some kind of construction
out of the range of private linguistic practices, conformity to the
public regularities providing a constraint on the adequacy of private
practices. One is using the language correctly if one's linguistic behaviour conforms to the public regularities: the choice of analytical
hypothesis or theory of interpretation is a pragmatic matter. It would
not be irrational to choose a particular hypothesis while suspecting that
it differed from those used by others: the public meanings come out
the same, if the private ones differ.

The tension between public and private meanings is unsatisfactory.
We can respond to it by removing the private intuition of intentional
content, thus asserting the primacy of public meaning, or by attempting to establish a form of public intuition in order to render intentional specifications determinate. Quine responds in the first way:

Brentano's thesis of the irreducibility of the intentional idioms is of a piece
with the indeterminacy of translation...One may accept the Brentano thesis
either as showing the indispensability of intentional idioms and the importance

[27] R. Chisholm, 'Sentences about Believing', *Proceedings of the Aristotelian Society*, n.s.,
56 (1955–6), 125–48.

of an autonomous science of intention, or as showing the baselessness of intentional idioms and the emptiness of a science of intention. My attitude, unlike Brentano's, is the second.[28]

There are philosophers who introduce the notion of a rule grounded in some kind of social practice, and claim that these rules render intentional characterisations determinate. At considerable risk of unfairness, we can cite Wilfrid Sellars and Peter Winch as examples of this trend.[29] If a speaker's use of an expression is to be guided by a rule, then it must surely be possible that the speaker be reflectively aware of what the rule demands. He has a belief about how the expression ought to be used, and this permits him critically to assess his linguistic behaviour. He must be aware, then, of the two possibilities of criticising his own conception of the rule in order better to conform to the linguistic practice of his community, and of criticising his own linguistic practice in accordance with the rule. In each case, it appears that this can be achieved only by establishing whether a public regularity conforms to the rule. But any public regularity conforms to many rules. Furthermore, as the rule is merely specified linguistically, determinate meanings are provided by the notion of a rule only if the two translation problems involved in rule use can be resolved and the meanings of the expressions used in the rule formulation are determinate. So, at first sight, there are problems for an attempt to use the notion of a rule to render meaning determinate. The notion of a social practice or 'form of life' is often introduced to resolve this difficulty. However, if the practice only shows itself as a regularity in social behaviour, it is difficult to see how it resolves the problem: the epistemological gaps remain. Unless a bizarre form of intuition of rule contrasts is introduced (as by Sellars's adversary Metaphysicus),[30] the possibility of indeterminacy seems to be provided for by the notion of a rule.

This becomes clearer if we consider a possible objection. A child is *taught* to use an expression in accordance with a particular rule. Thus, the argument for indeterminacy is just the claim that it is always conceivable that the child's practice has changed, which involves scepticism of the futile Cartesian variety. If semantical determinacy is established in the case of one's own linguistic behaviour, or that of someone one has taught – if he was taught in order that his behaviour be translatable homophonically, then there are only sceptical reasons

[28] Quine, *Word and Object*, p. 221.
[29] W. Sellars, 'Some Reflections on Language Games', in *Science, Perception and Reality* (London, 1963); Winch, *The Idea of a Social Science*.
[30] Sellars, *op. cit.*

for doubting that that scheme is not still correct – that provides a basis for empirically grounding psychological generalisations which can be employed in interpreting the linguistic behaviour of other members of the community, particularly because there will be a network of pupil–teacher relations connecting them. The weakness of the objection lies in its assumption that the teaching process produces determinacy. Of course, if the meaning of the rule formulation itself is indeterminate, that indeterminacy will be transmitted to the meanings of expressions used in accord with the rule. But what is more important is that the fact that the child's behaviour is conditioned so that the homophonic translation system will work does not entail that no other system will work or, if there are alternative systems, that only the homophonic system will be correct. Rather, the practice can be described in a number of different ways, and we may use different descriptions for different explanatory purposes. What emerges supports the indeterminacy thesis: teaching merely has to make possible the use of a particular translation theory.

How does this affect Winch's position? He seems to hold that the social context renders the rule formulations determinate, and concludes that there are difficulties facing one who attempts to interpret the behaviour of a society from the outside. If this is what he holds then we may object that he does not justify this theory of meaning, and that there is reason to think that the notion of rule cannot be made to do this kind of work. If we acknowledge that meaning is indeterminate, the problem he envisages disappears. However, there is a difficulty in this area, and possibly it is that with which Winch is concerned. We have noticed a difference between interpretative exercises directed at members of societies similar to one's own, and those directed at members of radically different societies, and we claimed that there is good reason to expect one theory of interpretation to be optimal in the first case – to have most of the virtues we seek in such theories. When the speakers whose language is being interpreted belong to a society radically different from our own, there is much less reason to expect this to be so. It follows from this that only in the first case is familiarity with the theory of interpretation likely to enable us to participate in the life of the community in question. Suppose, then, we wish to understand the behaviour of the community as they understand each other. We can do that, for we can provide a rationalising interpretation just as they do: but at the same time we cannot, for we cannot provide an interpretation that facilitates participation in their way of life. Winch appears to claim that an understanding that does not facilitate participation (where a strong notion of participation is involved) is necessarily distorting. But without the argument from the theory of meaning which we have seen reason to reject, it is far from clear why that is so. So while the indeterminacy thesis does not itself provide answers to the central questions of the philosophy of anthropology, it does enforce a certain perspective upon them which rules out some otherwise fruitful lines of approach.

Rational Man Theory[1]

PHILIP PETTIT

Every explanatory practice is the implementation of an explanatory theory, for if we are in the habit of invoking A-events to make sense of B-events, this means that we have a theory which countenances such events as items of substantive interest, and which construes regularities in their succession as matters of significance. My concern in this essay is with the practices of explaining human action represented by common sense and social science. I assume (1) that the theory of the human agent generally supposed in commonsense explanation depicts man as rational, and (2) that such a theory is that which social-science explanation of action ought also to suppose. What I wish to do is to give a sketch of 'rational man theory' and to impart a sense of the role it should play in social science. A full defence of my assumptions, and a full development of the view which they imply, is beyond the scope of a short paper.[2]

There are three sections to the essay. In the first I look at the *nature* of rational man theory, asking in particular about its structure, its status and the method of its selection. In the second I turn to the *function* of the theory: that is, the role which it serves within the ordinary organisation of our affairs. And, finally, in the third section I take up the question of its *application* in social science. Here I try to show that, even though it is implicit in common sense, rational man theory may underpin significant social-science inquiries.

[1] I would like to acknowledge the value of the criticisms that I received when this paper was read at a meeting of the Thyssen Philosophy Group in March 1976; I hope that I have gone some way towards meeting them in this revised version. I was also helped by discussions with Attracta Dunlop, Ross Harrison, Chris Hookway and Graham MacDonald.
[2] For some supplementation see P. Pettit, 'The Life-World and Role-Theory', in E. Pivcevic (ed.), *Phenomenology and Philosophical Understanding* (Cambridge, 1975), and 'Making Actions Intelligible', in R. Harre (ed.), *Life Sentences* (London, 1976).

I

A person's theory on any topic is the set of beliefs which he is prepared to avow about it plus those beliefs which he could be brought to recognise as implicit in his avowals. Or, to recast this in less psychological terms, a man's theory on any subject is the set of sentences in a specialised vocabulary (appropriate to the subject) which he is prepared to assert plus those sentences which follow from them by the man's own principles of inference.

There are three main questions to be raised about the make-up of any theory, and they are nicely formulated as inquiries after its structure, its status and the method of its selection. The problem with structure is to say how the sentences in the theory are internally ordered. The problem with status is that of how the theory should be thought of in relation to its subject matter – is it *a* picture of how things are, perhaps even an attempt at *the* picture, or something altogether unpictorial? And the problem with selection is: How do we argue that the theory should be chosen above its competitors – by appeal to the facts, by reference to formal or procedural criteria, or in some other manner?

In this discussion our concern is with a set of beliefs which is maintained by members of the commonsense community and upheld by social scientists who attach themselves to the image of rational man. We shall raise the questions of structure, status and selection in connection with the theory though we shall be able only to touch on many of the issues involved. The main fruit of the discussion will be the discovery that rational man theory is unusual in respect of its method of selection. This will lead us into the consideration, in the next section, of the function which such an unusually grounded theory can serve.

On the question of structure the first move suggested by the orthodoxy of positivism is to divide within each theory between analytic and synthetic – and, a crossing distinction, theoretical and observational – truths. The first distinction supposes that there are some truths imposed on a theory by its language, the second that there are some forced upon it by experience. But neither language nor experience has the independence of theory which these suppositions imply. If a theorist accepts truths which are tied up with his very use of words this does not mean that the truths are conventions about which he may have no choice: how he uses his words reflects his theory. And if on the other side he accepts truths which are directly borne out by experience this does not connote helplessness either, for how experience presents itself is determined by the theoretical assumptions on the basis of which it is described, assumptions which the theorist is free – at least in principle – to revise.

These points, without our enlarging on them further, give us reason to put aside the traditional distinctions within the sentences of a theory. But what divisions should we recognise then, if indeed we recognise any? Well, if we were to set out rational man theory in ordered fashion – say, in axiomatic form, in which we isolate a subset of sentences from which we show that the others follow by certain rules of inference – then it is likely that we should want to distinguish among at least three main classes of sentences. The first would be the set of logical truths determining what is implied in what within the theory, and we do not need to say any more about it in the present context. The second and third would be what I shall call, respectively, rational man postulates and rational man laws.

The best way of explaining what is meant by 'rational man postulates' is to give a list of propositions which might be accorded that title. Here I shall give a sketch expression of five postulates to which I believe that reflection will bring most of us to assent. Notice that they are propositions which, it is held, are at least implicit in commonsense beliefs; they need not be propositions which are explicitly avowed.

(1) Every human action springs from a desire or set of desires which, in view of the agent's beliefs, it promises to satisfy ('satisfy' defined in postulate 4).

(2) Every agent's desires, so far as they are properly human, are explicable by public standards of normality (see section II).

(3) Every agent's beliefs, so far as they are properly human, are explicable by public standards of normality (see section II).

(4) Beliefs and desires lead to action by familiar rational principles which it is the job of decision theory to spell out.[3]

(5) Beliefs, desires and decision principles can sometimes be construed in advance of action from past behaviour – assuming personal consistency – and from present circumstances – assuming commonness of response. Other factors, such as emotional expression, may also facilitate this sort of interpretation.

The distinction between rational man postulates and laws is essentially one of degree: in a strict sense of the term, the postulates count as laws of the theory too. But I shall reserve this term for the potential

[3] See Richard Jeffrey, *The Logic of Decision* (New York, 1965).

PHILIP PETTIT

infinity of true universal sentences which follow from the postulates
– or at least from the firm postulates, 1 to 4 – as theorems from axioms.
In each of these sentences a certain action situation is described, the
description presupposing a given pattern of beliefs and desires, and
a choice of action – the rational choice – is predicted. (Such laws presuppose procedural truths about how to establish beliefs and desires
– e.g., those employed in the Ramsey method described by Jeffrey[4] –
and these must derive from postulate 5. For simplicity's sake we leave
them out of our account of rational man theory.)

It is convenient to imagine rational man laws as conditionals in which
the antecedent is a matrix describing an action situation and the
consequent is the prediction of a rational choice. Whenever an agent
goes into action he is presented, in view of his *beliefs*, with (a) an array
of options, (b) a set of outcomes which he associates with each option,
and (c) an assessment, if such is available, of the likelihood of any
outcome ensuing in the event of the associated action being chosen.
The agent's *desires* enter this picture to determine the relative attraction or utility of each of the outcomes, the strength of which we may
suppose to be numerically representable. Thus the antecedent of any
rational man law may be expected to look something like this:

Option 1	First outcome	Second outcome	Third outcome
	Probability 0.25	Probability 0.25	Probability 0.5
	Utility 0.5	Utility 0.4	Utility 0.2
Option 2		First outcome	Second outcome
		Probability unknown	Probability unknown
		Utility 0.8	Utility 0.1
Option 3		Only outcome possible	
		Probability 1	
		Utility 0.45	

With such an antecedent the law will link, as consequent, the prediction
that a particular member, or at least a member of a particular subset,
of the options will be chosen, the option or options being indicated
by the decision-theoretic principles mentioned in postulate 4.

After structure the question which we must raise about rational man
theory is that of status. The debates involved in the status question
are between realism and anti-realism, conventionalism and essentialism, and monism and pluralism, but we shall only be concerned with
the first and third. The issue in the first debate is whether to take
rational man theory as a set of true or false sentences which say how
things, even perhaps unobservable things, are in the world. Anti-

[4] *Ibid.*

46

realism, which would deny the theory such a representational status, may take either of two forms: a reductionist one according to which the sentences are true or false but bear only on what is strictly observable, and an instrumentalist one which denies that they have truth values and claims that they are nothing more than convenient ways of organising expectations.

Let us take as our example not a sentence from within rational man theory but a sentence representing an application of it: the explanation that a particular agent chose A rather than B because he believed that it would satisfy, on any outcome, the desires that any outcome of B could be expected to satisfy. The realist would take this to attribute to the agent a strictly unobservable state of mind – whether or not reducible to a brain state – the occurrence of which is named as the cause of the choice of A. The reductionist would take it to be nothing more than the redescription of the choice of A as the attempt to satisfy the desires mentioned, a redescription without implications bearing on unobserved matters. The instrumentalist would take it as a way of engendering expectations about what might have happened had some condition been unfulfilled, or about what may yet happen should the agent be presented with a related decision – this without implying any factual truth connected with the agent or his action.

If we are to judge on the issue before us by reference to our intuitive sense of linguistic practice, then realism must surely come out as the doctrine to be espoused. When we give an explanation of the sort mentioned then we certainly commit ourselves to more than an account of how things observably are with the action performed. We at least imply, as the instrumentalist insists, that certain counterfactuals are warranted: we suggest, for example, that had the agent not believed that A had the property imputed to it he might not have acted in the way he did. But if this gets rid of reductionism, we get rid in turn of instrumentalism when we reflect that we would not hold by such a counterfactual unless we believed that there was something about the agent – something factually, but perhaps not observably, true of him – which explains why the hypothesis is defensible. Our practice in assigning rational man explanations and in drawing implications from them suggests that realism is the proper view to take of the theory.

There are arguments why we should revise our linguistic practice – or at least our assumptions about what it commits us to – taking on an anti-realist view of language, but we cannot try to review or counter them here.[5] Assuming that realism is an appropriate view to

[5] See John McDowell's paper in this volume.

adopt of rational man theory, the other question of status to which we must attend is whether to construe the theory on monist or pluralist lines. (The question, it may be noticed, arises in particularly acute form for someone who has judged for conventionalism rather than essentialism, but we have agreed not to consider that debate.)[6]

The issue between monism and pluralism may arise in connection with a single theory or a number of theories. Granted that we think of our sentences realistically, the question is: What view should we take of a case where a given body of data allows us to assert any one of a number of competing sentences, S1, S2 or S3? Pragmatically, we shall probably have to adopt one or other of the sentences as the thing to say, and in that case how should we think of those that we reject? If they are made from within the same theory and are incompatible with our chosen proposition, or if they translate from another theory so as to seem incompatible, should we simply say that they are false, thus espousing monism? Or should we perhaps refuse to mark off such sentences as true and false, taking reality to conform in some mysterious way with all?

When it is stated in this way, it should be clear that the issue engages our commitment to realism – at least so long as we take truth in the natural sense of correspondence with reality[7] – and that it allows us only to take a monist position. Incompatible sentences have truth conditions which we cannot conceive of as being simultaneously fulfilled, and if we assert one of the sentences we must deny the others. May we conclude then that we should view our rational man theory not just as a realistic representation of things but as one to which we must ascribe unique accuracy, to the extent that we endorse it? The answer is Yes, but in qualification it must be added that theory endorsement is compatible with reservation: we may believe in the possibility of an alternative which our ordinary criteria of theory selection would lead us to prefer. And may we conclude that if within the theory – that is, in applying it – we adopt one of a number of underdetermined but incompatible sentences, we should regard the chosen sentence simply as true and the others as false? Again the answer is Yes, but in qualification of it we must say something more than in the other case.

In particular it must be said that where we reject such sentences as being on the face of it incompatible with our chosen statement of

[6] For a conventionalist view, see W. V. O. Quine, *Word and Object* (Cambridge, Mass., 1960); for an essentialist view, see Hilary Putnam, 'The Meaning of "Meaning"', in Putnam, *Philosophical Papers*, vol. 2: *Mind, Language and Reality* (Cambridge, 1975).
[7] See John Mackie, *Truth, Probability and Paradox* (London, 1973), chap. 2.

things, we should be slow to declare them to be downright false. Quine's argument for the indeterminacy of translation, while it does not lead to pluralism in any strict sense, has shown that appearances of incompatibility can be seriously misleading in the ascription of propositional attitudes.[8] Such ascription is involved in the rational explanation of action, for such explanation imputes propositional attitudes to the agent – the belief or the desire *that such-and-such* – which parallel the attitudes ascribed in translation – the assertion, the request or the wish *that such-and-such*, for example.

The essence of Quine's case is that if we grant that there are no such language-independent objects as propositions – there are only language-specific sentences in which to express a man's propositional attitudes – then we must view many apparent incompatibilities of translation with a generosity which approximates to that of the pluralist. For consider a case where all the data available – and perhaps all the data imaginable – allow us to translate somebody's utterance in one of two incompatible ways, saying that he means that such-and-such or that not-such-and-such: we may assume that, as Quine argues, the case may indeed arise, and not just on exotic but on everyday occasions. If we reject the idea that there is a proposition lurking beneath the sentence used by the man, and if we decide that the sentence itself, and all the attendant translational evidence, is compatible with either construal, then what we have accepted is that there is no factual issue about which the rival translations into our own language are right or wrong. We must say that reality – all there is of it when we banish propositions – is indeterminate so far as the competing interpretations go or, less mischievously, that reality does not go so far – that it is determinate, but not up to the difference between the interpretations.

If we go along with Quine's rejection of propositions – as there seems every reason to do – we must be prepared to countenance not just underdetermination in the ascription of propositional attitudes, but also indeterminacy. However this does not make us pluralists in our view of rational man theory. It means only that we must allow that some choices within our application of that theory to another person or group of persons may be other than options about how to conceive of objective reality. They must now appear to us as choices with a practical significance only, like the choice between whether to make measurements in imperial or metric units.[9]

With the problems of structure and status behind us we turn finally to the question of how rational man theory is selected. The selection

[8] See Quine, *Word and Object*, chap. 2, and Christopher Hookway's paper in this volume.
[9] See Christopher Hookway's paper in this volume.

of theory is nicely represented by Mary Hesse in terms of an analogy with a learning machine.[10] The idea is that we think of a theory as a machine whose learning develops in interaction with an environment which provides a continual flow of data. What the theory has to do is to record and classify the data, subsume the observations made under a manageable set of general laws and use these laws to project future data, predicting what is likely to happen under different circumstances. The theory will be successful, establishing a stable equilibrium with its environment, if it develops such laws that it can handle any new piece of data coming in and if the projections which it makes on the basis of those laws do not fail to be fulfilled.

The analogy with the learning machine suggests that we think of the theory as having at least three distinct components: a receptor, a theoriser and a predictor. The receptor takes in the data provided by the external environment and processes it, delivering to the theoriser a set of sentences which represent in terms of a given stock of predicates the events observed. The theoriser – the theory proper – takes in these reports and seeks to display them as instances of general truths so that something like 'A P was found to be a Q' gets marked off as yet another example of the law that 'All Ps are Qs'. Finally, the predictor takes these generalisations from the theoriser and applies them to predictive purpose, spelling out what may be expected to happen in various concrete circumstances. These predictions, corroborated or undermined, become part of the empirical input which is delivered to the receptor: when they are borne out the theory's representation of the environment is vindicated, and when they are falsified the picture must be looked at again and amended.

The amendment of theory – the heart of the selection process – may be carried out, roughly speaking, at four different levels, as we can see if we imagine the different possible responses to the observation, contrary to the theory's laws, that a P is not a Q. (1) A first possible response is simply to amend the observation report, putting it down as a mistake: what was observed was not really a P or not really a Q. (2) A second reaction is to revise the stock of predicates on which the receptor draws, stipulating for example that a P of the sort that was found not to be a Q will no longer count as a P: the whale, not breathing through its gills, will no longer pass as a fish. (3) A third answer to the anomalous observation is to revise the law to the effect that 'All Ps are Qs' until it squares with the observation, amending it for example to 'All Ps under condition C – or of variety V – are Qs'.

[10] Mary Hesse, 'Models of Theory Change', in Patrick Suppes *et al.* (eds.), *Logic, Methodology and Philosophy of Science* (Amsterdam, 1973).

(A variant of this answer is where a law which is crucially related to the original one is revised, restoring correspondence with the data. It may be that the P in question was held not to be a Q on the grounds that it was an R, 'No Qs are Rs' being a law of the theory: in this case revision of the latter law will have the same effect as revision of the original one.) (4) Finally, if none of the other three responses proves capable of re-establishing a stable relationship with the environment, one of the set of suppositions within which the theory was conceived – something as deep as the physicalistic prejudices of natural science or the postulates of rational man theory – may be held up for question: this last move may entail a paradigm shift of the sort described by historians of science.[11]

The question which we must ask about rational man theory is whether we can imagine that it has come to be selected in the manner we have described. Does it look as though it is the product of amendment which has at last secured a stable equilibrium between the theory and its environment? The answer, to be quite curt about the matter, is that it does not. Rational man theory is 'soft-edged' in the sense that every apparently anomalous observation can be handled by response 1. The slightest reflection will bear this out. If we come across someone to whom we ascribe certain beliefs and desires on the basis of the factors mentioned in postulate 5, and we then find that he acts in a way which does not rationally accord with those psychological dispositions, we do not consider for a moment that the case provides a serious challenge to our rational man view of normal behaviour; we conclude without hesitation that we got the dispositions wrong in the first place or that they altered between the time of our imputation and the agent's action. And this is to say that we put down what seemed like an anomalous observation as being merely a mistake: we discount it and continue to cling to our theory. The move is one which is always at our disposal and, more than this, it is one to which we are always forced. For we cannot begin to imagine what it would be like to resort to any of the deeper responses in squaring rational man theory with observed behaviour. Someone sceptical about this point is invited to construct a plausible amendment on the lines of responses 2, 3 or 4, to which resort might be made in face of the appearance of irrationality.

It must be presumed that rational man theory fits human behaviour fairly well, since otherwise it would hardly be upheld in common life: indeed it may even be that people make it into a useful representation, matching their behaviour to the expectations it engenders. Being soft-edged, however, the theory cannot ever be shown not to identify

[11] See Thomas Kuhn, *The Structure of Scientific Revolutions*, 2nd edn (Chicago, 1970).

the springs of action accurately, and this fact makes espousal of the picture seem to be dogmatic and uncritical. We are thus led to inquire after the function which the theory serves in people's lives.

But before we do so it is necessary to consider an objection which could be raised against what we have just argued. It might be said that rational man theory comes out as soft-edged only because of the way in which we have divided it up, identifying the theory with general postulates and laws and distinguishing it from applications to particular persons or groups. If we identified the theory of nature with our most general beliefs concerning bodies – such as that if A and B and C are rigid bodies, and A is longer than B and B than C, then A is longer than C – perhaps it too would present itself as soft-edged, for we could scarcely consider revising such general beliefs in the light of empirical discoveries?

The suggestion is that rational man theory, so far as we apply it indiscriminately to other people, is a set of suppositions under the guidance of which we construct, for each individual person or group, a theory proper, this proper theory being in no way distinctive in its method of selection. We are no longer to think of there being one theory, consisting of logical truths, rational man postulates and rational man laws, but of there being a theory for each subject we try to understand. This theory contains in addition to the common stock of general propositions a set of ascriptions of specific beliefs, desires and decision principles. If we conceive of our theory in this way we are promised that we shall find nothing unusual about the way in which it is selected.

There is nothing to be said against the proposed way of counting our beliefs in theories other than that it is unorthodox, allowing propositions about individuals to be part of a theory, but it does not supply the promised rectification. For let us ask what happens to our theory of John Smith if we find on a given occasion that he acts quite irrationally so far as the beliefs and desires ascribed to him go. What can we do but, leaving the general postulates and laws untouched, revise one or other of the troublesome ascriptions? And while such a revision is on the face of it something deeper than response 1, it proves on a little reflection to be only a trivial variation of that response. It may now be that we are prepared to change our theory when confronted with unfulfilled predictions, but the only change we will allow is confined to the part of the theory consisting of specific ascriptions, and this costs us very little. The soft edge of rational man theory, as we choose to individuate that theory, reappears under the new dispensation as a soft centre.

II

We have given ourselves some idea of the nature of rational man theory: its structure, its status and the method of its selection. The topic to which we now turn is that of its function. By the function of a theory I mean the role which it plays within our way of organising our affairs, so far as this role is something invariant between people. The function of a theory in this sense may be expected to justify the interest taken in it, and to explain certain aspects of its nature.

Traditionally the function assigned to theory, at least within science, is that of prediction. That prediction is the overall end explains why theory conforms to the learning-machine model: the proof of the laws, but also their purpose, is that they enable the predictor component successfully to foretell what will happen under different specified circumstances. And that prediction is the overall end justifies the interest that we take in theory, for prediction is an attractive accomplishment, being a *sine qua non* of control.

Is prediction the primary function of rational man theory? A reason for saying that it is not is that, as we have seen, the theory does not lend itself to the sort of amendment by means of which it might become a really efficient predictive machine. The antecedents of its laws are held to be fulfilled in advance of action by reference to the sorts of factors mentioned in postulate 5, but the failure of the consequents to follow is always sufficient reason for withdrawing the claim that the antecedents were fulfilled. This means that the factors named in postulate 5 are not, and could never be, as tight as the indices by which the laws of ordinary scientific theory are held to apply. Even if the predictions which they lead us to make are often successful, these indices are not firm enough to allow us to make predictions with the confidence that we invest in the theory itself.

But if rational man theory is not designed after the manner we would expect in a streamlined predictive machine, it does still serve a predictive purpose. When I propose a rational explanation of a given piece of behaviour, attributing certain beliefs, desires and decision principles to the agent, I project associated behavioural patterns as likely to occur in succeeding and similar situations. This is because the explanatory factors invoked are all understood by us precisely as dispositions to do certain things in certain circumstances: thus, to believe that the cat is on the mat is to be disposed not to walk there, assuming at least that one desires not to trip, and not to disturb the cat.

The secondary predictive utility of rational man theory might well suggest that the function of the theory is still prediction and that it just happens in dealing with human beings that the function is best served by a soft-edged theory. Thus the complexity of human behaviour might be invoked to explain our resort to such a theory. It might be said that behaviour resists prediction on the basis of observable antecedents and that, as an alternative ploy, we work with the assumption that in every case it has unobservable antecedents – specifically, those which we would expect in a rational man. The utility of imposing the assumption is that if we find the antecedents in a given case then we lay hold of factors which we may expect to operate elsewhere in producing corresponding actions. Thus it gives us a certain predictive competence.[12]

This account of the function of rational man theory has the merit of not making such theory distinctive. And, besides, it gives due emphasis to the significant predictive utility attaching to rational explanation. But it is unsatisfactory in so far as it suggests that if we could find a hard-edged theory with which to make successful predictions about one another's behaviour, we would give up rational man theory in favour of it. The suggestion is unconvincing, for it is arguable that to give up treating people as rational would be to treat them exactly as natural causal systems, and that it is inconceivable that we should adopt this disposition towards one another – and if not towards one another at least towards ourselves. And if this claim is not granted, it must at least be acknowledged that we could not expect a hard-edged theory to be a very successful instrument of prediction, so long as the theory is a common possession: knowing the prediction which someone is bound to make about him, an agent might always set out deliberately to frustrate it. These considerations indicate that there is more to be said about rational man theory than that it constitutes the best instrument for predicting behaviour that we have been able in the history of the human race to devise.

Before following this thought through it may be useful to block the claim which someone might enter at this point, that we just *know* that rational man theory is the only possible way of explaining and predicting other people's behaviour, because in our own case we see that it is externally unobservable factors like beliefs and desires which produce behaviour. By this approach to the question, rational man theory is conceived as an instrument of prediction which we know from our own case to be the best available. Indeed, what applying the theory presumably amounts to is simply working out what one would do oneself in the circumstances of another agent, and why one might do it.

[12] See D. C. Dennett, 'Mechanism and Responsibility', in Ted Honderich (ed.), *Essays on Freedom of Action* (London, 1973).

The appeal to what one knows of oneself will not serve to bolster the view that rational man theory is merely the best predictive machine available because it relies on an uncritical notion of the sort of access we have to the sources of our behaviour. Beliefs, desires and decision principles are dispositions, and it is unclear how reflection could reveal to someone what he is disposed to do, other than by reference to behaviour he recalls or anticipates. Does he see into the grounds of the dispositions – the features of his mental or physical make-up which may be supposed to underlie his beliefs, desires and principles, being related to them as the molecular structure of glass is related to its fragility? Hardly, since no one ever thought that he could give an intrinsic description of those features on the basis of looking into himself.

It must be granted that a man does not have to rely on observing his own behaviour, in the way that others have to do, in order to learn what he believes or desires. But this can be explained without postulating any direct access to those psychological dispositions. To put the explanation in a few words, I maintain (1) that every agent has an immediate awareness under some description of what he has done, is doing or means to do; (2) that being informed in rational man theory he knows how what is done should be described and explained; and (3) that the combination of this awareness and this knowledge enables him to attribute beliefs and desires to himself without observing his behaviour as another might – indeed, in view of his awareness of his future actions he can ascribe them in advance of acting. The reference to future behaviour is important, for it means that when an agent says what he believes or wants he is not so much making a guess as giving a guarantee. He is committing himself to the course of action which will, by the criteria of rational man theory, vindicate the ascription of those psychological dispositions.

To return to the thought raised before this discussion of self-knowledge, I wish to propose that more can be said about rational man theory than that it is the best instrument available for predicting behaviour. An important feature of the theory which is neglected in this account may give us the cue for further ruminations: it is that by adopting a soft-edged theory of the kind in question we allow an agent control over the expectations that are formed of him. The grounds on which expectations are formed are not, as they would be with a hard-edged theory, objective indices which are realised independently of the agent's will. Rather they are the actions which the agent chooses to perform, for as we know it is ultimately his actions which decide what beliefs and desires we attribute to him.

PHILIP PETTIT

The agent's control over the expectations formed of him is explicitly exercised in the communicative act, where his primary aim is to invite a certain ascription of beliefs and desires, and the means on which he relies to secure it is the revelation – usually by conformity to a convention – of the aim itself.[13] But even in acting non-communicatively it may be presumed that the agent concerns himself in some measure with securing the ascription of certain psychological dispositions. Certainly this will be so where the action is performed in the known presence of other people, for he must take an interest in the expectations that they will form of him. And in so far as each agent is an audience to himself, forming expectations on the basis of his actions, rather than on private and inaccessible grounds, it will always be so. No agent can afford to disregard the expectations which his actions merit, for he has always at least to come to terms with his own assessment of himself.

The control of an agent over the expectations formed of him is not total, for if it were deception would be undetectable. Indeed, not only may we decide that a man does not mean to fulfil the expectations which he clearly intends us to form of him; we may also judge on occasion that though he does mean to fulfil them, accepting himself the ascription of belief and desire which he presents for our acceptance, he will not do so: he is not so much deceiving us as deceiving himself. Such a judgment we may present for the agent's own consideration, and, especially if his behaviour bears it out, it may be that he will accept it.

We have said that rational man theory is distinctive, not just in providing the best-laid expectations we are liable to get of someone else's behaviour, but specifically in providing expectations which *in general* may be presumed to carry the man's licence, being those which he assumes will be formed of him. But why is it significant that the theory engenders such licensed expectations: why may it give us some further insight into the theory's function? The answer is that only when we have licensed expectations of someone's behaviour – though we may also have expectations which we think the man ought to license – can we think of entering into interaction with him.

In interaction we form expectations of what the other person will do in various circumstances, particularly circumstances associated with certain overtures of ours, but these expectations must in general be such that we can take our respondent to recognise and ratify them, if only mischievously: for otherwise there is nothing to distinguish our

[13] See H. P. Grice, 'Meaning', *Philosophical Review*, 66 (1957); and P. F. Strawson, 'Intention and Convention in Speech Acts', *Philosophical Review*, 73 (1964).

disposition from that which we take towards a natural system at which we poke inquiringly. The significant thing about the licensed expectations given by rational man theory is that they fit the bill for interaction since, being precisely licensed, we may take the agent to be aware of them, and to acquiesce in their being formed of him. This we could not assume with the predictions that a hard-edged theory might have yielded of his behaviour. The indices at the root of such predictions would be firm and objective, and even if we had reason to believe that the agent was aware of the predictions, we would have no grounds for thinking that he meant to fulfil them.

The upshot of these remarks is that it would be seriously misleading just to say that rational man theory is a second-rate instrument for predicting human behaviour: we must also add that it is a predictive instrument specifically suited to giving those expectations required for interpersonal interaction. This is to say that there is sense in distinguishing the function of rational man theory from the function served by theory of the more familiar kind. Where ordinary theory gives predictions of the sort required for control, our theory gives expectations of the kind that interaction demands. Ordinary theory is designed to reveal its subject matter as a field for technological intervention; rational man theory is built to represent people as potential interactants.[14]

There are other matters which should be raised in connection with the function of rational man theory. It might be worth asking, for example, why the theory trades specifically in beliefs and desires, and whether its connection with interaction explains our often-remarked compulsion to view human behaviour as rational.[15] But it is not possible for us to pursue these questions here. Instead we must turn to the third topic which we said we would discuss, the place of rational man theory within social science.

[14] For a similar view, see Jurgen Habermas, *Knowledge and Human Interests* (London, 1972).
[15] See Quine, *Word and Object*; and cf. also Donald Davidson, 'Radical Interpretation', *Dialectica*, 27 (1973); Davidson, 'Belief and the Basis of Meaning', *Synthèse*, 27 (1974); Davidson, 'Psychology as Philosophy', in S. C. Brown (ed.), *Philosophy of Psychology* (London, 1974); Richard Grandy, 'Reference, Meaning and Belief', *Journal of Philosophy*, 70 (1973); David Lewis, 'Radical Interpretation', *Synthèse*, 27 (1974); Martin Hollis, 'The Limits of Irrationality', in Bryan Wilson (ed.), *Rationality* (Oxford, 1970).

III

We have discussed the nature and the function of rational man theory, and we come finally to the question of how it may be scientifically applied. The problem here is whether we undermine the prospect of significant social inquiry if we demand that the inquiry implement a theory which is already present in common sense.

Well, there are three traditional disciplines which remain substantively interesting even when it is recognised that the theory which they generally suppose is the rational man model: these are history, anthropology and economics. History and anthropology are distinctive disciplines because they apply the model at a chronological or cultural distance. Economics is distinctive because it uses the model to a special predictive effect: specifically, it postulates in economic men such beliefs, desires and decision principles as enable it to explain the actions and the (perhaps unforeseen) outcomes that characterise the economic world, thus providing itself with a means of predicting, within certain limits of accuracy and assurance, the economic results to be expected under various imagined circumstances.

If history, anthropology and economics have always tended to apply the rational man model of the human agent, traditional sociology has often rejected it, picturing man as a cultural dope, an ideological dolt or a role-bound dimwit. This however has begun to change with the appearance, often in widely divergent schools, of a new sociological individualism.[16] The question which we must ask in connection with a rational man sociology is whether we see a role that it can play, distinct from the role played by common sense.

Macro-sociology, when it is done in an individualistic fashion, can claim much the same justification as that attaching to economics, for its attempts to explain certain institutional features as the (perhaps unintended) result of rational human action, thus making prediction possible in some limited cases. But micro-sociology or social psychology – the study of human beings in their social milieux – is a different matter. Some of it may count as the quasi-anthropological description of unrecognised codes and conventions, but the most ambitious part, the social psychology of behaviour, resists any such characterisation. It presents itself as an attempt to do something which it may be thought that common sense does perfectly well already: to explain patterns of behaviour that are native to our society and familiar to

---

[16] See, for example, James Coleman, 'Social Structure and a Theory of Action', in P. M. Blau (ed.), *Social Structure* (London, 1976), and Anthony Giddens, *New Rules of Sociological Method* (London, 1976).

everyone within it. The problem here is to explain how such a rationalistic social psychology can hope to provide something that is not already available to every man of common sense. We shall devote the remainder of this essay to a discussion of it, for it raises difficulties in the relationship between social science and common sense which are at once pervasive and elusive.

For an example of a social-psychological account of behaviour we may take the explanation given by Stanley Milgram of the response manifested by the subjects in his famous experiment; the account, as it happens, is derived from Erving Goffman, one of the best-known exponents of a rationalistic approach to action.[17] In Milgram's experiment innocent volunteers were recruited for what was alleged to be an attempt to measure the effect of punishment on learning. Each volunteer turned up with someone who presented himself as another volunteer but who was in fact a hired actor. The actor was selected by the experimenter to play the experimental part of learner – the selection appeared to be determined by drawing lots – and the volunteer was given the role of teacher. Under the instructions of the experimenter the volunteer administered learning tasks to the actor and punished each mistake. The punishment consisted in the application, by a complex remote control, of ever more severe electric 'shocks': the actor was strapped in a chair and, it seemed, just had to undergo these. The lesson of the experiment was that most of the volunteers were prepared to obey the experimenter to the point of ignoring the simulated protests, and eventually the ominous silence, of the actor, giving him what they took to be shocks of up to 450 volts.

Milgram's account of the obedient behaviour of the volunteers is nicely summed up in this passage:

Goffman...points out that every social situation is built upon a working consensus among the participants. One of its chief premises is that once a definition of the situation has been projected and agreed upon by participants, there shall be no challenge to it. Indeed, disruption of the accepted definition by one participant has the character of moral transgression. Under no circumstance is open conflict about the definition of the situation compatible with polite social exchange.

...Since to refuse to obey the experimenter is to reject his claim to competence and authority in this situation, a severe social impropriety is necessarily involved.

The experimental situation is so constructed that there is no way the subject can stop shocking the learner without violating the experimenter's self-

[17] E. Goffman, *The Presentation of Self in Everyday Life* (Harmondsworth, 1969).

definition. The subject cannot break off and at the same time protect the authority's definitions of his own competence. Thus, the subject fears that if he breaks off, he will appear arrogant, untoward, and rude.[18]

The sort of rationalistic social psychology invoked by Milgram has an intuitive interest and validity. The problem before us, however, is to explain how it can claim to be anything more than common sense, since it has neither the predictive potential of economics nor the exotic appeal of history or anthropology. Two propositions which we can extract from our earlier discussion will be helpful in dealing with the question. The first is that the best explanation of a particular action is not definitively settled by the conditions mentioned in postulate 5 and/or the physical nature of the behaviour itself; and the second, that among the explanations which these factors leave us free to contemplate, that one is preferable which maximises the potential for interaction. The first proposition comes from our account of the nature of rational man theory: the action itself in any instance must leave us free to consider explaining it by one belief–desire matrix or another, and the conditions mentioned in postulate 5, being of necessity loose, cannot be expected to constrain our further choice to one option; this indeed is the reason why we may reject the explanation invited by the agent in favour of a candidate of our own. The second proposition springs from our ruminations on the function of rational man theory, for if the guiding interest of that theory is to represent people in a way which allows us to see how we might enter into interaction with them, it must be that of a set of plausible explanations of an action we should select that one (where there is such) which lets us best see how to interact with the agent.

What the first proposition entails, for our purposes, is that the application of rational man theory, the pursuit of rational man explanations, is not a science so much as an art. Within the traditional sciences it is characteristic of theory that it provides laws with such conditions of application that in a given instance there is no doubt about which of the laws applies. The feature of rational man theory, by contrast with this, is that it leaves the individual theorist room for imagination and initiative when it comes to selecting the law – if we should still speak of laws – by which to explain a particular event. There is an art to the explanation of action; it is not something constrained by exact manuals.

This, it should be remarked, does not make rational man theory unique. Elsewhere I have argued that a narrative – or, more generally,

---

[18] S. Milgram, *Obedience and Authority* (London, 1974), p. 150: Milgram writes 'subject' for 'learner' – an obvious slip – in the next-to-last sentence. See also Goffman, *op. cit.*

an aesthetic – theory such as structuralism provides cannot generate a science, but only an art, of narrative analysis (see Pettit, *The Concept of Structuralism*). The structuralist theory, consisting in something like the postulates we isolated in the rational man case, gives a novel framework within which to view narratives, identifying certain properties and elements as the objects of theoretical interest. However, two individuals may bring the framework to bear on the same text without having it force them to the same analytical conclusions. The theory leaves them discretion in how to apply it, making narrative analysis an enterprise of art, not a matter of following an algorithm.

Because the application of rational man theory is an art, we can begin to understand why there should be room for a social psychology, side by side with common sense. Just by being possessed of common sense, we are equipped to practise the art of rational man explanation. But common sense, proverbially, is narrow. The justification of a rationalistic social psychology can only be that it provides a broader vision of the springs of action than that which people usually attain. The claim is that just like a Jane Austen, a George Eliot or a Henry James, someone like Goffman expands ordinary horizons and lets us see at the origin of human behaviour concerns to which the habit of common sense normally blinds us.

But it is not enough to say merely that the explanations offered in social psychology are broader than those of common sense; some more specific mark of their alleged superiority needs to be named. And here we may make use of the second proposition mentioned above. If the social-psychological explanations really are superior then it is natural to claim that their particular virtue lies in the fact that they create a greater potential for interaction.

A distinguishing mark of commonsense accounts of action is that when the ordinary patterns of accepted behaviour are broken, they resort quickly to what may be called quasi-rationalistic explanation. In such explanations an action is traced in the familiar way to a belief–desire matrix, but some aspect of this configuration is explicable only on the assumption that the agent is under an influence that pushes him towards the margins of normality. Typically, to suggest some examples, he is taken to be overcome by passion, to be blinded by a physiological condition, to be the victim of some habits or illusions or to be the product of a deprived or brutalising environment. By invoking such factors quasi-rationalistic explanations have the effect of distancing us from the agents whose behaviour is explained: if we enter into open exchange with them then we must make manifest an assumption of dissimilarity which redounds to our credit rather than theirs, casting them in the role of being relatively deviant. This parallels in a minor way what happens when we give up on the assumption of rationality altogether and treat some people as mad.

Rationalistic social psychology, I suggest, is a significant discipline because it often succeeds in providing full rational man explanations of human behaviour where common sense resorts to quasi-rationalistic ones. Thus, for example, it seeks to account for the actions of football hooligans or street vandals in a manner which reveals greater possibilities of interaction than the traditional 'They're just delinquents'. This latter story gives us no idea of how we might begin to have an exchange with the people in question, suggesting that the only possible reaction is the impersonal 'They need to be taught a good lesson': the point becomes not to communicate with the offenders but to change them. A rationalistic social psychology would presumably take a different tack from this since it would strive to relate the behaviour to beliefs and desires which, granted the circumstances of the agents, we find readily explicable. The account it offered might be less comforting for us, forcing on us the recognition that we are no different from them; and it might also be less flattering for the offenders, representing their behaviour as calculating rather than spontaneous, for example. Its virtue would be that it let us see the agents as potential if not appealing interactants; however unpalatable the fact, it would allow us to recognise them as ordinary men.

This would be a fine moral note on which to end but, by way of a coda, I would like to add that there is a pattern in the sort of rationality which social psychology usually unearths, a pattern to which we may give the name of 'reflexivity'. The insight which has dominated recent writing in the field is that common sense, in its rational man explanations of behaviour, does not give sufficient recognition to people's reflexive habit. This is the habit of concerning oneself not just with something straightforward like pleasure or money or power but with the effect – on one's self-image or on the image formed of one by others – of being seen to have that straightforward desire.

It is assumed within the tradition represented by Goffman that human beings are consummate and incorrigible game-players who, if they explain each other's behaviour at one level, are always themselves a level higher. If they invoke concerns A, B and C in explanation of action, they open themselves thereby to the influence of further unavowed concerns – desires to be seen to have, or not to have, A or B or C. This reflexivity, which it is of the essence of common sense to overlook, is what creates an opening for rationalistic social psychology.

The claim may be vindicated by reference to our original example. When Milgram explains the obedient behaviour of his subjects by their concern with maintaining frame – that is, the definition of their situation – we see art in action, liberating us from common sense. Without this explanation we might have been forced to describe the subjects as sadistic, thus minimising the humanity of their desires and making it difficult to see how we should communicate with them. But the inspiration behind this art is no capricious muse; it is the idea of reflexivity. As Milgram says, the subjects' concern is that, if they break off, they will appear arrogant, untoward, and rude. Rather than appear to act out of such dispositions, they prefer not to act at all, and so they continue with the experiment.

The concern with maintenance of frame is just one example of a reflexive concern. Another is the concern which ethnomethodologists invoke with doing things that are 'accountable'. And yet further examples, drawn from a wide range of literature, are concerns with conformity to role, position among peers, reference-group approval, and so on. Goffman may be the messiah of rationalistic social psychology, but there have also been other prophets.

Enough has been said to vindicate the claim of social psychology, even when it trades in rational man explanations, to have a distinctive contribution to make to our stock of knowledge. And what, in con-clusion, is the destiny of such social psychology? It can only be to vanish into common sense, as the lessons of the discipline are popularly learned. In those enlightened days there is little saying what will happen, for men will have put themselves in a position to go a reflexive level further, acting out of a concern with being seen (or not being seen) to act out of a concern with being seen (or not being seen) to act out of a concern...Perhaps it will be the time when another Goffman, his hour come round at last, slouches towards Bethlehem to be born.

Maximising, Moralising and Dramatising[1]

ALAN RYAN

Towards the end of *The Presentation of Self in Everyday Life,* Erving Goffman writes, 'The claim that all the world's a stage is sufficiently commonplace for readers to be familiar with its limitations and tolerant of its presentation, knowing that at any time they will be able to demonstrate to themselves that it is not to be taken too seriously.'[2] The object of this essay is to ask, How seriously is too seriously? Since one perfectly plausible answer to that question is offered both in *The Presentation of Self in Everyday Life* and in *Frame Analysis* – an answer which reminds us that what goes on on the stage isn't *real* – some justification is needed for making more fuss than that about so-called dramaturgical explanation. If we know why we should not take the dramatic analogy too seriously, do we need to take it seriously at all?

The justification for doing so runs something like this. A large part of social science requires us to explain why actors act as they do in the situations in which they find themselves. To explain their behaviour is to reconstruct what Popper terms 'the logic of the situation'.

---

[1] I have to apologise for what follows on two not unrelated counts. In the first place, this is a very unfinished essay, in which many more hares are started than are caught, where several swans turn out to be wild geese, and where in short an area in the philosophy of the social sciences which desperately needs a good deal of tidying up is left as scruffy as before. In the second place, I have not made much effort to incorporate the discussion to which the paper was subjected at the meeting of the Thyssen Philosophy Group at Easter 1976 in the body of this revised version. The explanation of this lamentable omission is this: the bulk of the paper was intended to offer something which both Professor Goffman – who was at the meeting – and philosophers not primarily interested in the philosophy of the social sciences might find relevant. It emerged, however, that, like other social scientists, Professor Goffman found philosophical discussions useful as a source of empirical hypotheses (cf. E. Goffman, *Frame Analysis* (Cambridge, Mass., 1974)), or as sketches of mechanisms to be found in social life, but that, again like most social scientists, he was not much concerned with problems in the logic of explanation, not much concerned to distinguish one kind of explanation from another. To that extent, therefore, the hope that one could so to speak try out a first draft on Professor Goffman, and clear one's mind in the process, was not fulfilled. Accordingly, I have added a short concluding note to summarise some issues which the discussion seemed to raise. Otherwise, I have simply tried to make this essay as lucid as I can.

[2] Goffman, *The Presentation of Self in Everyday Life* (New York, 1959), p. 254.

This, again, can plausibly be represented as explaining their behaviour in terms of their doing what is, in some sense yet to be explained, 'the thing to do'.[3] It is a commonplace of recent sociology that the concern of traditional sociologists with social structure, with invariant relationships rather than varying personnel, often led to the assumption that 'the thing to do' and the actor's belief that it was indeed 'the thing to do' could be read off from some universally agreed description of the social role occupied by the actor. Hence, one mode of explanation by situational logic would simply be that of discovering an actor's role, and inferring what it required him to do on a given occasion. To understand what an agent did would simply be to understand what role he was filling. There are, no doubt, far more questions raised than answered by such a claim. It tells us nothing about why a given society recognises the roles it does; it does not suggest any way of discriminating between those bits of activity which are role-fulfilling and those bits which are not. All this is commonplace.

Appeals to roles leave out questions of motivation in particular. That is, at one level, we may suppose the question 'Why did Smith shoot himself after he had been slapped by the pork butcher?' is answered when we are told that Smith was an officer in a crack regiment. To be slapped by a social inferior with whom it was impossible to settle the matter by duelling would be to be dishonoured; only suicide could restore his honour and that of the regiment. But, what we do not know is why he was so committed to the code that he was willing to accept death rather than dishonour. This suggests that if we want to know why someone does what he does, we must look to the goals he is seeking, and to his beliefs about their rewardingness to himself. The assumption underlying the demand is the belief that men do what they find it most rewarding to do – even if, to paraphrase Homans, they find the damnedest things rewarding.[4]

This assumption provides the general structure of an answer to the question about an actor's motivation for doing what, as we say, 'the role requires' him to do. The answer to the question of why Smith shot himself is that he found death more rewarding than dishonour, or that, of all the actions available to him, death by his own hand was the most rewarding. This still leaves unanswered the question of why he finds death the most rewarding of the available options; none the less, we should have no trouble in principle, at least, in providing a genetic account of how he came to feel that he would rather die than live dishonoured. The structure of explanation would be to assume

[3] I. Jarvie, *Concepts and Society* (London, 1972), chap. 1.
[4] G. C. Homans, *The Nature of Social Science* (New York, 1967).

that what was done was the most rewarding thing to do, and to answer questions about how it can have been such in terms of the individual's socialisation. Sometimes we are unlikely even to be tempted to invoke the role a person occupies, when explaining his behaviour in maximising terms. The man who is dying of a painful disease and who therefore shortens the process by taking an overdose of sleeping tablets is quite readily represented as calculating that if the returns on being dead are zero, the returns on dying slowly and painfully are negative, so that the rational choice is to be dead sooner rather than later.

There is some tendency for writers to oppose role-filling and returns-maximising models, as if the fact that one account talks about 'officers' and the other about Smith, Jones and Wilkinson placed them in competition. Of course, this isn't so. There is much to be said about an excessive reliance on the concept of a role or, relatedly, on the concept of a norm, and the dangers of assuming that men will just do what they think they ought, or what their role requires; and there is much to be said about the dangers of tautology in the returns-maximising model, as well as more sophisticated things about which elements of a theory of motivation we can safely agree to be tautological and which elements we must at all costs preserve as vulnerable to empirical test. Still, the immediate point is simply to observe that there are both actors and roles, that *Smith* is an officer, and that *an officer* is what Smith is.

It is this insistence on preserving both aspects of the role-filling and returns-maximising model which lets in the third view of how to determine what 'the thing to do' is. We accept both premises of the previous models; there are roles with rights and obligations attached to them, and rights and obligations do provide *reasons for action*, and can, therefore, feature in the explanation of why an actor did what he did: but there are also agents who are individual, flesh and blood creatures who are not bundles of rights and duties, and who have goals, wants, wishes, purposes of their own. Explanations of social behaviour must accommodate both persons and parts, just as an explanation of a game of chess needs to accommodate not only the rules which lay down what moves each piece can make, and what counts as victory and defeat, but also the aims of the players, their skills, their temperaments and so on. The sociologist may, perhaps, rest content with giving a structural description of a society's role structure – and no one reading Siegfried Nadel could be in any doubt about the importance and the difficulty of so doing.[5] But, if we want to explain what

[5] S. F. Nadel, *The Theory of Social Structure* (London, 1957), pp. 20ff.

happens during some strip of social interaction, we need both roles and actors, both the recognised rights and obligations and the hopes, fears, skills and weaknesses which the actor brings with him in filling his roles.[6] It is an insistence on this which seems to mark out the 'dramatistic', 'dramatic' or 'dramaturgical' approach to the study of social interaction.[7] (I'm not sure that anything hangs on which of these expressions one adopts.)

I now broach the question which will haunt what follows, even though little of what follows tackles it explicitly. This is the question whether the dramaturgical model insists on the theatricality of social life merely in the sense of insisting that *people* fill roles, just as persons act parts in a play; that they can, therefore, cease to fill them, can at all times fill them with more or less commitment to the standard goals and purposes which the roles appear to presuppose; that they can, at least sometimes, stand back from their own performance of the role and ask themselves why they are bothering to go on with it when they could be doing something more interesting or more agreeable; that they can take advantage of the role to indicate to others that they are not quite the people they seem from the performance they are putting on.[8] That is, it is the question whether the crucial element in the dramaturgical picture is that cluster of insights which goes under the general heading of 'role distance'. Or is the crucial element the claim that style is the man; that we leave out the *aesthetic* dimension of social life at the risk of misunderstanding much of what goes on; that when people put on a good performance of some social part, this is not simply a device for leaving in other people's minds the impression that they are peculiarly estimable or admirable, nor necessarily to plant in other people's minds false beliefs about the terms on which they are prepared to co-operate in the projects of others, to exchange benefits with them or whatever? Is it, perhaps, the claim that the only way in which we can accommodate the twin pressures of social life on the one hand and of our private selves on the other is by turning that process of accommodation into a work of art, into a project which is better understood by poets, playwrights and novelists than by cost–benefit analysis or the functionalist analysis of roles?

Antoine de Saint-Exupéry was very fierce about a young man who pulled on a pair of white gloves before blowing his brains out.[9] Was he complaining of the 'theatricality' of the gesture? If he was, are we

[6] Goffman, *Frame Analysis*, pp. 573ff.
[7] Cf. S. M. Lyman and M. B. Scott, *The Drama of Social Reality* (New York, 1975), and R. Harré and P. F. Secord, *The Explanation of Social Behaviour* (Oxford, 1972).
[8] E. Goffman, *Encounters* (New York, 1961), chap. 3.
[9] Saint-Exupéry, *Sand, Sea and Stars* (Harmondsworth, 1966), p. 25.

to infer that there is a distinction between serious matters and matters susceptible to dramatic renditions; or are we to infer that serious matters are susceptible to dramatic rendition, precisely because theatricality is a vice which destroys good drama and only good drama?

So much by way of introduction. I now want to say something – though I do not know how to say enough – about the peculiarities of rational explanation, and about the role of reconstructions of 'the thing to do' other than the role of explaining an action or series of actions. To do this, I take a brief look at the perhaps overworked problem of accounting for voting behaviour in the terms proposed by Anthony Downs's *An Economic Theory of Democracy*.[10] All this leads on to the suggestion that if the world both is and must be rather short of people who are rationally maximising values – either returns to themselves or some other value[11] – it is no wonder that social scientists should turn their attention to some of the non-maximising activities in which people are engaged, such as staging social dramas or planning their lives as works of art. This remains nothing better than a suggestion, for reasons which become sufficiently obvious when we turn to some recent accounts of the phenomenon of suicide (and of Durkheim's *Suicide*).

It would be pointless to adduce as an explanation of an action the good reasons for doing it unless we accepted something like 'the principle of rationality'[12] which Popper calls 'false but indispensable' to the social sciences. Yet, as Popper's characterisation of it suggests, it is a strange principle; it can hardly be a generalisation from particular cases, for all the familar reasons about the impossibility of identifying the explanandum in particular cases without already presupposing the principle. Thus, we seem to be left to read the principle as a conceptual truth, or as a heuristic principle. That is, we might construe the principle of rationality not as saying that by and large men do the thing to do but as the conceptual claim that what a (rational) action *is* is what an agent does because it is (in some sense or other) the thing to do; to read it thus would be to take it in something like the way Kant takes the principle of universal causality. Or we might treat it as a heuristic principle, which tells us not to give up trying to find reasons for a piece of human behaviour, not to rest content with any explanation that does not show how what happened was at least subjectively the thing to do. People who are sceptical about

[10] A. Downs, *An Economic Theory of Democracy* (New York, 1957), pp. 261 ff.
[11] Cf. A. Heath, 'The Rational Model of Man', *European Journal of Sociology*, 15 (1974), 200ff.
[12] J. W. N. Watkins, 'Imperfect Rationality', in R. Borger and F. Cioffi (eds.), *Explanation in the Behavioural Sciences* (Cambridge, 1970), pp. 172–9.

ALAN RYAN

heuristic interpretations of such principles might reflect on the work
of, say, R. D. Laing, where the principle is adopted in very unpromis-
ing circumstances, in order to try to render the behaviour of
schizophrenics intelligible.[13] The attraction of this is that it brings back
into the fold of human actions events which would have to be taken
otherwise as things which merely *happened* to the schizophrenic
patient.

If the rationality principle is not a conceptual truth or a heuristic
principle, it is hard to know what else it might be. As an empirical
generalisation about men generally doing the right thing it is pa-
thetically false, in view of the unfortunate human proneness to error.
If it is to be read more narrowly, as it would be, for instance, by many
sociologists when they claim that rational behaviour is common in
economic matters but not in social life generally, then 'rational' is
clearly being interpreted much more narrowly than it is here – either
in such a way as to fulfil Weber's account of *Zweckrationalität*, or in some
sense equivalent to Pareto's account of logical action.[14]

What this means is that, on one view, to show that an action was
in any sense 'the thing to do' just is to show that it was the rational
thing to do, for showing that it was the thing to do is rationally
explaining it. On the other view, to show that it is the thing to do is
to render it intelligible; to show that it is the *rational* thing to do is to
go one step farther. There is no easy way to tell what hangs on the
choice of a more or less restrictive account; if we want to insist on the
significant differences between explanations in terms of people's goals
and knowledge on the one hand and straightforward causal explanation on the other, presumably we shall have no objection to the wider
usage; if we want to insist on how differently the artist, poet or priest
shapes his means to his ends from the way the entrepreneur and
engineer shape theirs, we shall presumably want to narrow the notion.

Downs's book, *An Economic Theory of Democracy*, illustrates some of
the problems we are faced with here. Downs's book expands on a
suggestion implicit in Schumpeter's *Capitalism, Socialism and Democracy*
to the effect that political parties and voters can be understood as if
they were firms on the one side and consumers on the other.[15] Voters
spend their votes to secure the greatest possible flow of utilities from
the policies which political parties will implement if they gain office.
Political parties are assumed to have only one aim, that of securing

[13] R. D. Laing, *The Divided Self* (Harmondsworth, 1965), pp. 18–38.
[14] I. Jarvie and J. Agassi, 'The Problem of the Rationality of Magic', in B. R. Wilson
(ed.), *Rationality* (Oxford, 1970), p. 173.
[15] Downs, *Economic Theory of Democracy*, p. 29n.

power by selling their policies to as many voters as possible. Initially, Downs credits all parties with much the same omniscience that the theory of perfect competition assumes in orthodox economics, but the analysis gets exciting only when real-life phenomena analogous to brand loyalty and information costs are allowed to intrude. The best-known crux, however, arises when we make only the assumption that voting is an activity with opportunity costs; for, once voting is allowed to have costs, Downs sees that it is very hard to explain why people vote *at all*. The rational voter operates with some estimate of what difference it will make to his overall utility if one party rather than another should win; what he then has to work out is whether the chance that his vote will make all the difference between the 'right' and the 'wrong' party winning, multiplied by the difference it makes for the 'right' party to win, is a larger sum than the cost of voting rather than doing any of the things he would rather do. Now, it is evident that in a large electorate the chances that any given individual's vote will make all the difference are tiny; the value of the voting act, therefore, is tiny also, since it is unlikely that the party differential is so enormous that it would make a serious difference to the result. Hence, if voting has any cost at all, the voter won't vote – not if he's rational, that is.

Downs begins his book by suggesting that the only point of a theory is to predict what happens, and therefore commits himself to the view that the only proper course of action when we are faced with such a divergence between what the theory demands voters should do and what voters actually do do is to junk the theory. One would suppose, therefore, that Downs would simply throw out the hypothesis that voters are acting to maximise their utility flow. In fact, he does not do so. So strong is the grip of the theory that he looks round for something other than the party differential to supply the voter's pay-off. Thus, he suggests that the voter is not just voting for the party which offers him the better deal, but also voting to sustain democratic government too. If fewer than a certain number of voters turn out, democracy will collapse; the voter, therefore, has to consider the costs to himself if the whole system were to collapse. This, in essence, is a way of pushing up v (the utility of an outcome) to compensate for the smallness of p (the probability of its occurring under specified conditions). And like other arguments addressed to self-interested persons in order to induce them not to free-ride, it is bound to fail if the odds against their individual contribution being decisive one way or the other are very high. The odds against any single voter's participation or abstention being decisive are so enormous that the self-inflicted costs of abstention are bound to be very low, no matter how much the individual may dislike the prospect of the collapse of democracy.[16]

Now, here two avenues open up which we ought to keep distinct. The first is that which leads us to investigate what decision rules people do use, in order to see why they make decisions which pure utility-maximisers might not make – supposing they were infallible in their estimate of the probabilities attaching to the various outcomes. In essence, we should stick to the view that people were acting self-interestedly, but look more closely at how they did so, in order to see whether they were, perhaps, satisficers rather than maximisers, or whether they were intendedly maximisers but had curious views about probability. Now, along these lines there are many interesting results we might want to investigate. For instance, the phenomena of football pools and insurance companies suggest two things – that when we are faced with the prospect of really large losses we overestimate the danger of their occurrence and thus accept odds which a true utility-maximiser would not, and that when we are faced with a really large gain we are prepared to gamble a small amount at odds which the utility-maximiser strictly ought to reject. Downs might, along these lines, have argued that voters will overestimate the possibility of system collapse, or else that there is a threshold below which they do not count costs at all, and would happily vote in the same frame of mind as they would spend fivepence on a lottery ticket. But Downs takes the second line, which is to treat as sacrosanct the assumption that men are utility-maximisers, and to then look round to see *what* yields them a utility. Downs tinkers with the pay-off to the voter by suggesting that the pleasures of a satisfied conscience make it worth the voter's while to go and do his duty and vote. It is, of course, an empirically well-confirmed view that people's disposition to vote at all correlates much more closely with the strength of their sense of 'citizen duty' than with their perception of the differences between the parties. This certainly suggests that the first version of Downs's theory is less likely to hold water than the second version.[17]

But, of course, once we allow 'doing one's duty' to feature in the desires of the agent, we run into exactly those troubles which Macaulay so enjoyed pointing out to James Mill.[18] The theory that men maximise their flow of utility loses its explanatory stuffing. We begin with the

[16] B. M. Barry, *Sociologists, Economists and Democracy* (London, 1970), pp. 45f.
[17] *Ibid.* pp. 17f.
[18] T. B. Macaulay, 'Mill on Government', in *Works*, vol. 7 (Edinburgh, reprint of 1902), p. 354.

belief that when rational behaviour is thought to be utility-maximising behaviour, we can find some simple constraints on the sort of thing which will yield men a utility – such as money income. We then find ourselves baffled, because if men were acting to maximise money returns, say, they would not vote at all. Now, when we stand by the notion that they must be maximising something or other, we end up with a different theory and a different empirical task. We do not have a predictive, falsifiable, and indeed falsified theory; what we have is an analytical framework into which we try to fit a rather different predictive theory, if we can find one.

Faced with the failure of utility-maximising models to do as much as they promised to tidy up the explanation of choice, one can see why people have been attracted to alternative models, such as the dramaturgical. But it can hardly be said that the model has received what one might take to be a definitive statement, or to have been spelled out in such a way as to achieve consensus on what its scope and limits are. The situation is not helped by the fact that the writer with whom the model is most frequently associated, Erving Goffman, has more than once done his best to get out from under its shadow. That is, a good deal of *Frame Analysis* is devoted to denying that everything is a piece of theatre; Goffman insists that events in everyday life have *real* consequences in a way that events depicted on the stage do not, and he spends the bulk of a particularly engaging chapter elaborating the devices by means of which we make sure that what happens on the stage is *not* taken to be part of real life.[19] The topic is not an easy one to keep clear; but a small start might be made if we were careful to distinguish between *pretending* and *depicting*. It is important that the actor who plays Othello does not *pretend* to be Othello in anything like the sense in which the con-man pretends to be a gas-meter reader; his playing of Othello is not at all intended to mislead anyone into supposing that he *is* Othello, whereas it is of the essence of the con-man's activity that he should induce us to believe that he really is the gas man, and just as it is an essential part of the fraudulent claimant's activities that he should be taken to be the very same person as the legitimate heir. It is an important consequence of Goffman's analysis of, for instance, the occasion when a member of the audience leaped onto the stage and began to attack the 'hero' of *Look Back in Anger* that whatever sort of suspension of disbelief it is that the theatre requires, it cannot be one which requires us to think that we are really seeing Othello strangle Desdemona.[20] The proper response to Othello's strangling Desdemona would be to stop him.

[19] Goffman, *Frame Analysis*, chap. 5.   [20] *Ibid.* pp. 362f.

ALAN RYAN

Now, it is certainly true that in the world which Goffman shows us there is a great deal of pretending going on. People are constantly pretending to be acting in good faith when they are not, pretending to competences they do not possess and to commitments they do not feel. At any rate one aspect of the notion of role-distance – though not, perhaps, the most important – is its reminder of the way we often pretend to be more at ease in a given task than we are, the way we try to mislead others about our ability to perform the task in hand with something to spare. To that extent, it may be thought that the element of deception is crucial, and that 'putting on a show of doing...' is the central notion in dramaturgical analysis. This, I think, is to chase too hard in only one direction. For the notion of depiction, which is more obviously dramatic in its connotations, has a role to play. We do not need to suggest that a man who plays the role of surgeon is only *pretending* to be a surgeon; what he really is is a surgeon all right. But, we might well want to say that what he does *qua* surgeon also depicts what a surgeon does, in spite of the obvious awkwardness of saying any such thing. The awkwardness is, of course, that it seems odd to say that a thing might be both itself and a picture of itself; but there is no particular awkwardness in saying that a given piece of behaviour might be both that piece of behaviour and a picture of pieces of behaviour of that sort. A cricketer who plays an admirable cover drive both plays that particular drive and displays an image of the good cover drive. So on this view we ought not to be unduly alarmed by the suggestion that a given activity is both the real-life activity of saving lives by surgery and an exemplary picture of what it is like to do the job conscientiously, efficiently, skilfully and so on.

Nor does the argument end there; we might go on to claim that it is just because the activity can be seen as an image of that sort of activity that it allows room for considerations of style, for an aesthetic dimension. That a man fills the role at all is not usually a question of style; to *be* a surgeon at all is mainly a question of ability, or qualifications, or what he usually does to the patients confided to his care. Doing the job is a technical matter; but the surroundings in which the job is done offer the chance to do it *in style* rather than *merely*. In something like surgery, style is very much the man – bound up with how an individual manages the demands on him; but it is also an element in the role, in the sense that an account of the style in which a role can be filled is one of the things we would want to know about any role before we felt we understood it. It would be a thin knowledge of cricket which did not include the insight that Hammond was, and Barrington was not, a stylish player.

74

This is by no means all there is in Goffman's accounts of 'strips' of social interaction, and a worrying aspect of Goffman's habitual offhandedness about his theoretical commitments should be broached now, before we push on to take a closer look at dramaturgy. This is the ambiguity between a disposition to see 'what's going on' as something played as a drama, and a disposition to see it as a game in the games-theoretical sense, a game in which we are standardly beset by something like Prisoners' Dilemma problems, and in which we are constantly trying to get as much as possible for ourselves out of an essentially fragile co-operation with others. In this second reading, the importance which Goffman attaches to the control of information about ourselves has a much more obvious explanation than it would on a more committedly dramaturgical view. It is the object of each of us to convey an impression of himself which will make the terms of co-operation more favourable to himself. On this view, the surgeon who does his job stylishly is concerned not to make the terrors of dying and causing death more bearable by distancing them in an aesthetic framework, but to secure his dominance over the rest of the surgical team, to induce in them the belief that he is vital to the success of the operation and that to secure his co-operation they have to yield to him. Or, more generally, what the actor is up to is trying to rig the social terms of trade by engendering the appropriate beliefs in everyone else. This, of course, requires what Goffman always insisted on, the essential gap between agent and role. *Everyone* in everyday interaction knows that social life is possible only if everyone is kept sweet enough to be willing to do his bit in the social undertakings on which we all depend; so everyone is watching out for signs that other people are reliable or unreliable, competent or incompetent. A feature of Goffman's work which is apt to offend people is the apparent implication that we spend so much time either sneaking a look at the shortcomings of others or trying to tart up the image we ourselves present. A good many of his readers protest that they rarely, if ever, think about putting themselves over to an audience, and never, or at least very rarely, entertain doubts about the sanity, sexual normality, good temper or whatever of their associates. If they are outraged, and are also attracted to one of the contemporary versions of Marx, they may insist that these anxiety-ridden phenomena are typical of a society whose values are corrupted by commodity production, and where therefore we worry incessantly about what price our virtues will fetch, and about whether we shall be sold a pup by others. I am not at all sure that anything so sinister ought to be read into it all; though it does appear that there is a genuine puzzle about the generalisability

ALAN RYAN

of Goffman's work, a genuine puzzle whether what he says is true of
Americans and not of the British, as Banton suggests,[21] or whether
it is true of advanced industrial societies and not of simpler pre-
industrial societies. The only question at issue here is whether we
should treat his account of social interaction as a story about how we
rig the market, or as a story about how we engage in putting on a good
show.

In *The Drama of Social Reality*,[22] Lyman and Scott suggest that they
have something of the same anxieties about Goffman's theoretical
commitments. But they regard themselves as thoroughly committed
to the view that life really *is* theatre. The question then arises to what
are they thus committed, seeing that G. H. Mead and Freud are
invoked along with Goffman to explain what the dramaturgical standpoint is, even though Goffman is then dismissed as a non-fully-fledged
dramaturgical theorist. The obvious considerations on which they
draw are such things as our ability to rehearse *in foro interno* what we
are going to do before we do it – but that in itself scarcely seems
enough, since the mere fact that I work out a calculation in my head
before I write it down will qualify as an instance of rehearsing what
I'm going to do without tempting many of us to see it as the rehearsal
of a drama. Again, they seem to suggest that in all aspects of social
life we follow a script; but for the reasons suggested above, it's not
clear whether this is a script or a game plan, whether it's a script
containing technical instructions or the lines in a tragedy. I'm following
a text when I follow the instructions in the car's handbook, and change
a wheel; but Goffman's insistence that there's a difference betwen
changing a wheel on the road and changing a wheel in a play still makes
one want to say that even if the two activities looked like each other,
we are miles from showing that all life is theatre.

It might be said that changing a wheel is not a social interaction,
being a matter merely of the driver and inanimate matter locked in
combat; but merely introducing another character to assist one in
following the instructions does not seem to alter the analysis much.
More plausibly, we might say that only where we do what we do in
front of an audience, real or imagined, is there room for the theatrical
analogy to operate. Thus, where it isn't simply me, or me and a mate,
wrestling with the beastly wheel, but me representing myself to some
audience or other in the guise of 'one who is wholly incompetent, but
through no fault of his own', we might say I am putting on a little
drama. But at just this point the ambiguity we noticed above comes

[21] M. Banton, *Roles* (London, 1965).
[22] Lyman and Scott, *The Drama of Social Reality*, n. 1 to chap. 5, pp. 168f.

back: can we not equally well say that what I am doing is telling people that my imposing upon them the burdens of assisting me is not the result of a flaw in my character, or of mere idleness? If we can, we are back where we were with the question of how we are to distinguish an insistence on social life as a drama from an insistence on attending to the ways in which people set out to secure a *definition of the situation*, either co-operatively or in competition with each other.

There is one hint which might suggest that the attractions of the emphasis on aesthetic explanation rest on something other than the false claim that all the world is really a stage. The suggestion stems from Freud's concern with art, and at best it surfaces briefly in the analysis offered by Lyman and Scott. The hint is that the enjoyment which we get from art, which lies at the root of all aesthetic activity, is to be explained by the role of artistic transformation in making the pains and anxieties of life more bearable. In Lyman and Scott's account, it sometimes looks as if it is Freud's *theory* which is the drama, with Id, Ego and Superego playing parts in a tragi-comedy;[23] the more interesting notion is that within the theory, Ego is to be recast, not as an economic calculator trying to maximise psychic gratification in a dangerous world, but as a poet or dramatist making life bearable by giving it a unity which is not itself explicable in economic terms. That is, even preserving the claim that in some sense the task of the ego is to adjust the dealings between the organism and the environment, the claim would be that the nature of this adjustment was *essentially* rather than contingently to be understood by invoking considerations appropriate to the evaluation of a work of art. It is a striking claim, and it goes much beyond anything to be elicited from, say, Mead's observation that behind the social Me there lies the personal I; for it is a claim, however inexplicit, about how the I shapes what happens to the Me, and about why the I is prepared to put up with all sorts of misadventures to the Me, so long as they are organised in the right way.

Still, this is no more than a speculative throwaway. If we go back to our earlier anxieties, there is one further issue to settle before ending with a confession of bewilderment. It is sometimes said that dramaturgical explanation must be parasitic on other sorts of explanation, in the sense that what goes on in the theatre is already parasitic on what goes on in the non-theatre. There are two rather different points to be made. The first is that some versions of everyday behaviour depend for their effect on being copies of what goes on in a film or in a play or whatever; the surgeon who puts on the manner

[23] *Ibid.* p. 102.

ALAN RYAN

of Gary Cooper for some particularly grim operation is plainly borrowing from the realm of the theatrical in the strictest sense. But this is not to say that the dramatic qualities of real-life behaviour depend on our lifting the script from a drama – what goes on in plays, films and the rest is a heightening and a concentration of what goes on elsewhere. But, secondly, there is certainly a sense in which dramaturgical explanations are parasitic on other explanations. In any case where a dramatic explanation is in place, there is some other explanation in place as well. The woman who commits suicide and represents herself as having been truly broken-hearted, therefore, may be said to be performing the last lines of a tragedy of blighted love.[24] But we have two explanations pinned to one action here. The reason for committing suicide might be to make a coherent ending to an otherwise intolerably muddled existence; but the misery which needs resolving is a misery in its own right. The woman may be engaging in a *dramatic rendering* of 'I am really broken-hearted', and the half-intended impact of her death may be to ensure that the blame for it falls squarely on the man who jilted her; but none of this would make any sense unless being broken-hearted was already understood to provide adequate reasons for putting an end to oneself. If we invoke the analogy of the drama only to suggest that her suicide was a saying as well as a doing, the passing of a message as well as an act of self-destruction, the burden of the explanation falls as much on those motives to which she is drawing attention as it does on the dramatic presentation of them. To get extra mileage out of the dramatic analogy, we have to suggest an explanation of why only a drama will put across the message; otherwise, the drama is not merely, as it must be, parasitic on the other account of motivation, but also thoroughly uninformative.

This point is important and general. When Lyman and Scott apply their talents to the analysis of Shakespeare's most famous plays, the result is oddly unimpressive. They may be right to suggest that what *Antony and Cleopatra* is in part concerned with is the rise of bureaucratically rational administration; but what we want to know is why should Shakespeare write a *play* about a phenomenon which is handled so differently in, say, *The Social System*?[25] The distinction this rests on, between the message and its vehicle, is one which is crucial to the anxieties I have expressed about separating out the information-passing account of behaviour from a genuinely dramaturgical account. When Durkheim attends to moments of social effervescence and explains how religious rituals enforce, symbolically, the moral re-

[24] J. D. Douglas, *The Social Meanings of Suicide* (Princeton, 1967), pp. 315ff.
[25] Lyman and Scott, *op. cit.*, pp. 66f.

78

lationship between individuals and society, one feels inclined to ask why *this* way of telling the individual these things is *the* way to do it. Even in Weber's account of *wertrational* behaviour, something of the same difficulty recurs; a given action is thought to be the only possible way of expressing a particular value, or of driving home the point of a given way of life. And we are left anxious about the way the values and the expression of them are connected, and left to look for some account of how a mode of expression is or is not adequate to what it has to express.[26]

A last look at three sorts of suicide, in the light of the anxieties of what has gone before, may sum up the doubts of this paper, even if it will not lead to any conclusions. The three cases we might contrast are a man killing himself to avoid dying of a painful, wasting illness, a captain going down with his ship, having been forced to scuttle it, and the jilted woman who drowns herself. It does not seem at all difficult to account for the first in value-maximising terms; the only awkwardness is posed by the values of the man's society and the extent to which they restrain the pursuit of self-interested goals of this sort. The man certainly *has* good reasons, in self-interested terms, to take his own life, but in terms of the local norms he may have good reasons not to do so. I do not have anything to say about when a man will *take as his reasons* for acting one set of reasons rather than another, but it is obviously a topic of central importance in accounting for rational explanation.[27]

The second case is analysable so simply that it explains why role theory has been the object of some derision; that is, we might simply adduce in explanation the convention or norm that disgraced captains go down when their ships go down. If we want to know why Jones chose to drown, we simply point out that he was a captain who had been forced to scuttle. We have, as was suggested at the beginning of the paper, a problem which is the converse of that which the first case presented. That is, the first case raises the question of how norms constrain the acceptance of self-interested reasons; here we have the question of how self-interest constrains the acceptance of altruistic norms. The captain has a good, selfish reason for not going down with his ship, but he does not take it as his reason for action.

Although, as suggested just a little earlier, it is the third case which raises the question of how to apply dramaturgical concepts, it might be argued that they are at home here too. For what is it to go down with one's ship except to end one's career in style, to leave the stage

[26] *Ibid.* chap. 2.
[27] D. Richards, *A Theory of Reasons for Action* (Oxford, 1971), pp. 3–71.

ALAN RYAN

in the grand manner? This is not, of course, to say that there is any room here for such a notion as role-distance, for the thing about the captain is he does not distance himself from the role – he identifies himself with it so completely that he never thinks of doing anything but going down with his ship. But the suggestion raises the question whether the role of captain is sustained by the opportunities it offers for *displays* of heroism and so on.[28] And one then has to decide how an act's heroism refers to its 'desirability characteristics': is heroism to be explained simply in terms of altruism, endurance of pain and so on, or in terms of the show a hero can put on in front of an appreciative audience?

In the third case, there is no temptation to suggest that the woman played a role, so long as roles are thought of as bundles of rights and duties, though if we want to run the dramaturgical model for all it's worth, we may well say that 'Sheila, the jilted woman' is a part, a *dramatis persona*. But just as we worried earlier about the tendency of dramaturgical images to boil down to stories about how behaviour conveys information, getting a certain definition of the situation established and so on, so here we may end up feeling that she hasn't put on anything interestingly analysable as a drama, but has done something, part of the point of which was to establish *why* she had done

[28] It is impossible to do very much to take advantage of the discussion which the paper received. The main point to make is, perhaps, that not only Professor Goffman's work but also Professor Goffman himself resists the attempt to erect a general theory on the basis of his observations, and any further attempt to draw strenuous morals from them. It appears that the only general moral to which Professor Goffman might be willing to subscribe is that social life is very much more intricate than the naked eye tends to notice, and that we employ a remarkable range of communicative skills, and rely on all sorts of hidden communicative conventions, to facilitate even the most everyday activities. There are gestures which the man standing on the kerb employs in order to signal his intentions to car-drivers; there are hosts of gestures which pedestrians in a busy street employ in order not to collide with one another, in order to keep each other in invisible lanes – invisible to the pedestrian, but detectable by careful plotting. The suggestion which some of us had thought we detected in *Encounters* and elsewhere, to the effect that social life is hard and emotionally wearing work, is not part of Professor Goffman's case. There is a great deal of *busy* work, but not in any plausible sense hard work.

This suggests that the information-transmitting aspect of behaviour is, indeed, the central aspect of the argument. In this case, the idea that 'dramatic' explanations are parasitic on other sorts of explanation is reinforced, for what a drama turns out to be is a particular mode of telling a story. The story itself must, presumably, have a coherence of its own already which is, in principle at least, there to be elicited before the dramatisation occurs. But we are still left with the question with which the paper ended – a question which, of course, is one which literary theorists have wrestled with for ages – namely, what makes a particular form of presentation uniquely, or specially, apt to transmitting a given sort of information, and why should it satisfy individuals to learn, or remind themselves of, truths about themselves to express them in this fashion? Whether this is a question for sociological theorists I do not know.

80

it. What she was up to was, in part, telling us why life seemed to her to be so intolerable.

All of this raises far more questions than it answers, and this in spite of the fact that innumerable issues have not been raised at all, although a full analysis would require their resolution. Thus, nothing has been said about distinctions between rituals, dramas, different kinds of games, interior monodramas and so on; nothing has been done to resolve the doubts of those who think that all this suggests that the only sort of theatre ever devised is the naturalistic drama of recent western European culture. Again, nothing has been done to spell out the differences between those theorists who insist on our need for an audience to appreciate our activities and those who insist on our need to retreat 'backstage' and put on consolatory shows in private. Indeed, the upshot of what has gone before is perhaps this only: first, to raise the question whether in appealing to the dramatic or stylistic component of social behaviour we have invoked a distinctive kind of explanatory framework for activities otherwise misunderstood, or merely noticed what was noticed before the Flood – the importance of impression management; and second, to raise the question of the indispensability of particular symbols, particular modes of passing information and so on – the question, perhaps, whether in this area the medium and the message are distinguishable.

The Meaning of Another Culture's Beliefs

JOHN SKORUPSKI

My topic – very generally stated – is the relation between the theory of meaning and the sociology (history etc.) of thought. Within this very broad territory, however, I shall concentrate on an exemplary and much-debated set of problems which put some of the dependencies between the two areas in a particularly clear light. These problems centre on the translation or interpretation of the beliefs of a culture very different from our own: in particular, of the religious world-view of such a culture. Although distinctive methodological issues are no doubt raised by ethnographic interpretations of this kind, the philosophical questions I shall discuss in connection with theories of religion in social anthropology are mainly such as might also arise in broadly parallel ways in connection with, for example, the history of ideas. I shall generally be more interested in contrasts between more or less familiar, but idealised, philosophical positions than in the nuances of particular authors' views.

A convenient method of approach will be to outline a specific mode of interpretation of religious beliefs in a primitive culture, and to examine the various philosophical difficulties which have been thought to stand in its way. We shall not for this purpose need to go into very precise details about the beliefs which are the object of interpretation: they are, let us say, the beliefs of an isolated, pre-literate, clan-based tribal culture, somewhere in sub-Saharan Africa. The religious practices of this culture centre, let us suppose, on a high god and an extended pantheon of godlings, ancestor spirits, heroes, personal guardians, etc. There is divination, and acceptance of and precautions against witchcraft and sorcery; there are magical practices in cultivation, crafts, curing and so forth.

One method of interpretation of these practices and beliefs proceeds as follows. (1) It treats the magical and, by and large, the religious practices as 'instrumental': as attempts to control the course of events in such a way as to bring about this-worldly ends which the actors seek. (2) It takes such actions to be broadly rational applications of the magical/religious beliefs received in the culture, and thus treats these beliefs as amounting to an (at least potentially) systematic conception of the world, of its constituents and dynamic principles. Primitive[1] religious beliefs, on this view, are characteristically deployed to provide explanations of, and a rationale for attempts to control, aspects of the natural environment; and (3) not merely do these beliefs actually serve these functions: they initially emerge out of the need to comprehend and control natural phenomena, and their other possible functions derive from or modify this initial goal. The gods and spirits are, in short, the theoretical entities of the culture's 'transcendental hypothesis'.

I shall call this position 'intellectualism'.[2] A position which accepts points 1 and 2 I shall call (for reasons which will appear in section I) 'literalism'. The synchronic analysis of the literalist obviously builds up some momentum towards the diachronic thesis of the intellectualist, but it does not entail it. It is possible to believe that, while primitive religions are characteristically preoccupied with the activist, this-worldly goals of explanation and control, other needs and preoccupations are from the beginning more important in shaping their content and form.

In the following sections we shall consider three kinds of philosophical difficulty which have been thought either to undermine completely, or to place *a priori* constraints on, the intellectualist approach. If they do affect it, they affect it independently and at different points – in principle they are linked only in so far as they can all be seen as stemming from considerations about meaning and translation which belong to the philosophy of language. However, they can also be linked by a slogan – that one can understand a belief or an assertion only in its relevant cultural context – and perhaps have sometimes been linked in this way in people's minds. In section I, I sketch out two modes of interpretation of ritual which differ radically from the literalism which provides a basis for the intellectualist approach, modes of interpretation which, if correct, undermine that approach completely. In the next section we move on to issues, concerning conceptual relativism, which threaten to constrain the intellectualist's account of conceptual development and change. Again my aim here is primarily expository rather than critical. Finally in section III I examine a much less general question. A straightforwardly literalist interpretation of primi-

---

[1] I use the term 'primitive' rather than 'traditional' to distinguish 'primitive' religions – small-scale, culture-specific, typically pre-literate – from the 'world-systems' (Islam, Christianity, etc.) which in a given culture may also have a 'traditional' character in an obvious sense.

[2] Following E. E. Evans-Pritchard, *Theories of Primitive Religion* (Oxford, 1965).

tive religious systems of thought often results in an account which makes certain beliefs in these systems of thought incoherent, or at least to us bizarre. (These anomalies have characteristic forms noted by Lévy-Bruhl.) The question arises whether an interpretation which has this consequence is acceptable, and indeed whether the notion of an incoherent belief is an intelligible one at all.

I. FORMS OF LIFE

In what one might call 'classical' modern anthropology, the intellectualist has been largely cast in an adversary role, as a figure epitomising shallow nineteenth-century rationalism (though more recently intellectualism has had its defenders).[3] If the intellectualist's key interpretative concept in respect of primitive religious belief is 'theory', the key concept of what may fairly be described as the orthodox modern anthropological account of 'ritual' is that of 'symbolic expression'. This approach (1) denies that magical or religious action is (primarily) instrumental, (2) assumes no simple explanatory priority from magical/religious *belief* to *action* and (3) teaches that such beliefs and actions are alike to be understood hermeneutically, as belonging to a system of symbolic expression, where (4) what is symbolically expressed (so it is most typically claimed) is a representation of the *social* order.

It will be noted that the 'symbolist' does not deny that primitive religious beliefs, when taken literally, have the appearance of a cosmological system – a conceptual framework within which the *natural order* is understood. Nevertheless his position is incompatible not merely with a fully intellectualist approach but also with literalism: for he denies that these beliefs are ultimately to be understood or explained at this level. Variations on some such position, all more or less acknowledging the influence of Durkheim, are familiar in anthropology (though they are rarely worked out explicitly or clearly). I shall not examine the methodological difficulties they involve; I want instead to consider the contrast they afford with another approach to the same range of issues, which is more familiar in philosophy and acknowledges the influence of Wittgenstein. Peter Winch's 'Understanding a Primitive Society'[4] is an example. Winch's account of the meaning of Zande magic is ultimately not at all unlike that which some

---

[3] Robin Horton, 'African Traditional Thought and Western Science', *Africa*, 37 (1967) is an imaginative and influential extended exploration of the interpretative possibilities of intellectualism.

[4] In *Ethics and Action* (London, 1972).

symbolist writers might give; but it gets to this endpoint by a very different semantic route.

A metaphorically or symbolically expressed thought is a thought expressed in a statement which (at least in most cases) has a literal meaning: what makes the statement symbolic or metaphorical is just that (i) its literal meaning (if any) is not the meaning to be understood, and (ii) the literal meaning of the words constituting it must be grasped if one is to 'decode' the meaning which *is* to be understood. In a strict sense, therefore, the literalist and the symbolist are agreed on what the *translation* of ritual statements is. The difference between them is that the symbolist insists on the need for further hermeneutic interpretation of this translated corpus of statements, while the literalist takes them at face value: that is, he accepts that they do express, as understood literally, beliefs which it is then his business to try to explain.

Acceptance of the Wittgensteinian position, on the other hand, would lead one to question whether ritual statements do have the meaning which both literalist and symbolist are agreed upon at all, and to suggest that the translation which gives them this meaning misunderstands the language games – the forms of life[5] – in which magical and religious statements are made. (A person who held this position might well, of course, question literalism's right to its name.) But one has to be careful here in talking of translation. The need for translation, or rather correct understanding, arises for the Wittgensteinian as much with the modern English-speaker's religious language as with that of our traditional African culture. He need not question, therefore – though he might – the rendition of sentences from the latter language into English sentences on which symbolist and literalist alike agree. He may instead deny that these renditions have the (literal) sense which both the others take them to have.

Of course, on the Wittgensteinian's view it is not particular mistakes of translation which give rise to this divergence (as is clear in the case where all are agreed on an English rendition); it is rather an inadequcy in the general conception of meaning and language with which the other two approaches implicitly operate. A classical programme in the

[5] Here I take 'language game' as the linguistic correlate or dimension of 'form of life'. In Wittgenstein's writings 'language game' and, to a lesser extent, 'form of life' often refer to minutely discriminated patterns of activity involving distinctive uses of language: in this spirit one would not talk of the 'religious' language game or of religion as a form of life. Religion would, rather, encompass a congeries of language games and perhaps forms of life. On the other hand there seems to be no settled principle in later writers' use of these terms; they are used at varying levels of discrimination, though 'form of life' tends to be broader in application than 'language game'. These variations do not I think affect the issues discussed here.

theory of meaning envisages the possibility of giving a unified account of strict meaning and truth for sentences in a natural language, invariant in respect of their subject matter. The Wittgensteinian certainly rejects this possibility – he denies that one and the same general account can be given of how meaning and truth are determined, say, for sentences which convey observational reports, the sentences of a scientific theory, sentences in mathematical discourse – and, in particular, sentences in religious discourse. Each of these language games (or congeries of language games) involves *sui generis* forms of understanding.

But it would be a mistake to infer from this that the Wittgensteinian notion of a language game can be correctly represented simply as the idea of a set of sentences of whose meaning a unified type of semantic account can be given. Such a notion would remain a purely *semantic* one in that sense which relies on a distinction between the 'semantic' level concerning what a sentence 'strictly means' and the 'pragmatic' level which concerns what its use might in typical contexts express, convey, make clear to the hearer and so forth. But the Wittgensteinian is not interested in an amendment of the classical programme which would involve rejecting the idea of a unified semantic treatment independent of subject matter for a language, in favour of giving separate types of semantic account for different areas of discourse in the language: he rejects the classicial programme outright by rejecting *any* fundamental distinction between what is 'strictly meant' by a sentence and what a speaker conveys or accomplishes by its use on a given type of occasion. (An example of his approach might be this: nothing is conveyed or accomplished by saying 'This is my head', or 'I have a head', except, let us suppose, in those contexts in which the utterance serves as some kind of linguistic elucidation. The sentence itself therefore has no sense outside such contexts, and in them has the sense of a linguistic elucidation, for example, of the term 'head'.) Just this is one main ingredient in the injunction to look to the use of an expression for a grasp of its meaning: what is said in a language game has the meaning it has in that context; to understand its meaning one has to grasp the use of an utterance in the language game of which it is a part.

There is obvious artificiality in imputing philosophical conceptions of meaning to approaches in social anthropology. Nevertheless it may be illuminating to treat the symbolist as sharing with the literalist an implicit semantic assumption, viz. what I have called the 'classical' view that a unified semantic account can be given of all the sentences in the traditional religious believer's language. The account will take the form of outlining how the meaning of a sentence is determined by the meaning of its constituent expressions and (an important issue, as will be seen in the next section) how the meaning of such constituent expressions is determined. Hence the meaning of sentences spoken in religious discourse can be ascertained when the meaning of their constituent expressions is known; and given the assumption of unity, this knowledge can be acquired from another, more easily translated area of discourse, or, in the case of expressions specific to the religious context, by direct questioning which elicits an answer in terms of expressions already understood. Given this approach the symbolist finds himself in agreement with the literalist as to the manifest meaning of religious and magical statements in our notional culture: his next step is to insist on a symbolic understanding of what is latently expressed by their use.

The Wittgensteinian's criticism of this should now be clear. He approves the symbolist's stress on looking to the social context of the form of life in which ritual utterances are made, and ritual actions performed, for a grasp of what is conveyed in them; but on his view this approach should be extended to include the very meaning of what is said in such contexts: the symbolist goes wrong in interpreting the ('literal') meaning of ritual statements by projecting the meaning of their constituent expressions from the function which these have in other areas of discourse. For their role in sentences in the language game of ritual cannot be deduced indirectly from their role in other contexts (of factual reportage, for example) – it must be established directly, *in* the ritual context. The idea that these sentences have a cosmological level of meaning *at all* is therefore an illusion engendered by a bad theory of meaning. If the symbolist followed his approach right through he would be freed from the false dialectic of 'literalism' and 'symbolism'.

II. RELATIVISM

Both symbolist and Wittgensteinian attack intellectualism at its literalist base, in its analysis of the meaning – or, for the symbolist, of the underlying or sociologically privileged meaning – of magical or religious statements in our thought-experimental culture. Both characteristically attack on internalist or contextualist grounds: we must make sense of primitive belief in its own terms, in its own context, we must avoid the mistake (allegedly made by the intellectualist) of trying to force it into categories of our own culture which it does not properly fit. Thus stated, the slogan is unexceptionable. But as with most slogans of this kind, a variety of contestable, and certainly not truistic, claims can be offered under its truistic form. Two such have been described. At a quite different level, the slogan can get a relativist twist. Here the literalist claim – that magico-religious beliefs in our postulated culture amount to a thought system among whose primary functions is the explanation and control of natural phenomena – is not questioned. The difficulty for intellectualism is thought to lie not at the synchronic level, in its analysis of the meaning and function of these beliefs, but at the diachronic level, in its account of their development and of change in them.

Discussion of these issues has been bedevilled by, on the one hand, modish idealist rhetoric in the sociology of thought[6] and, on the other, solemn refutations of the absurd world-proliferating forms of empirical idealism which this rhetoric, taken literally, would imply. A more powerful and serious relativism, which avoids such empirical idealism, threatens to place limits on the intellectualist approach. I propose in this section to give a (very sketchy) outline of its foundations and form.

The relativism I have in mind is based on the thesis that theory is underdetermined by experience. This form of relativism has seeds in the intellectualist programme itself: namely, in the intellectualist's account of the *persistence* of magical (or primitive religious) beliefs, of practitioners' failure (in Evans-Pritchard's words) to 'perceive the futility of their magic'.[7] Thus one can observe how Tylor's discussion of the 'intellectual conditions accounting for the persistence of magic',[8] with its brief recitation of the blocks to falsifiability which explain the continued acceptance of such beliefs, is developed by Evans-Pritchard into a much more serious and extended analysis of the 'circle' of magical or 'mystical' beliefs;[9] how this account in turn, which originally was offered as marking a contrast with scientific thought, has more recently developed into a sense that *all* generalising systems of thought involve such 'circles'; and how, finally, this has led to relativist doubts

[6] 'At the very least, as a result of discovering oxygen, Lavoisier saw nature differently. And in the absence of some recourse to that hypothetical fixed nature that he "saw differently", the principle of economy will urge us to say that after discovering oxygen Lavoisier worked in a different world.' T. H. Kuhn, *The Structure of Scientific Revolutions*, 2nd edn (Chicago, 1970), p. 118. 'The selections offered here draw out of sociological theory of knowledge a certain thread. The theme goes back to Hegel and Marx; that reality is socially constructed. Every thinking sociologist would now agree it [sic] in principle. But how far dare they follow it?' Mary Douglas (ed.), *Rules and Meanings* (Harmondsworth, 1973), pp. 9–10.
[7] E. E. Evans-Pritchard, *Witchcraft, Oracles and Magic among the Azande* (Oxford, 1937), p. 475.
[8] E. B. Tylor, *Primitive Culture*, 2 vols. (London, 1891), vol. 1, pp. 134ff.
[9] Evans-Pritchard, *Witchcraft, Oracles and Magic*, pp. 475ff.

about the possibility of explaining changes of overall belief in rational terms.

The conclusion is unpalatable to the intellectualist since it is precisely such an overall framework of belief (the agency-based cosmology of primitive religious thought) that intellectualism seeks to explain – and it explains it as an intellectual reaction: an application of reason, at a given level of inherited knowledge, to experience. Furthermore, it is a natural extension of this approach that the transition from, let us say, traditional magico-religious curing to modern Western medicine is capable of being explained at least in part as the result of a more or less reasonable assessment of their comparative effectiveness. Hence if the conclusion is to be that moves between overall cognitive frameworks are intrinsically non-rational, the whole programme seems undermined.

Let us examine the step from the underdetermination of theory to relativism. The fundamental premise here is that any one belief in a system of beliefs can be defended against any possible experience by suitable amendments in the rest of the system. For then, with the choice of different beliefs to be defended come what may, can come different systems, all of which may be stated in such a way as to be falsifiable, but between which experience cannot discriminate: it falsifies one if and only if it falsifies all. How then does a particular belief get falsified? For experience to score a direct, disconfirming hit on a particular target, there must be a framework, not itself in question, which sets the target firmly in place. From this a further step takes us to a relativist position: the truth value of the belief is itself relativised to the framework within which it is assessed.

But, even given the structuring of the belief system into a stable framework and a set of beliefs within the framework, the fact that the method by which we assess the truth value of a belief within the framework *presupposes* the truth of the beliefs making up the framework does not at first sight entail that the truth-value of the belief is itself *relative* to the truth of those beliefs. The conditional character of our knowledge does not obviously entail the relativity of its object. The one is an epistemological matter, concerning the inferential relations which must hold between various parts of our knowledge; the other is an ontological matter, concerning the character of what is known. How does the relativist bridge this apparent gap?

Let us talk very abstractly of 'world-views' (Ws). They come in various versions, where each version is a set of sentences sharing with every other version of the same world-view a proper subset of sentences which are not questioned or tested; these are called 'core sentences'. *Assuming* overall preservation of meaning, we have a different world-view if and only if the core sentences change. (If we drop the idea of a sharp class distinction regarding proneness to revision between core sentences and others, and replace it by a completely classless society, or a hierarchical continuum of tenure, we make the relativist's life more difficult. For in that case it becomes more difficult to separate a change of opinion where the conditions to which truth is relativised remain constant from a change of these conditions. At the classless extreme, there can be no difference between cognitive moves within a world-view and changes of world-view, and hence it becomes difficult to see how, on a relativist conception, any pair of opinions would ever be inconsistent. But I want to consider the relativist's case on its most favourable ground.)

The relativist's position can now be stated thus:

(i) If S_i and S_j are sentences in W_i and W_j (S_i may be S_j), such that S_i is synonymous with S_j, then S_i may be true/false-in-W_i and S_j may be false/true-in-W_j.

(ii) The core sentences of $W_1, \ldots, W_n$ cannot be said to be *true* (except in an honorific sense) or *false* at all.

It is evident that the relativist needs a theory of meaning which will do a number of jobs. It must bridge the gap from conditionality of knowledge to relativity of truth. It must show also how sentences can be compared in meaning across world-views. Do W_i and W_j differ, for example, if their core sentences, as *structurally characterised*, differ? Not necessarily. For if these different sentences have the same meaning, W_i is W_j.

The kind of theory of meaning which can produce the results that the relativist wants I shall call 'anti-realist'. ('Verificationism' and 'constructivism' are also familiar labels, but each has further distinctive connotations.) The meaning of a sentence, on this account, is determined by what possible experiences (and, if necessary, inferential procedures) would establish its truth (warrant one in counting it true). Let us call this set of possible experiences (etc.) the 'assertibility conditions' of the sentence. But now since different such conditions may become associated with a sentence when there is a change in the core sentences, it looks as if the meaning of a sentence will depend on the world-view in whose context it appears.

However this conclusion itself presupposes that world-views, and thus the meaning of their core sentences, can be distinguished. But the core sentences of various world-views are alike in being accepted come what may. They are thus limiting cases: either one can refrain from saying that any experience would *establish* their truth, or one can say that *any* experience does. In either case, there is on the present approach no way of distinguishing between core sentences in respect of meaning, and hence no way of distinguishing co-falsifiable world-views. There is, given this approach, neither underdetermination nor relativism.

We can avoid this conclusion, and at the same time give the anti-realist approach greater verisimilitude, by splitting it into two levels:

(1) The meaning of a sentence is a function of the meaning of its constituent expressions.

(2) The meaning of a constituent expression is its contribution to determining the assertibility conditions of all the sentences in which it appears.

We can now say that core sentences, and generally any sentences with the same assertibility conditions, may nevertheless differ in meaning by dint of differing in their semantic structure and constituents.

However, this revised approach still needs to take serious account of the underdetermination of theory: a sentence on its own does not have determinate assertibility conditions – it has them only in the context of a theory or world-view. Consequently a constituent expression can make a determinate contribution to the assertibility conditions of a sentence in which it appears only in the context of a world-view. One possible moral to draw from this is that meaning is incommensurable across world-views (cf. Feyerabend's incommensurability thesis). But such relativism about meaning is incompatible with relativism about truth: there is then no identifiable item of which it can be non-trivially said that it is true relative to one W and false relative to another. Another way to draw the moral, however, is to say, as Quine has said, that while Frege was right in pointing out that the unit of meaning is not a word, he should have gone further than he did – and taken as the basic unit of meaning not the sentence but the theory (world-view). For anti-realism the unit of meaning is that which has assertibility conditions. Frege's doctrine of asking for the meaning of a word only in the context of a sentence is expressed in (2). But now that the unit of meaning has shifted up from sentence to world-view we must apply this approach to world-views themselves, or rather versions of them. So we finally arrive at a holistic form of anti-realism.

(1a) The meaning of a given version of a W is a function of the meaning of its constituent sentences.

(2a) The meaning of a constituent sentence is its contribution to determining the assertibility conditions of all the versions of Ws in which it appears; and this contribution in turn is a function of the meanings of its constituent expressions.

(3a) The meaning of a constituent expression is the systematic part it plays, for any sentence in which it appears, in determining the contribution of that sentence to the assertibility conditions of the versions of Ws in which it appears.

This somewhat mind-boggling position is, as far as I can see, the one required to yield the relativism formulated in (i) and (ii) above. For a sentence now preserves a definite meaning through the various world-views in which it may appear just as an (unambiguous) word preserves a definite meaning through all the sentences in which it appears. At the same time, however, while preserving its meaning, a sentence may be true in one world-view, false in another, and core-true in a third.

To see more clearly how anti-realism is required as an additional premise in the move from underdetermination to relativism, let us consider what happens when it is replaced by realism. The fundamental concept is now not of assertibility conditions but of truth conditions – sets of possible states of affairs given which the sentence is respectively true or false. The realist's conception of sentence-meaning is given by (1) together with:

(2b) The meaning of a constituent expression is its contribution to determining the truth conditions of all the sentences in which it appears.

The underdetermination of theory now no longer drives us to holism. For the realist the question whether a sentence is true or false is determined by whether the states of affairs which make it so obtain, quite independently of whether we are in a position to find out whether they obtain. The fact that we *can* consistently retain a sentence in the face of any possible experience does not in any way affect the fact that that sentence is, taken on its own, true or false depending on how the world is. In particular, that we decide to treat a sentence as true, come what may, is quite compatible for the realist with its being false. The realist does not accept, as does the anti-realist, that a sentence for which such a decision has been made is by that very fact rendered true by convention. If it already has meaning, then its truth value is already determined by how the world is, and there is no room for stipulative convention. What is conventionally determined for him is always meaning and never directly truth. Underdetermination then shows at most that there must be choice; it does not show that the question whether the choice is correct – in the specific sense of whether the framework chosen is *true* – is senseless.[10]

For the anti-realist, the core sentences of a world-view – 'propositions', in Wittgenstein's phrase, 'which have the form of empirical propositions'[11] – function in a substantial sense as 'criteria of rationality' within the world-view. They play an essential role in the procedures whereby hypotheses within the world-view are to be rationally assessed, and one cannot significantly ask of them while remaining within the same world-view whether they may not themselves be false. The relativism which has been set out here, then, carries with it a relativism about criteria of rationality. For the realist, on the other hand, core sentences are no more the criteria for, rather than the objects of, rational assessment than any other sentences of the world-view.

The move from the underdetermination thesis to relativism requires, then, a particular conception of meaning as an additional premise. So far I have tried to show that we can go a certain distance in describing what form this conception must take – it will have to be holistic and anti-realist. It is developed by taking seriously the dictum that the unit of meaning is the theory and then pushing the analogy between the meaning of a word as its contribution to sentence-meaning, and the meaning of a sentence as its contribution to theory-meaning. I am not suggesting that this conception can be worked out coherently – I suspect, on the contrary, that it cannot be. One large difficulty for it is likely to stem from its holistic character – that is, from the fact that it takes the 'theory' or 'world-view' rather than the sentence as the prime bearer of assertibility conditions. What is puzzling is how, on this account, it is possible for a language to be learnt. The normal (realist) picture is that we learn the truth conditions of a sample of sentences, taking them at this stage as syntactically unanalysed blocks, then break them up and hypothesise constituent meaning and syntactic structure, achieving in this way a compositional understanding of the

---

[10] I realise that the terminology used here – of *sentences* being, and accepted as being, true or false – is potentially misleading. The points being made in this section could, however, be made, in a more circumlocutory way, without using it. In section III we shall have cause to distinguish between *believing that S* and *believing that the sentence 'S' is true*.

[11] L. Wittgenstein, *On Certainty*, repr. with corrections (Oxford, 1974).

old sentences and of new ones whose truth conditions we have not directly learnt. If the view that the prime unit of meaning is the world-view is taken seriously, it would seem to imply that what we learn *en bloc*, as the initial step in learning a language, are the assertibility conditions of sample *world-views*: but this seems an unintelligible project.

I shall not pursue this difficulty, however. Instead I want to consider how much of intellectualism can survive if a relativist framework is accepted. As has already been noted, relativism of the kind described here, if applied to primitive religious thought, is not merely compatible with but presupposes a literalist account of it: for literalism merely asserts that such thought constitutes a framework of belief within which people seek to understand and control natural events. It says nothing of how this framework evolved or of its rational comparability with other frameworks. When we turn to the intellectualist's picture the situation is more complex. Rationality in the 'context of discovery' is a different matter from rationality in the 'context of justification'. This is well recognised in contemporary versions of intellectualism, such as Horton's.[12] The fundamental notion that primitive religious cosmologies are the products of rational 'theory-building' is in this version maintained, but the kinds of factors which are taken as counting towards the rationality of a process of theory-development – an interest in accounting for experience in an economical, simple, consistent way, in terms of a basic analogy which is familiar and well understood, and so on – can apparently be accepted as playing a role in the development of a theory, consistently with a relativist view of the theory itself. On the other hand, I remarked earlier that it is a natural part of intellectualism to suppose that a change in, say, our notional African culture from traditional magico-religious curing to Western medicine can be seen as resulting from a rational assessment of their comparative effectiveness. Now here rationality is involved in the context of a comparative evaluation of frameworks which compete at a fundamental level, involving presumably a 'clash of paradigms'; it is therefore unclear whether relativism could accommodate such an explanation of the change from one framework to another even as an *a priori* possibility.

The overall picture, then, is that philosophical relativism, founded on an anti-realist conception of meaning conjoined with the thesis that belief is underdetermined by experience, does impose some cutbacks on the full intellectualist project, but that a pretty substantial part of it could survive. Indeed my impression is that the controversy between

[12] Horton, 'African Traditional Thought and Western Science'.

JOHN SKORUPSKI

'symbolist' and intellectualist approaches to primitive thought is to a considerable extent being replaced, at least among social scientists interested in the sociology of thought and influenced by the writings of Kuhn, by what is in fact an essentially philosophical controversy between realist and relativist forms of intellectualism. For example, Barry Barnes, a sociologist of science interested in the comparative study of scientific and primitive belief systems, seems to adopt a position of some such 'relativist/intellectualist' kind.[13] Here again, of course, I am not imputing to these social scientists explicit positions on the theory of meaning. The suggestion is, rather, that an attempt to work out the philosophical basis for the kind of position they seem to adopt would lead in the direction described in this section: though, as I have said, there seems to be good reason to doubt whether following it up can in the end result in a consistent and intelligible account at all.[14]

The connection the anti-realist makes between the meaning of a sentence and what counts as evidence for it leads him, if he is to avoid the apparent underdetermination of belief and thus of sense by evidence, to the view that certain 'propositions which have the form of empirical propositions' are not empirically grounded at all. 'If the true is what is grounded, then the ground is not *true*, nor yet false'[15] – however, it is only in the context of propositions which stand in no need of a ground but which form part of the ground of other propositions that we can determine the truth value of those others; and if the context of ungrounded propositions changes so to do the grounds and truth value of the rest. Although I cannot argue this here, I believe that Wittgenstein was wrestling with thoughts of this kind about meaning, evidence and truth in *On Certainty*, and that the implications of the anti-realist position he was there developing are relativistic in the sense described in this section.[16] On the other hand

[13] E.g. in Barry Barnes, 'The Comparison of Belief-Systems: Anomaly versus False-hood', in R. Finnegan and R. Horton (eds.), *Modes of Thought* (London, 1973).
[14] The actual source of this relativism, as opposed to the underpinning it requires, may not have much to do with an explicit philosophical conception of the notions of meaning and truth. The idea which plays a major role in current sociology of thought is that belief is underdetermined by evidence; its appeal to liberal tolerance of other cultures' world-views is obvious – and after all, if belief is underdetermined by evidence, that leaves room for its determination by sociological variables. Writers struck by this idea are led in realist mood to a position of radical doubt, and in anti-realist mood to one of relativism. Realist scepticism, however, tends to go over into anti-realist relativism, which affords a more comfortable resting point.
[15] Wittgenstein, *On Certainty*, § 205.
[16] On the anti-realism of *On Certainty*, see e.g.: 'If everything speaks for an hypothesis and nothing against it – is it then certainly true? One may designate it as such. – But does it certainly agree with reality, with the facts? – With this question you are

96

I do not claim that the Wittgensteinian position developed, for example, in Winch's 'Understanding a Primitive Society' is relativistic in this sense. It is one thing to assert that forms of life with quite different aims than those of explanation and control involve different criteria of rationality to those of science, and to argue – on the basis of considerations about meaning of the kind described in section I – that religion, or magic among the Azande, correctly understood, are seen to constitute such a form of life: concerned not so much with influencing the contingencies of human experience as with arriving at an acceptance of them. It is quite another thing to accept that Zande magic is in the same business of explanation and control as science, but to argue on relativist grounds that it involves its own contextually determined criteria of rationality (e.g. 'The poison oracle is always right'). The two claims are in fact incompatible. It must be admitted that much of the discussion of 'agreement with reality' and 'criteria of intelligibility' in Winch's paper, and his criticism of Evans-Pritchard's 'metaphysical claims', itself suggests the adoption of a radical metaphysical position of an anti-realist kind. ('Reality is not what gives language sense. What is real and what is unreal shows itself in the sense that language has.')[17] But in the last pages of his paper, in which Winch tries to give some positive account of Zande magical practices, it is the first claim which comes to the fore.[18]

already going round in a circle...' (§ 191). 'What does this agreement consist in, if not in the fact that what is evidence in these language-games speaks for our proposition?' (§ 203).

In the discussion of anti-realism in this section I am indebted to Michael Dummett's writings, particularly to *Frege: Philosophy of Language* (London, 1973), chap. 17. For the later Wittgenstein's anti-realism, see P. M. S. Hacker, *Insight and Illusion* (Oxford, 1972), or G. Baker, 'Criteria: A New Foundation for Semantics', *Ratio*, 16 (1974).

[17] Winch, 'Understanding a Primitive Society', p. 12.

[18] A similar ambiguity affects a more recent paper by Winch ('Language, Belief and Relativism', unpublished). Here he says 'I have tried to undermine the seductive idea that the grammar of our language is itself the expression of a set of beliefs or theories about how the world is, which might in principle be justified or refuted by an examination of how the world *actually* is.' (He goes on to remark, citing *On Certainty*, that the boundary between 'grammar' and 'theory' is neither clearcut nor stable.) Winch's position nevertheless is that 'belief' in witches or oracles is part of the 'grammar' of Zande language and thus not open to *refutation*, although it may become – for reasons which remain mysterious – untenable. This is precisely the position of the anti-realist, if the 'grammar' of a 'language' is understood as what I have called the 'core sentences' of a 'world-view'; and it is a relativist position. If, on the other hand, 'grammar' is understood in the non-philosophical sense of 'set of rules characterising syntactic well-formedness', then naturally the idea that belief in oracles belongs to the 'grammar' of Zande language is unintelligible. In fact the difficulty in understanding Winch's position boils down to the obscurity of the term 'grammar' as he uses it.

III. INCOHERENT BELIEFS

To many people brought up in modern Western societies one of the most compellingly mysterious features of primitive modes of thought – at least as these have been presented to them – is their apparently bizarre, often downright paradoxical content. Lévy-Bruhl built this feature into a scheme of contrast between the modern and the primitive – 'pre-logical' – mentality. Subsequent reactions to the essential ideas embodied in his early work – particularly to the idea that pre-logical thought contains distinctive types of anomaly centring on the logic of identity and change – are interesting as measures of a growing awareness of the problems of method involved in the interpretation of primitive thought. For many modern anthropologists, I suspect, Lévy-Bruhl epitomises the weird and wonderful misconceptions of primitive thought into which a ploddingly literalist approach falls. Divergences from such literalism come in degrees. Suppose, for example, that our African culture believes, as do the Nuer in Evans-Pritchard's account,[19] that rain is Spirit. Someone who interprets this apparent Lévy-Bruhlian 'mystical participation' as a purely symbolic identification is not thereby committed, of course, to the symbolist approach of section I. But suppose our culture also believes that the lesser godlings, while in no sense identical with each other, are nevertheless all identical with the high god. A symbolist account of the doctrine might interpret it for example as symbolically affirming or representing the unity or integration of clans in the overall society. In any case a radical divergence from literalism seems at first sight required to expel all appearance of incoherence from such a belief.

The symbolist would either deny that people in our culture strictly and literally *believe* that *rain is Spirit*, or that *the godlings are identical with the high god*, or else explain the beliefs as the result of some kind of reification. For the Wittgensteinian approach, too, the apparent paradoxicality of such beliefs, as they are presented in the literalist account, would probably amount to further evidence of the inadequacy of the principles on which literalism bases its understanding of them. With Quine he might well claim that 'pre-logicality is a trait injected by bad translators'.[20] But of course his grounds for making the claim, resting as they do on his 'decentralised' conception of language (a language game looks after itself), would in no way be Quine's.

[19] E. E. Evans-Pritchard, *Nuer Religion* (Oxford, 1956).
[20] W. V. O. Quine, 'Carnap and Logical Truth', in *The Ways of Paradox* (New York, 1966), p. 102.

Quine is concerned simply with trading off the probability of incoherent beliefs against the probability of bad translation – his interpretative charity puts the price of incoherent beliefs unattainably high. Such interpretative charity, just because it is not tied in to non-literalist principles of translation like the symbolist's or the Wittgensteinian's, is of some importance for assessing intellectualism. Let me explain why.

If a literalist account of religious beliefs, say in our notional African culture, does present it as containing characteristic paradoxical elements in its ideas about the nature of spiritual beings and their relation to the world, then these must in turn be explained by the intellectualist, because intellectualism bases itself on a literalist account. On the face of it, they pose some difficulty for the view that primitive religious beliefs evolve and persist as an attempt to comprehend and master natural phenomena. For if primitive religious thought pre-eminently devotes itself to making experience intelligible and controllable, why should it develop and retain strikingly anomalous doctrines about the character and relationships of its theoretical entities? On the other hand, of course, if it could be shown that these doctrines are *inevitably* generated by the attempt to explain experience in terms of a theory which goes beyond experience, then their presence would on the contrary be a strong point in favour of the intellectualist account. Just this is in fact Horton's strategy:

the sciences are full of Lévy-Bruhlian asertions of unity-in-duality and identity of discernibles. These assertions occur whenever observable entities are identified with theoretical entities . . . I shall argue, not only that they are irreducibly paradoxical, but also that their paradoxicality is integral to their role in the process of explanation . . . I shall try to show that in their nature and location, the paradoxes of African religious discourse are very similar to those of scientific discourse. I shall also try to show that, as in the latter, the occurrence of paradox can only be understood in terms of the quest for explanation.[21]

But now if apparent paradoxes, incoherences etc. in the belief system of a culture are in reality always traits injected by bad translation, then they can provide no challenge for intellectualism: neither fences for it to fail nor points for it to score.

We shall examine Quine's principle of charity below. But some further considerations which seem to reinforce the tendency to place incoherences at the door of the translator should first be noted.

In the first place, talk of 'understanding' or 'making sense of' another culture and its beliefs, common in both philosophy and

[21] Robin Horton, 'Paradox and Explanation: A Reply to Mr Skorupski', *Philosophy of the Social Sciences*, 3 (1973), 232.

JOHN SKORUPSKI

anthropology, facilitates an important equivocation. A careful distinction must be drawn between 'understanding' a thought system (i) in
the sense of giving an accurate descriptive account of it as it is held
by those who hold it – a phenomenology of that system of thought
– together with some account of why it should be thus held; and (ii)
in the sense of making it fully intelligible, of interpreting out any
apparent obscurity of content. Simply to run these two projects together is to prejudge the question we are presently discussing, of
whether incoherence must necessarily be the product of bad translation. Here again the dictum that one should 'make sense' of another
culture or way of life in its own terms is likely to crop up;[22] grounds,
however, must be given for making the achievement of (ii) a *sine qua
non* of success in achieving (i).

Such grounds may centre on the thought that an attempt to report
a belief by means of an incoherent or unintelligible sentence may result
not in the reporting of an incoherent belief but in failure to report
a belief at all. As Bernard Williams remarked in 'Tertullian's
Paradox',[23] the difficulty for a religious man required to believe an
unintelligible doctrine seems to lie in knowing *what it is* that he is
supposed to believe. Analogously, when another man's belief is reported by the use of an unintelligible or incoherent sentence the
problem seems to be one of identification – of knowing what it is, if
anything, that he is being said to believe.

A number of distinguishable issues are implicit in this way of
putting the point. One rests on a semantic consideration: a man cannot
have beliefs which are unintelligible in the *strict* sense of being
reportable only by sentences which *lack sense*. We report N's belief by
embedding a sentence in the context 'N believes that. . .'. But if what
is embedded has no sense, no report has been made: the whole
sentence lacks truth conditions. The same point is put in another way
if one says that a sentence has sense if and only if it expresses a
proposition, and that belief is a relation to a proposition. Then a
sentence lacking sense expresses no proposition and hence cannot be
used to report a belief.

Now within the general approach which treats sentence-sense as
explicable in terms of truth conditions, a strict account (e.g. Wittgenstein's, in the *Tractatus*) insists that the sense of a sentence is given
by the boundary line which its assertion draws through the totality of

[22] As noted by Ernest Gellner, 'Concepts and Society', reprinted in B. Wilson (ed.),
Rationality (Oxford, 1970).
[23] In A. Flew and A. MacIntyre (eds.), *New Essays in Philosophical Theology* (London,
1955).

possible worlds. The boundary line must both include and exclude: a line which excludes nothing or everything is not a boundary line at all. On this account sentences which might be said to express necessary falsehoods or truths are in fact strictly senseless. They cannot be used, it accordingly follows, to report a person's beliefs. Incoherent sentences, on any characterisation of incoherence, would in this account be senseless; hence there could be no incoherent beliefs.

However, while it is indeed impossible on this account that anyone should believe that rain is (literally) Spirit, it is also and equally impossible that anyone should believe that rain is not Spirit, or that vixens are female foxes, or that there is a construction for trisecting any angle, that Hesperus is Phosphorus and so on. Our problem on the other hand stemmed from the feeling that a *specific* philosophical difficulty lies in the supposition that another culture (another person) has *incoherent* beliefs: the feeling, that is, of some *special* impossibility in the idea of an incoherent belief, and thus of a 'pre-logical mentality'. (Of course the term 'pre-logical mentality', with its suggestion of a *system* of incoherent beliefs and non-logical modes of thought, also raises further puzzles about the limits on what can be described as a 'belief system' or a mode of 'thought', which are not raised by the supposition of localised and non-ramifying incoherent beliefs.) The very strict conception of meaning which has just been noted does not isolate this special difficulty which seems to reside in the idea of an incoherent belief. And in any case a more liberal conception of sense, which distinguishes between significant sentences whose truth conditions are such that they are true of all or no possible worlds, and sentences to which no truth conditions are assigned – senseless sentences – is much more natural. But on this more liberal conception, the difficulty about incoherent beliefs will not be a semantic difficulty; any difficulty which remains will arise because the limits on what can be believed are tighter than the limits on what has sense.

I do not in fact believe that when the semantic issue is set aside there remains any clearcut limitation on the possibilities of belief which is grounded on *conceptual* considerations. The claim that another culture's beliefs are in certain respects incoherent is not itself incoherent; it gives rise, rather, in given cases, to problems of imaginative understanding – of understanding what it is like to have such-and-such a belief; of dispelling the opacity which a culture or a mind in which such a belief is held has for an observer who finds the belief incoherent. At its limit this opacity might reach a point where the observer's problem could be described – compatibly with his being able, in one sense, to give a strictly complete and accurate report of what was believed – as that of not knowing *what* was believed. Truistically, the opacity of the mind or culture which held the belief could be dispelled, if at all, only by information about the context of institutions and activity in which the belief was held. This process *might* to some extent relieve the obscurity of the belief itself by making it, so to speak, more thinkable to the observer. There are gradations of thinkability, and differences of resonance, among incoherent – or just obscurely weird – suppositions: that this drawing pin feels pain when banged into the wall, that this drawing pin is an evil demon, that this drawing pin is the Empire State Building. (By 'supposition' I mean the envisaging of a counterfactual situation in which, e.g., this drawing pin is the Empire State Building; and not the taking it as actually *representing* the building for the purpose of a mimetic enactment – though supposition in the latter sense is of importance in the understanding of magical modes of thought.) With these gradations of thinkability go gradations of intelligibility as regards the corresponding beliefs: the mind of a child who believes that a drawing pin is in silent pain when hammered into the wall – e.g. the feelings and reactions which go with this belief – is open to us; whereas the mind of a madman – as he would presumably have to be – who believed that the drawing pin in his match-box was the Empire State Building is completely opaque. (Not even of this belief, though, could it be taken as a *datum* that it was a mad belief; independently, that is, of the social background against which it was held. Only a brave man would claim that *no* legitimating institutional context could be conceived in which a comparable belief might not be held by perfectly normal people. Given such circumstances, it might be easy for an outside observer to explain why rational persons held the belief; but what it was that was believed would remain opaque as ever.)

In practice, the material from primitive religious/cosmological thought which exemplifies a 'Lévy-Bruhlian' anomalousness that the intellectualist must explain or explain away – mainly consisting of paradoxical ideas about the identity and ubiquity of various spiritual beings[24] – is nowhere near the conceivable outer limits of unintelligible or opaque belief. It should not be unfamiliar in character and degree, for example, to someone brought up in orthodox Catholic doctrine. The latter in fact poses a special additional problem of its own. An opaque belief is as difficult to understand for the believer as for the observer; but the believer may simply fail to recognise that difficulty in his own belief, especially where the belief is legitimate

[24] I discuss some ethnographic material of this kind in 'Science and Traditional Religious Thought', *Philosophy of the Social Sciences*, 3 (1973), part III.

and accepted in his social milieu. But in the case of the Catholic Church certain doctrines are explicitly recognised as unintelligible. Specifically, they are categorised as 'mysteries in the strict sense'. (Naturally, 'unintelligible' does *not* here, or in my discussion, mean 'senseless'.)

Whereas an ordinary mystery is a doctrine whose truth has to be taken on faith but whose content is perfectly intelligible, in the case of a 'mystery in the strict sense' the believer is required to accept on faith not merely that it is true, but that, understood literally, it has content at all. The problem is therefore that of understanding what the Catholic believes when he believes that the consecrated Host is the whole living body of Christ – and also believes that that claim is not fully intelligible to the human mind. Such a person seems to be simultaneously in the position of naive believer and perplexed observer – but can he be? A linguistic account of the belief involved is very tempting – surely what the Catholic believes is that the doctrine of the Eucharist has a literal sense and in that sense expresses a truth. Yet in general there is all the difference in the world between believing that a sentence expresses a truth and believing the proposition expressed by the sentence. Should one then say that the Catholic does not believe that the consecrated Host is Christ, but rather that the sentence 'This consecrated Host is Christ' is true? Obviously, what this would leave out of account is the fact that the Catholic understands the constituent expressions of the sentence and its syntactic structure, and has that grasp on the proposition he takes the sentence to express which this understanding allows. But the relation between his belief in the Eucharist and that of a naive believer is a difficult one to portray – it is not obvious that the situation is happily captured, although this is how we do put it, simply by saying that while both *share* a certain belief, one has a belief about that belief which the other just does not have.

Let us return from the question whether there can *be* incoherent beliefs, and the problems of understanding them given that there are, to the question whether anything could count as evidence warranting the claim that a person or culture holds an incoherent belief. What is indisputable is that if an incoherent belief is to be attributed to someone, the improbability of his holding such a belief must not outweigh the probability that the translation scheme which reads his utterances as evidence of such a belief is a good one. Thus a principle of interpretative charity which directed one to eliminate incoherence in every case in which it arose by adjusting one's translation scheme could be rationally founded only on the view that the improbability of such incoherence must always be so great as to be decisive. (By incoherence I here mean actually held beliefs which are in and of themselves incoherent, not potential incoherence under deductive closure of beliefs. No one would regard the latter as improbable enough to justify retranslation in every case.) In the case of a similar argument (Hume's) about miracles, the probability that the report of a miracle is correct is reduced against the improbability of the miracle reported by our knowledge of the vagaries of information transmission, of the likelihood of 'channel noise' as the message moves from person to person, and the relatively low determination of the final message output by the original message input. Analogously, the probability of correct translation is reduced against the improbability of incoherent beliefs by Quine's considerations on the looseness with which translation schemes are constrained by the input sample of linguistic behaviour, however large.

But these considerations cannot justify total interpretative charity. (I am not suggesting that Quine thinks they can.) In the first place, people can have beliefs about the intelligibility of their own beliefs. We have seen, for example, that the orthodox Catholic believes the doctrine of the Eucharist and also believes it to be a 'mystery in the strict sense'. A retranslation which removed any appearance of paradoxicality from the doctrine would make the fact that it was regarded by the believer himself as a strict mystery itself mysterious.[25] But the main point to be made is more general. Quine remarks that 'the more absurd or exotic the beliefs imputed to a people, the more suspicious we are entitled to be of the translations; the myth of the pre-logical people marks only the extreme. For translation theory, banal messages are the breath of life.'[26] This is too simple. More correct is to say 'the more *inexplicably* absurd or exotic the beliefs imputed to a people, the more suspicious we are entitled to be of the translations'.[27] The degree of probability attaching to the claim that certain incoherent beliefs are held in a culture, and thus the degree of probability attaching to the translation scheme which supports the claim, cannot be assessed independently of the psychological and

---

[25] A related point is made by Susan Haack (*Deviant Logic* (Cambridge, 1974)) in connection with Quine's idea that the would-be deviant logician merely succeeds in changing the subject (compare W. V. O. Quine, *Philosophy of Logic* (Englewood Cliffs, N.J., 1970), pp. 81 ff). The verdict delivered by the principle of charity is, as she says, 'quite ambiguous where the Deviant logician holds, besides his (apparently) idiosyncratic logical beliefs, the further belief that he disagrees with the classical logician' (Haack, *op. cit.*, p. 200).

[26] W. V. O. Quine, *Word and Object* (Cambridge, Mass., 1960), p. 69.

[27] The point is agreed on in discussion by Donald Davidson, David Lewis and Quine in *Synthèse*, 27 (1974): see e.g. pp. 328, 346.

sociological story we may be able to tell as to why people in that culture should hold such beliefs, the comparative familiarity we may have with beliefs of the kind in question from our knowledge of other cultures, and so forth. The plausibility of the translation scheme is determined in the context of our general sociological and psychological knowledge, and in conjunction with the particular psychosociological account we may be able to give of the culture concerned.

The point applies also to the conception of meaning which determines the principles underlying the translation scheme. The symbolist's principles of translation were those of the literalist up to a literal translation; but in the case of 'ritual' discourse the symbolist then went further, seeking to establish a symbolic level of meaning on contextualist grounds – thus his distinctive semantic notion was that of symbolic representation. The Wittgensteinian's divergence from the literalist is more radical: he applies contextualist principles to the elucidation of the – 'literal' – sense of ritual utterances itself. Each of these two positions may suffer from its own internal difficulties: it is questionable whether either can provide sufficient controls for assessing the correctness of a given account of the meaning of ritual discourse. For example, the Wittgensteinian's presentation of his case is that his interpretation of ritual in a given culture starts without preconceptions from the same material as the literalist's (Evans-Pritchard on the Azande, say); the divergence between his and the literalist's final account of the meaning of ritual being the result of their different conceptions of meaning and 'translation'. But do the Wittgensteinian's principles lead determinately from the material to any one interpretation at all? At least on the face of it, fewer constraints are placed on translation if one allows that the same expressions can function differently and thus have different meaning in different 'language games' than if one requires a unified account of how a given expression contributes to the meaning of a sentence. What determines the meaning of an expression in a language game – in a request for protection to an ancestor spirit, for example, as against a request for protection to a chief – is of course supposed to be its use-in-that-context. But a detailed example of this approach at work has yet to be given. Pending that, one can be excused for thinking that it is not so much a case of distinctive semantic notions and principles leading the Wittgensteinian to a distinctive account of the meaning of ritual as of a familiar modern idea of the meaning which primitive ritual must have leading him to exploit such notions as that of a 'language game' in order to underwrite an account which will give it that meaning.

But let us put aside difficulties which cast doubt on whether a symbolist or a Wittgensteinian account of the meaning of ritual is workable at all, and suppose that each can be made to supply a translation or interpretation of religious and magical actions and utterances in our notional African culture. Each of these overall accounts, together with the literalist's, involves distinctive semantic principles of translation and understanding. But as in natural science the choice of geometry is not independent of the choice of physics, so in the sciences of man the choice of a theory of meaning – of semantic principles of interpretation – is not independent of the psychology and sociology of thought. So the adjudication between these overall accounts cannot be conducted in terms of rough and ready rules of thumb such as an incoherence-avoiding principle of interpretative charity. Certainly 'the trouble with such all-embracing logical charity is, for one thing, that it is unwittingly quite *a priori*: it may delude anthropologists into thinking that they have found that no society upholds absurd or self-contradictory beliefs';[28] more directly the trouble with it is that, taken as a principle, it is simply wrong. The adjudication must turn on a different, more complex question: can what people in a given culture mean, on the given theory of meaning/principles of interpretation, by what they say, be linked with a plausible psycho-sociological theory which tells us why they should be given to saying what – so understood – they do say? When this question is properly posed, then the candidacy of that account of primitive cosmology which we have been considering – classical and realist in its semantic principles of interpretation, intellectualist in its sociology of thought – looks much stronger than some of the orthodoxies of modern social science and philosophy have allowed.

[28] Gellner, 'Concepts and Society', p. 36.

'Realistic' Realism and the Progress of Science

NICK JARDINE

I

To be a realist is to adhere to a correspondence theory of truth: to hold that to speak truly is 'to say of what is that it is'. To be a relativist is to deny the correspondence theory of truth: to deny the legitimacy of invoking, in the face of the diverse interests, ideologies, cultures, and systems of belief of speakers, a single external reality as the measure of truth. Recently the historiography of science has been widely exploited as a source of ammunition in the perennial strife between realists and relativists. Each party has sought to convict the other of a distorted interpretation of the succession of scientific theories. Realists charge relativists with commitment to an account which in explaining succession unduly subordinates human rationality to external sociological and ideological factors, and which by denying that it makes sense to talk of cumulative growth of true scientific belief renders the fact of human technological progress inexplicable. Relativists charge realists with 'the chauvinism of time', with commitment to accounts of the contents of past theories and of their succession which are distorted by the imposition of *our* present conceptual framework and *our* present criteria for the assessment of theories. Alas, in this dispute there is often a distressing lack of clarity both in exposition of the alleged disparate historiographical commitments, and in explanation of the way in which they reflect the fundamental disagreement about the nature of truth.

It is the great merit of Hilary Putnam's recent paper 'What Is "Realism"?' that it attempts to say precisely what is the strategy for the interpretation of the history of science to which the realist is committed, and how the commitment arises. Here is the crux of Putnam's argument:

What if *all* the theoretical entities postulated by one generation (molecules, genes, etc., as well as electrons) invariably 'don't exist' from the standpoint of later science? – this is, of course, a form of the old sceptical 'argument from error' – how do you know you aren't in error *now*? But it is the form in which the argument from error is a *serious* worry for many people today, and not just a 'philosophical doubt'. One reason this is a serious worry is that eventually the following metainduction becomes overwhelmingly compelling: *just as no term used in the science of more than 50* (or whatever) *years ago referred, so it will turn out that no term used now* (except maybe observation terms, if there are such) *refers.* It must obviously be a desideratum for the Theory of Reference that this metainduction be blocked; that is one justification for the Principle of Benefit of the Doubt.[1]

According to Putnam the Principle of Benefit of the Doubt (hereafter 'PBD') allows us to equate the referent of a term 'ψ' of our science with that of a term 'ϕ' of a past science provided only that the descriptions which the protagonists of the past science used to characterise ϕs would, when 'reasonably reformulated', characterise ψs. It allows us to say that although Bohr's beliefs about electrons are not precisely satisfied by any kind of entities recognised in our physical theory, nevertheless his term 'electron' and ours have the same referent. The same goes for Dalton's 'atom' and ours, for Mendel's 'formative element' ('*bildungsfähig Element*') and our 'gene', and so on. Only when no 'reasonable reformulation' would turn their descriptions into a characterisation of a kind of entities we recognise are we bound to say that a term of a past science has no referent. 'Phlogiston' is such a term.

Should the PBD succeed in assigning referents to enough of the terms of past sciences, the disastrous 'metainduction' is blocked. And the mode of operation of the Principle is such that if it succeeds it will reveal in the history of science a cumulative growth of knowledge of the world, a convergence of belief about the kinds of things we recognise on the beliefs we hold about those kinds. Should the PBD fail to secure referents for enough of the terms of past sciences the disastrous metainduction goes through. The realist will have cause to doubt all our scientific beliefs, not on the reasonable ground that things may not be quite as we describe them, but on the 'unrealistic' ground that our fundamental terms may have no referents so that we fail to describe anything. The 'realistic' man should be prepared to abandon realism rather than have to entertain such a fantastic doubt. Fortunately for the realist, however, common sense indicates that the PBD would succeed, thus vindicating realism.

[1] Putnam, 'What Is "Realism"?', *Proceedings of the Aristotelian Society*, n.s., 76 (1975–6), 183–4. This scepticism-inducing argument does not wear its logical form on its sleeve. I take it to be of the form 'if T, then probably not T; so probably not T', where T is 'our' scientific theory. To see that it is not a direct induction on the falsity of past scientific theories, it suffices to note that the falsity of a past theory by virtue of empty reference of its terms is supposed to be premised on a theory of reference *plus* 'our' scientific theory.

From this point on I shall drop Putnam's terminology, replacing his claims about the *referents* of *terms* by entailed claims about the extensions of predicates. When Putnam writes of the *referents* of terms he intends *kinds* – gold, atom(kind), etc. – and *properties* – mass, length, etc. It is not my concern in this paper to attack Putnam's ontology, or to deal with justifications for the Principle of Benefit of the Doubt which he has offered elsewhere which depend upon that ontology. Provided one takes it, as one surely must, that if terms 'ϕ' and 'ψ' have the same referent then the corresponding predicates '— is ϕ' and '— is ψ' are coextensive, my replacements are harmless.

I find much to applaud in Putnam's argument. The transcendental strategy is appealing. We do indeed have scientific knowledge, and if our philosophical tenets conspire to cast doubt on this, so much the worse for them. And the conclusion is nicely in the naturalistic spirit. Where others have sought to settle the realism/relativism issue *a priori* – for example, by arguing that the relativist cannot even state his position without making use of concepts which are coherent only if realism is true, or by claiming that the realist postulation of a single domain of quantification for all languages is nonsensical – Putnam seeks to show that the resolution is dependent on a contingency, on the contingent success or failure of a principle for the interpretation of past science.

Surely the realist who would be 'realistic' about our science must somehow evade Putnam's metainduction. And Putnam is surely right in suggesting that application of the PBD would enable him to do so.[2] If Putnam is also right in implying that this is *the only sensible way* in which the realist can escape the scepticism-inducing induction, then we are faced with a dilemma: *either* succumb to relativism; *or* accept a principle for the assignment of extensions to the predicates of past sciences which would reveal in the history of science Putnam's 'convergence' of knowledge. The dilemma is a harsh one for those who find uncogenial both relativism about truth and conceptual chauvinism.

I have two main aims in this paper:

(1) To show that the dilemma is a false one. There is a *tertium quid*.

(2) To provide grounds for accepting the *tertium quid*.

---

[2] Though, as Hartry Field has pointed out in 'Theory Change and Indeterminacy of Reference', *Journal of Philosophy*, 70 (1973), 462–81, there are cases in which the Principle appears to face us with an arbitrary choice. Is Newton's term 'mass' co-referential with the special relativity theorist's 'relativistic mass' (i.e. total energy/c²) or with his 'proper mass' (i.e. total non-kinetic energy/c²)?

The first of these aims is prosecuted by producing two Principles for the assignment of extensions to the predicates of past sciences – Principles whose application, whilst enabling the realist to evade Putnam's metainduction, would reveal in the history of science growth of a kind far removed from his 'convergence' of knowledge. The second and more ambitious of the aims is prosecuted as follows. In sections III and IV, I adumbrate an account of the nature of reference and argue that my two Principles for the assignment of extension must be accepted on pain of making reference miraculous. In section V, I seek to exhibit the picture of the growth of human scientific knowledge which my Principles would yield as an attractive one.

II

By way of introduction to the main constructive arguments of this paper, let us note some apparently curious consequences of application of the PBD. Consider chemistry in England around 1800. Let us focus on the predicates '— is an oxide', '— is an acid', '— is a muriate', and '— is phlogiston'. Applying the PBD we may well conclude that their predicates '— is an oxide' and '— is an acid' have the same extensions as our predicates '— is an oxide' and '— is an acid', '— is a muriate' the same extension as our predicate '— is a chloride', and '— is phlogiston' null extension. Now consider the reports offered by a Georgian chemist of two commonplace laboratory observations:

OR1 'On dissolving bleaching powder in water and heating the solution production of the oxide of muriatic acid was observed';

OR2 'On addition of concentrated vitriolic acid to granulated zinc production of phlogiston was observed'.

In each case it is obvious what was observed – what the report is 'about'. In the first it is the production of chlorine gas on heating a solution of bleaching powder; in the second the production of hydrogen on adding sulphuric acid to granulated zinc.[3] Yet in each case we must apparently deny that the description offered applies to the event observed. For by the PBD '— is oxide of muriatic acid' is coextensive with our '— is hypochlorous acid', and '— is phlogiston'

---

[3] Cf. M. B. Hesse, 'Truth and the Growth of Scientific Knowledge' (forthcoming). Further chemical examples are readily culled from M. P. Crosland's fascinating *Historical Studies in the Language of Chemistry* (London, 1962).

has null extension. So the first description applies to events of a kind quite different from the observed event, and the second applies to no events whatsoever.

Chemical examples have been chosen merely for ease of exposition. Analogous consequences arise if, for example, we equate the extensions of our predicate '— is a gene' and the predicate '— is a gene' as used by classical geneticists around, say, 1920; or if we equate the extensions of our predicate '— is a magnet' and Gilbert's. In each case the same pattern is exhibited. The PBD requires us to equate the extensions of a predicate '— is ψ' of our science and a predicate '— is ϕ' of a past science. But we then find that the predicate '— is ϕ' enters into descriptions of observed events offered by protagonists of the past science in such a way that:

(i) It is quite obvious what sort of events they observed;

(ii) Given that '— is ϕ' and '— is ψ' are coextensive, the descriptions do not apply to the events they observed.

As an objection to the PBD this is far from conclusive. The defender of Putnam's position might well reply as follows.

(1) There is nothing curious in these consequences of application of the PBD. Consider that notorious contemporary of the phlogiston theorists, the transvestite Chevalier d'Eon.[4] The fact that Englishmen of the 1790s concurred in using the predicate '— is phlogiston' in describing certain productions of hydrogen is strictly on a par with their having concurred in using the predicate '— is a woman' in talking about the Chevalier. It is just as ridiculous to infer that productions of hydrogen are to be included in the extension of their predicate '— is phlogiston' as it would be to infer that the Chevalier is to be taken as a member of the extension of their predicate '— is a woman'.

(2) Even if, for the sake of argument, we admit that their use of the predicate '— is phlogiston' in describing certain productions of hydrogen is not a straightforward case of misapprehension, do we really want to assign extensions in such a way as to make OR1 and 2, and the like, come out true? After all, our natural inclination is only to say that they 'contain an element of truth' or 'are true in a loose sense'.

These defences are well-taken. In the following sections I shall

[4] See E. A. Vizetelly, *The True Story of the Chevalier d'Eon*... (London, 1895).

attempt to undercut them by showing that it is a precondition for assignment of extension to the predicates of a past science that that assignment be such as to make many such observation reports as OR1 and 2 come out true.

III

For the realist reference is a relation between words and things. And unless he is prepared to deny the so-called 'trivial conventionalist' thesis that two languages might differ only by a permutation of extensions, he is bound to relativise the relation in some quite drastic way – to communities of speakers at a given time, say. Moreover, as Field, Friedman and Putnam have emphasised, though Tarski's theory of truth defines truth-in-a-language in terms of the reference of the non-logical primitives of the language, it is utterly non-committal on the question of the nature of reference.[5] To be sure, if (that's a big if) we had a Tarskian truth theory for a natural language, then the theory would specify the extensions of all complex referential expressions as functions of the extensions of their non-logical simple constituents. But it would tell us nothing further about what reference is.

I am going to consider the question in a restricted form: What is the relation between a predicate '— is ζ' (where 'ζ' is simple or complex) as used in a community of speakers at a given time, and the entities which belong to its extension? I shall be concerned throughout only with predicates of particulars (material objects, events, and instances of matter[6]). This is not the place to offer a comprehensive survey of theories of reference. For present purposes it suffices to note that they fall into two categories: those which make appeal only to the capacities, beliefs, knowledge, etc. of speakers of the language, and those which postulate other determinants of extension. An extreme theory in the former category is that which maintains that the extension of a predicate '— is ζ', as used in a community P, is determined by a subset of the beliefs the members of P hold about ζs, the analytic truths which together constitute the criteria of demarcation, identification and reidentification associated with the predicate. An extreme theory in the latter category – one which Putnam

---

[5] Putnam, 'What Is "Realism"?', *loc. cit.*; H. Field, 'Tarski's Theory of Truth', *Journal of Philosophy*, 69 (1972), 347–75; H. Friedman, 'Physicalism and Indeterminacy of Translation', *Noûs*, 9 (1975), 353–73.

[6] The type of entities such predicates as '— is gold' range over, e.g., the instance of matter the Pope's crown is made of; for the need for such a type see *Synthèse*, 31 (1975), which is devoted to the semantics of mass nouns.

appears to endorse[7] – is that which maintains that the extension of a predicate '— is ζ', as used by a community P, is determined by the essential nature of whatever objects are the causal ancestors of their use of the predicate.

We need to distinguish, sharply, two questions:

(1) What is it for an object to belong to the extension of a predicate as used in a community of speakers?

(2) How can we discover which objects belong to the extension of a predicate as used in a community of speakers?

An answer to the first question which must occur to anyone unpre-possessed by a philosophical theory of reference is:

C   The extension of a predicate '— is ζ', as used in community P, consists of just those entities which a suitable majority of members of P would identify as ζs.

This won't quite do as it stands, for it has the admittedly absurd consequence that the aforementioned Chevalier d'Eon is a member of the extension of the predicate '— is a woman' as used by Englishmen of the 1790s, provided only that most of them were fooled by him. But it is surely on the right track. Were we to adopt a philosophical theory of reference which could, in principle, divorce the extensions of all predicates used in a community from the objects to which members of the community would concur in applying them, we would face the possibility of finding ourselves *vis-à-vis* that community in the unenviable position of one who says, 'I'm the only one in step'.[8]

A second shot:

C'   As C but with the qualifying clause '..., were each member of P to know, of all that is known by any member of P, all that he would take to be relevant to the identification of ζs'.

This still won't do. With a little ingenuity we can tell a story in which no one, including the Chevalier d'Eon himself, knew anything that would have inclined anyone to decline to identify him as a woman.

A third shot:

[7] See 'The Meaning of "Meaning"', in H. Putnam, *Philosophical Papers*, vol. 2: *Mind, Language and Reality* (Cambridge, 1975), pp. 215–71.
[8] A jibe directed at Kripke's causal theory of names by M. Dummett, 'Postscript' (to papers given at a conference on Language, Intentionality and Translation Theory), *Synthèse*, 27 (1974), 523–34.

C″   As C but with the qualifying clause '..., were each member of P to know the answers to all questions that he would take as relevant to the identification of ζ s'.

C″ deals adequately with consensus based on straightforward shared misapprehension, but it raises some deep and tricky questions. For example, many of the predicates used in a community figure in the expressions of beliefs which have the form of blank cheques to be filled out in the light of future knowledge. Thus some eighteenth-century Englishmen believed there to be hidden particulate determinants of sex in organisms. In specifying the extensions of their predicates '— is a man' and '— is a woman', must we consider, as C″ would apparently require, how they would have applied those predicates had they had our knowledge of the genetic determination of sex and known the genetic constitution of each person? Suppose that the Chevalier d'Eon had indeterminate parts, but that we, on subjecting the Chevalier's pickled ear to microscopic examination, find a male genetic constitution. Are we to say that the Chevalier belongs to the extension of their predicate '— is a man' on the grounds that had they known what we now know they would thus have identified him?[9]

The oddity of such speculations is, I think, merely symptomatic of an underlying incoherence in C″. There is, of course, no incoherence in supposing an eighteenth-century Englishman to have had the capacity, in principle, to acquire our knowledge of the genetic determination of sex. But we cannot suppose him to do this without in so doing ceasing to share many of the beliefs which were in fact shared

---

[9] Along these lines one might even seek to use the consensus account of reference to vindicate the PBD. Thus Putnam writes (in 'The Meaning of "Meaning"'): 'In the view I am advocating, when Archimedes asserted that something was gold ($\chi\rho\nu\sigma\acute{o}s$) he was not just saying that it had the superficial characteristics of gold..., he was saying that it had the same general *hidden structure* (the same "essence", so to speak) as any normal piece of local gold'. Hence it may be argued that although in fact ancient Greeks concurred in identifying as instances of $\chi\rho\nu\sigma\acute{o}s$ many things which are not gold, nevertheless their predicate '— is $\chi\rho\nu\sigma\acute{o}s$' (pardon my Greek) and our predicate '— is gold' have the same extension, because had they known what we now know about the microstructure of matter they would have concurred in identifying all and only instances of gold as instances of $\chi\rho\nu\sigma\acute{o}s$. The 'reformulation' of the beliefs of others which the PBD allows can now be seen as the process whereby we honour their blank cheques drawn on future knowledge. Even if C″ is taken to be coherent this is fishy. One may doubt whether blank-cheque beliefs are really as prevalent as the argument requires if it is to get off the ground. Even if we suppose that they are, it is doubtful whether questions of the form 'How would they apply the predicate "— is ζ" were they to know Θ?' (where their coming to know Θ requires their acquisition of new theoretical knowledge) have determinate answers. Surely different answers will be appropriate given different hypothetical details about the way in which they acquire that knowledge. Far from vindicating the PBD, C″ threatens to render indeterminate the extensions of many predicates of past sciences.

by eighteenth-century Englishmen and acquiring a vast range of concepts and beliefs they did not in fact have. So, on any account which makes a substantial measure of shared belief a determinant of linguistic commonality, we cannot coherently suppose an eighteenth-century Englishman to have the capacity to acquire our knowledge of the genetic determination of sex whilst remaining a member of his original linguistic community.[10] C″ must be modified to:

C‴   As C but with the qualifying clause, '. . ., were each member of P to know the answers to all questions that he would take to be relevant to the identification of ζs and to which *qua* member of P he could have access'.

(In the following pages I shall abbreviate this qualifying clause to '. . ., were each optimally informed'.) C‴ remains obscure. Just what kinds of knowledge are accessible to a person *qua* member of a linguistic community? In the absence of a precise account of the way in which shared belief is a determinant of linguistic commonality, the question cannot be answered.

Though many such awkward questions must be answered in any full justification of the consensus account, this is not the place to pursue them further. For the present purpose it suffices to note that the consensus account can avoid the absurd commitment to actual consensus as the determinant of extension in cases in which that consensus rests on a shared misapprehension. It remains to be shown that, even in its present embryonic form, the consensus account, when combined with certain commonplaces about our application of predicates, yields powerful constraints on our assignment of extensions to the predicates of past sciences. But before embarking on this constructive task a few further notes and provisos are in order.

(1) What makes a language, L, syntactically and semantically specified, into the language of a community, P? Peacocke has suggested that to answer this question would be to convert the Tarskian theory

[10] The arguments for making a substantial measure of shared belief a determinant of linguistic commonality are, fortunately, too well known to bear repetition here. In the context of the present account, alas, a suspicion of circularity arises, roughly as follows. To ascertain the presence of whatever degree of doxastic homogeneity amongst persons is required for linguistic commonality we must have access to the content of the beliefs of those persons. But we cannot have such access unless we can understand the utterances they use to express their beliefs. And this in turn presupposes our ability to specify the extensions of some, at least, of the predicates they use. In reply it may be pointed out that interpretation of utterance is not a precondition for all ascriptions of belief, and that anyway there may be behavioural grounds for ascribing a measure of doxastic homogeneity prior to any particular ascriptions of belief.

of truth-in-a-language into a theory of truth, for we would have an account of truth in the language of P for arbitrary P.[11] On the consensus account it is at least a necessary condition for L to be the language of P that the referential scheme of L be that determined by C'''.[12]

(2) The consensus account belongs to the first of the two categories of theories of reference mentioned earlier, those which appeal only to the capacities, beliefs, knowledge, etc. of speakers. Let us call the capacity, if optimally informed, to identify as ζs the same objects as would a suitable majority of other members of P, similarly well-informed, 'the $C(\zeta)$-capacity'. We can identify having the $C(\zeta)$-capacity with grasping the sense of ζ, and submit to the Fregean slogan 'sense determines reference'. However, in an important respect the consensus account is un-Fregean. If we equate grasp of the sense of a predicate '— is ζ' with possession of the $C(\zeta)$-capacity, doubt is cast on the Fregean claim that the sense of a compound predicate is determined by its logical form and the senses of its simple constituents, which together stipulate a 'canonical' way of applying the predicate. The claim is seen to be plausible only for compound predicates for which the Fregean 'canonical' mode of application provides the only basis on which members of the community would, under any circumstances, apply it, (e.g., perhaps, '— is a cat or weighs less than 2 ounces' as used by us). Where other criteria of application for a compound predicate are, or might under certain circumstances be, used by members of a community, the Fregean doctrine is called in question (for example it seems implausible for the predicate '— is π-meson emission' as used by us, or for the predicate '— is a loss of phlogiston' as used by phlogiston theorists). To put it in a nutshell, the consensus account requires us to abandon the claim that the logically primitive predicates of a language are the only epistemically primitive predicates. This consequence of the consensus account has considerable ramifications which cannot be explored here.

[11] C. Peacocke, 'Truth Definitions and Actual Languages', in G. Evans and J. McDowell (eds.), *Truth and Meaning* (Oxford, 1976), 162–88.

[12] Any attempt to establish a precise 'degree of consensus' short of total consensus as the condition for membership of the extension of a predicate falls foul of the sorites paradox. Clearly the consensus account (like most other accounts of reference) demands a generalisation of the Tarskian schema which allows some sort of ordering of degrees of satisfaction. Great care would be needed in setting up such a generalisation. It is doubtful whether generalisations which, like many of those recently published, take degree of satisfaction to define a total ordering, or even a probability measure, on the domain of a model could be conjoined to the consensus account without running into second-order sorites paradoxes. It just won't do to be too precise about vagueness.

(3) The consensus account is compatible with Putnam's 'hypothesis of the socio-linguistic division of labour', a hypothesis which Putnam has claimed as a motive for adopting a causal theory of reference.[13] For in case a convention of deference to experts in the identification of ζs is subscribed to by members of a community, we are bound to consider *the identifications experts would arrive at* as constituting *answers to questions members of the community would take as relevant to the identification of ζs.*

(4) The consensus account suggests a much stronger version of Putnam's metainduction. To suppose that many of the predicates used in a community have null extension is to cast doubt on the possibility of successful communication within that community, and hence to cast doubt on their utterances as constituting the speaking of a language. I shall not press this line of argument, however, for Putnam's meta-induction already provides powerful enough grounds for the 'realistic' realist to insist that the majority of the predicates of any language have non-empty extensions.

IV

It might be thought that the consensus account of reference *per se* justifies assignments of extension that would render true such observation reports as OR1 and OR2. Remember, it might be said, that the account applies to both simple and complex predicates. Since optimally informed Georgian chemists would, for the most part, have identified as *productions of phlogiston* productions of hydrogen consequent on the addition of sulphuric acid to granulated zinc, then such events belong to the extension of their complex predicate of events '— is a production of phlogiston'. Alas, this short argument won't do. For our conviction that optimally informed Georgian chemists (or at least the pre-Lavoisierian ones) would, for the most part, have identified as *productions of phlogiston* productions of hydrogen consequent on the addition of sulphuric acid to granulated zinc depends upon our having at least a partial understanding of their chemical theory, an understanding sufficient for us to see why they applied that predicate to those events. But unless we can say in what such understanding consists without, in so doing, presupposing that we already know how to specify (in our language) the extensions of their scientific terms, our appeal to that understanding is circular.

How then are we to extract from the consensus account of reference

---

[13] On 'sociolinguistic division of labour', see Putnam, 'The Meaning of "Meaning"', *loc. cit.*, and Dummett, 'Postscript', *loc. cit.*

some positive guidance on the assignment of extensions to the predicates used by past scientists?

Suppose that one day we discover, at the level of the physical, chemical and neurophysiological processes involved, what constitutes a person's dispositions to make identifications and how such dispositions are inculcated. Then, perhaps, a physicalistic reduction of reference would be to hand. But though we lack such esoteric knowledge, we do have exoteric knowledge both about the way in which we acquire our dispositions to make identifications and about the ways in which we do, on occasion, make them. And such knowledge of ourselves, if extrapolated to others, constrains our assignments of extension to the predicates of others.

For example, we know that some form of imitation of the applications of predicates made by others in reporting their observations plays a (causally) important role in each speaker's acquisition of the disposition to apply predicates 'in harmony' with other members of his community. And the existence of such 'harmonious dispositions' is, on the consensus account of reference, a necessary condition for the predicates used in a community to have extensions. It would therefore be *miraculous* if the extensions of many of the predicates used by past scientists in reporting their observations consisted of objects which weren't there or of events which didn't occur on the occasions on which they so used those predicates. We should, therefore, adopt the following Principle:

PCO As far as possible specify the extensions of predicates which figure in the observation reports of past scientists in such a way as not to preclude the presence of members of the extensions of the predicates under the circumstances in which the observation reports were offered.

'PCO' is for 'Principle of Concession of Observations'. 'Concession', not 'Charity': it is we who are the losers if we go round postulating miracles. Application of the PCO does not presuppose initial understanding of the theories of past scientists. Absent from us though past scientists are, we can, without understanding their theories, gather from their lab notebooks, instruments preserved in museums, etc. something about the circumstances under which some of them used some predicates in reporting observations. However, the PCO is very weak. To really get a grip on the extensions of the predicates used by past scientists we need to combine it with some additional Principle or Principles with more guts. Further, our present justification for the

PCO is not altogether a happy one, for it depends upon 'armchair' learning theory. Fortunately a better justification is to hand.

What else do we know about our identificatory practices? Well, we know that our identifications are generally based on reasons. When a person identifies a material object as a ζ, his reasons generally include both beliefs about the thing in question, got by observation, and general beliefs about ζs:

a 'When heated it gave off a violet vapour'
   'Heating ζs causes them to give off violet vapour';

b 'It had red spots on its throat'
   'ζs generally have red spots on their throats';

c 'It seemed ζish to me'
   'ζs appear ζish to normal observers under normal conditions'.

It is not my intention to embark on a rigorous typology of reasons, or to make claims of a normative kind about the conditions under which a person's beliefs constitute adequate or sufficient reasons for making an identification. For my purpose it suffices to observe that the beliefs about ζs on which we do in fact base identifications of things as ζs fall into a number of broad categories.[14] There are beliefs about the observable behaviour of ζs under a variety of natural and contrived circumstances (as in *a*), there are beliefs about the observable properties of ζs (as in *b*), and there are beliefs about the ways in which ζs appear to observers under various circumstances (as in *c*). Let us call such beliefs, collectively, 'O[ζ]-beliefs' ('O' for 'Observation'). Further, we know that in our community, for almost all predicates that are actually used, identifications of any object may be based on a variety of O-beliefs from the first two categories; and that for few, if any, predicates are identifications based only on O-beliefs of the third category.[15] By extrapolation from our own case we may assume that these commonplaces hold for all human communities.

On the consensus account a predicate '— is ζ' as used in a community P has null extension unless there are objects which a suitable majority of members of P would, if optimally informed, identify as ζs. On our

---

[14] 'Base' is unforgivably vague. I am inclined to say that an act of identification is based on a belief just in case it would not have occurred had the identifier not come to hold that belief. But this introduces many more problems, problems on which I have nothing original to say.

[15] A stronger thesis – that in no language learned in anything like the way our language is learned could there be predicates for which all identifications are based directly on appearances – is ably defended by M. B. Hesse, 'Is There an Independent Observation Language?', in R. G. Colodny (ed.), *The Nature and Function of Scientific Theories* (Pittsburgh, 1970), 35–77.

assumptions about the role of O-beliefs in the making of identifications it would be *miraculous* were members of P to achieve consensus in their application of a predicate '— is ζ' if many of their $O[\zeta]$-beliefs are false. For on our assumptions it is clearly a necessary condition for achievement of such consensus that different members of P (and the same member on different occasions) should frequently identify the same object as a ζ on the basis of different $O[\zeta]$-beliefs. If we assign extensions to their predicates in such a way as to render many of their $O[\zeta]$-beliefs false, the satisfaction of the condition becomes inexplicable for us. And we now have a better justification for the PCO. For it would be equally miraculous were members of a community to concur in identifying objects as ζs on the basis of $O[\zeta]$-beliefs despite their being generally deluded in believing they had observed the requisite characteristics or behaviour of those objects.

Let us focus on the first of our broad categories of $O[\zeta]$-beliefs, beliefs about the observable 'behaviour' of ζs. For example, consider the predicate '— is (pure) gold'. Amongst our $O[(\text{pure}) \text{ gold}]$-beliefs are:

> 'heating of pure gold to 1,063 °C causes it to melt';
>
> 'dropping gold into *aqua regia* causes it to dissolve';
>
> 'heating of gold by 1 °C in the range 18–100 °C causes it to expand by 14.3×10^{-6}'.

The correct analysis of such sentences – let us call them 'OC-sentences' ('C' for 'Causal') – is a controversial matter. For my purpose, however, a single thesis suffices, the extensionality thesis brilliantly defended by Davidson.[16] The truth values of C-sentences are preserved under substitution of coextensive predicates for the (generally complex) predicates of events which figure in them. Thus, *if* all and only heatings of gold to 1,063 °C are heatings of matter composed of atoms with 79 protons each to 1,336 °K, *then* heating of pure gold to 1,063 °C causes it to melt if, and only if, heating of matter composed of atoms with 79 protons each to 1,336 °K causes it to melt.

We are now in a position to state the second of the promised Principles for the specification of extensions of the predicates of past sciences. We have established that it would be *miraculous* if the

[16] D. Davidson, 'Causal Relations', *Journal of Philosophy*, 64 (1967), 691–703. In a number of recent papers Davidson's extensionality thesis, and his refusal to admit facts, properties, states of affairs, etc. into the domain of the causal relation, have been ably defended against plausible objections. See, e.g., F. R. Bohl, 'On Sentences Referring', *Logique et Analyse*, n.s., 13 (1973), 345–57; D. V. Gottlieb and L. H. Davis, 'Extensionality and Singular Causal Sentences', *Philosophical Studies*, 25 (1974), 69–72.

predicates used by past scientists had extensions, but many of the OC-beliefs they associated with the predicates were false. So, on pain of postulating miracles we should adopt the following Principle:

PCC As far as possible specify the extensions of predicates which figure in the OC-beliefs of past scientists in such a way as to render them true.

'PCC' is for 'Principle of Concession of Causes'. Like the PCO, the PCC is such that its application does not presuppose our prior understanding of the theories held by past scientists. For the extensionality thesis assures us that to find out whether an assignment of extensions to the predicates of an OC-sentence renders it true we have only to see if substitution into it of the predicates we use to specify the extensions for the original predicates yields a true sentence. We do not have to 'understand' the original sentence; we do not have to worry whether or not the predicates we use to specify the extensions 'have the same meanings', 'have the same extensions in other possible worlds', 'play the same explanatory roles', as the original predicates.

  Together the PCO and PCC justify the 'commonsense' assignments of extension which earlier we used to cast doubt on Putnam's Principle of Benefit of the Doubt. In each case we satisfy PCO. Our assignment of extensions does not preclude the past scientists' having observed what they said they had observed under the circumstances under which they offered the observation reports. And in each case we satisfy PCC. Our assignment of extensions renders true their sentences 'addition of vitriolic acid to granulated zinc causes production of phlogiston' and 'heating of bleaching solution causes production of the oxide of muriatic acid'.

V

There can be little doubt that in practice application of the PCO and PCC, like application of Putnam's PBD, would yield specifications of non-empty extensions for many of the predicates, both technical and commonplace, used by past scientists. But the consequences of application of the PBD and of my Principles of Concession ('PC' for short) are otherwise diametrically opposed.

  (1) According to the PBD, whenever we ask about the extension of a simple predicate '— is ϕ' of a past science we face a dilemma. *Either* we must equate its extension with that of some simple predicate '— is ζ' of our science, *or* we must admit that it has null extension.

NICK JARDINE

According to the PC we escape this dilemma. We are allowed in specifying the extension of simple predicates of past sciences to use exceedingly complex disjunctive predicates. For example, an approximate specification of the extension of the predicate '— is phlogiston' as used by Georgian chemists might be: 'occurrences of matter which are *either* hydrogen resulting from the addition of an acid to a metal *or* oxygen which combines with a substance when it is burnt or fermented *or*...'. Note that it is not just 'technical' predicates of past sciences which are thus fragmented. The extension of the commonplace predicate of events '— is a *loss* of...', as used by phlogiston theorists, would turn out to include certain kinds of *accession*; for the PC would urge us to include in the extension of the predicate '— is a loss of phlogiston' certain kinds of accession of oxygen. Of course the fragmentation of the predicates of past sciences need not always be *so* drastic. Consider the predicates '— is a gene' and '— is a chromosome' as used by classical geneticists. Though the PC would yield a rather complex specification of extension for the classical geneticist's predicate '— is a gene', all the things thereby specified as members of its extension would be segments of DNA or RNA (the operons, cistrons, recons and mutons of the molecular geneticist).[17] And the PC would probably specify the extension of the classical geneticist's predicate '— is a chromosome' as consisting just of chromosomes.

(2) The ways in which we approach past sciences for the purpose of specification of extension using the PBD and PC are very different. Using the PBD our attention is focused on the predicates which figure as primitives in their most fundamental theoretical laws. Using the PC our attention is focused on complex predicates which figure in the derivative causal laws on which their expectations about observable successions of events depend. Where the PBD comes crashing down on top of past sciences the PC sneak up underneath them.

(3) The PBD urges us to assign null extension to a predicate of a past science just in case the theoretical beliefs of the past scientists in which the predicate figures cannot be exhibited as approximately true of entities of some kind we recognise. The PC, on the other hand, will always urge specification of a non-empty extension provided we can detect a consistent use of the predicate in observation reports and OC-beliefs. Despite the strangeness of Newton's mystical beliefs about the star regulus, application of the PC to the content of his alchemical notebooks would unromantically reveal the extension of his predicate

[17] For evidence for this claim see K. F. Schaffner, 'The Watson–Crick Model and Reductionism', *British Journal for the Philosophy of Science*, 20 (1969), 325–48.

'— is the star regulus' to be a subset of the extension of our predicate '— is copper/antimony alloy'.[18] Only when a predicate never figures, or figures in no consistent way, in past scientists' observation reports and OC-sentences will the PC suggest a null extension. Gassendi's predicate '— is an atom', and perhaps even Dalton's, may be such cases.

(4) The overall views of scientific progress which the PBD and the PC would yield are diametrically opposed. Application of the PBD would reveal that science shows a convergence of knowledge, offering an ever more complete inventory and accurate description of the fundamental *kinds* of things. Anaxagoras was the first to talk about (?discovered) atoms, but we know far more than he did about them; Gilbert was the first clearly to discriminate (?discovered) electricity and magnetism, but we can make that discrimination far more accurately. Such a picture of scientific progress may encourage, though it does not entail, a Peircean vision of an ultimate science, an omega of human knowledge in which the essences of all things are revealed. Application of the PC would reveal no such convergence. The simple predicates of one science become – are found to be coextensive with – vastly complex disjunctive predicates of subsequent sciences. The progress which the PC would reveal is progress in the domain of low-level causal beliefs, the beliefs on which identifications of things are based and on which men's expectations of regularity in observed successions of events depend. Such a picture encourages, though it does not entail, a vision of science as endlessly tentative and open-ended.

The view of scientific progress which the Principles of Concession encourage may be called a 'Duhemian view', not because it embodies any specifically Duhemian theses about the structure and epistemology of science, but because of the way in which it contrasts progress at the level of the beliefs which yield predictive control over nature with instability at the level of the concepts we use to explain and systematise those beliefs.[19] I find that the Duhemian vision of scientific progress yielded by the PC – a vision of experimental groping forward amid conceptual chaos – is eminently commonsensical; Putnam, likewise, finds that the vision of scientific progress yielded by the PBD – a cumulative discovery of, and convergence of knowledge about, natural kinds – is implicit in science 'viewed diachronically' and 'taken at face value'. What apart from bare common sense, then, makes the Duhemian vision plausible?

(1) It assimilates 'the acceptable face of relativism'. The relativist

---

[18] See B. J. T. Dobbs, *The Foundations of Newton's Alchemy* (Cambridge, 1975), pp. 146–56 and Appendix B.

[19] P. Duhem, *La théorie physique, son objet et sa structure* (Paris, 1906).

NICK JARDINE

claims that speakers of different cultures, having different *Weltan-schauungen*, ideologies, interests, paradigms, etc., 'carve up the world differently', 'see the world through different categories', 'create incommensurable worlds', etc. And these differences are all-pervasive, not restricted to specialised, technical concepts. On the Duhemian view these metaphors have a straightforward interpretation. There is no reason to expect, and plenty of reason not to expect, an extension-preserving 1 : 1 correspondence between the simple predicates used by speakers of different cultures, having different *Weltanschauungen*, ideologies, interests and paradigms. And this holds for all predicates, not just the technical and specialised. The Duhemian, indeed, is prepared to go further than many relativists, making drastic conceptual divergence a fairly domestic matter. No need to imagine tribes with weird interests and practices, just visit the older scientists in the lab next door. So we embrace the relativist's metaphors, but where he uses them to cast doubt on the legitimacy of quantifying over all there is, we take them to imply only that there are far more sorts of things than the ones *we* talk about.[20] This qualified admission of conceptual relativism is harshly opposed to a certain 'hard-line realist' view of the sources of scientific knowledge, a view which Putnam flirts with – the view that there is an absolute ontology of essential natures or properties whose causal efficacy is evident *both* in the observed behaviour of things *and* in the growth of our knowledge about the essential natures of things.[21] To the extent that such hard-line realism is objectionable – objectionable in its essentialism, and objectionable in its talk of *properties* causing *events* – it is to the credit of the Duhemian view that it militates against it.

(2) It assimilates 'the acceptable face of hypothetico-deductivism'. No one seriously doubts that there has been a cumulative, if sometimes uneven, growth in human technological and predictive control of nature. It would be strange indeed if this increase in efficiency in human action had not been accompanied by, and is not to be partially explained by, an accumulation of true belief about the outcomes of actions. The hypothetico-deductivist sees the requisite accumulation as an accumulation of belief in true 'experimental laws'; the Duhemian sees it as an accumulation of belief in true 'OC-sentences'. There is, of course, a crucial difference here. The hypothetico-deductivist's experimental laws are just those generalisations all of whose non-logical primitive predicates are, or are definable in terms of, *observation*

[20] Cf. D. Davidson, 'On the Very Idea of a Conceptual Scheme', *Proceedings of the American Philosophical Association*, 47 (1973–4), 5–20.
[21] The flirtation appears briefly in section 6 of 'What Is "Realism"?', *loc. cit.*

predicates: predicates whose applicability is always decidable by direct observation. No such limitation is imposed on OC-sentences. It suffices that the often complex predicates of events which figure in them be in fact used in reporting observations. 'Impact of a proton on a K-meson causes the production of three π-mesons and a stable baryon' is a perfectly good OC-sentence, given that scientists do in fact report what they observe (in cloud-chambers) in such terms. The fact that the descriptive use of such predicates presupposes a massive body of theoretical knowledge – that such predicates are, to use the current jargon, 'theory-laden' – is irrelevant.

VI

Putnam suggests that realism about truth, a 'realistic' attitude to our scientific knowledge, and an account of the nature of reference which appeals to causal chains and essential natures conspire to dictate a certain Principle for the assignment of referents to the terms of past sciences, a Principle which yields a vision of 'convergence' of human scientific knowledge. I have suggested that realism about truth, a 'realistic' attitude to our scientific knowledge, and a consensus account of the nature of reference conspire to dictate certain Principles for the assignment of extensions to the predicates of past sciences, Principles which yield a Duhemian vision of the progress of science.

At the very least we have an alternative package of philosophical prejudices for the 'realistic' realist. I believe that we have more than that, that we have here a programme for the vindication of realism about truth in an area in which it has recently come under heavy fire. I say 'a programme for vindication' because both the consensus account of reference and the Duhemian picture of the growth of science require far more in the way of justification than I have been able to offer in this paper.

Perhaps it is futile to seek to vindicate realism about truth in an area so far removed from the fundamental issue which divides realists from relativists. Perhaps it can be shown *a priori* that it is or is not legitimate to appeal, regardless of the diverse beliefs, cultures and interests of speakers, to a single external reality as the measure of truth. By induction on the history of philosophy from Protagoras and Plato to Dummett and Putnam, I doubt it.[22]

[22] I am grateful to Chris Hookway and Jonathan Lear for constructive criticism of an earlier draft of this paper.

On 'The Reality of the Past'[1]

JOHN McDOWELL

§1 Philosophers have found attractions in the idea that a theory of meaning for a language might include a component capable of specifying, for any indicative sentence of the language, a condition under which it is true.[2] But suppose we are dealing with a language which, like our own, permits formation of sentences with the following property: we have no method which we can bank on to equip us, within a finite time, with knowledge that a given sentence is true, or, failing that, with knowledge that it is not. Thus inability, however protracted, to detect that a sentence is true need not put us in a position to rule out the possibility that it is. It seems, then, that if we credit ourselves with a conception of conditions under which such sentences are true, we have to picture them as conditions which may obtain beyond all possibility of bringing them to our awareness. Now the idea that truth conditions may thus transcend possible verification is characteristic of a realism which Michael Dummett has urged us to find problematic.[3]

A theory of meaning for a language should be a theoretical representation of the practical capacity which constitutes understanding it.[4] The capacity would be perspicuously described by a theory which related the language, in detail, to the world, in such a way that

---

[1] The topic of this paper is not the reality of the past, but rather realism and anti-realism as discussed by Michael Dummett in his paper 'The Reality of the Past', *Proceedings of the Aristotelian Society*, n.s., 69 (1968–9), 239. I have been helped, in writing this, by Gareth Evans, Graeme Forbes, Colin McGinn, and Christopher Peacocke. My view of Wittgenstein is close to that independently adopted by Samuel Guttenplan in his *Meaning and Truth* (Milton Keynes, 1976).

[2] Donald Davidson has recommended the idea in a series of papers beginning with 'Truth and Meaning', *Synthèse*, 17 (1967), 304. For a sketch of the justification as I see it, see §1 of my 'Truth Conditions, Bivalence, and Verificationism', in Gareth Evans and John McDowell (eds.), *Truth and Meaning* (Oxford, 1976), p. 42. Indexicality dictates a modification (not sentences *tout court*, but sentences as uttered on occasions) which I have silently introduced at various subsequent points.

[3] As well as 'The Reality of the Past', see 'Truth', *Proceedings of the Aristotelian Society*, n.s., 59 (1958–9), 141; *Frege: Philosophy of Language* (London, 1973), *passim* (see the Brief Subject Index, under 'Verificationism versus realism, as theories of meaning'); and 'What Is a Theory of Meaning? (II)', in Evans and McDowell (eds.), *op. cit.*, p. 67.

[4] See, e.g., Dummett, *Frege*, p. 92.

JOHN MCDOWELL

someone who explicitly knew the theory (and knew enough about the
world) would be able to use the language as if he had an ordinary,
unreflective competence in it. Alternatively, we might conceive ordinary, unreflective competence as actually consisting in implicit knowledge of such a theory.[5] Now suppose the realistic notion of truth
conditions is employed in a proffered theory, implicit knowledge of
which is thus to be thought of as constituting competence in a language.
According to the anti-realist position which Dummett describes, it
is impossible to make sense of a speaker's possessing that state of
knowledge. All that can be imparted, by the training which results
in competence with a language, is an ability to suit one's linguistic
behaviour to circumstances which impinge on one's consciousness.
How can the capacity so acquired involve the idea of states of affairs
which may obtain even though they defeat all attempts to bring
them to our awareness? How could the training have given one
any conception of what it would be for such a state of affairs to
obtain?[6]

Some sentences with the problematic property – in particular, sentences in the past tense – are, however, quite intelligible. So the line
of argument I have just sketched motivates the aim of constructing
theories of meaning in a contrasting, anti-realist style: theories which
use – in their expression of the content of the implicit knowledge in
which (if we formulate their claims in that way) competence with such
sentences is conceived as consisting – not the notion of possibly
undetectable conditions under which the sentences are true, but rather
the notion of conditions guaranteed detectable when they obtain, to
which the language-learner has been trained to respond as making it
correct to assert the sentences.

§2 At the very least, then, anti-realism poses a challenge to a realist:
to explain how someone can acquire a realistic conception of truth
conditions from training which relates the correct use of sentences only
to accessible states of affairs.

Now, according to Dummett, a realist about the past might claim
to meet the challenge by an appeal to the 'truth-value link': the

[5] There are dangers here: see §9.
[6] Couching the anti-realist argument, as here, in terms of theses about the learning of
language makes it seem vulnerable, in ways that it should not really be, to accusations
of reliance on armchair learning theory: see Crispin Wright, 'Truth Conditions and
Criteria', *Proceedings of the Aristotelian Society, Supplementary Vol.* 50 (1976), 217. The
acquisition version of the argument is, however, the one most prominent in 'The
Reality of the Past', and it provides a natural context for my discussion of the appeal
to truth-value links (§§2–4). See, further, §§7 and 8 below.

128

principle, that is, that a suitably dated past-tensed sentence, uttered, say, now, is true just in case a suitably related present-tensed sentence, uttered at the appropriate past time, would then have been true.[7]

How is the truth-value link supposed to help? In the case of *present*-tensed sentences – so long as we waive anti-realist difficulties other than those which stem from the past's lack of guaranteed accessibility – a description of competence in terms of truth conditions can be seen, by an anti-realist, as a harmless variant of his style of theory. For whether those truth conditions obtain is always, in principle, ascertainable – if we waive those other difficulties – by the person whose competence is being described, so that no anti-realist query arises here about how the person can have a conception of what it is for such a condition to obtain. The realist's idea, now, would be that by way of the truth-value link one can transfer to applicability to *past*-tensed utterances the conception whose innocence is thus established for the case of the present tense. Equipped with a conception of what it is for, say, a sentence reporting rain to be true when the rain is falling now, the language-learner uses the truth-value link to project a conception of that very same circumstance – the falling of rain – into the past. What is required is a conception of the sort of state of affairs which would have made an utterance of 'It's raining now' true at some past time; and that is the very sort of state of affairs a conception of which we have already found it harmless to ascribe to our subject.

An anti-realist insists that linguistic competence cannot involve a conception of sorts of circumstance other than those which a language-learner had available to his consciousness in learning the language. Dummett's realist is attempting, with the truth-value-link manoeuvre, to respect that principle. His idea is that a circumstance of the relevant sort (say, an instance of the falling of rain) can indeed have been available to the language-learner's consciousness – namely, on occasions when the appropriate *present*-tensed sentence was correctly assertible; and that the truth-value link suffices to entitle a theorist, on the basis of that fact, to represent competence with *past*-tensed sentences as implicit knowledge whose content involves precisely those sorts of circumstance (rainfall or whatever) which would figure in a truth-conditions description of competence with the related present-tensed sentences – the difference being only that in the projected employment they are tagged as having obtained in the past. On these grounds, he disavows an obligation to restrict the materials of his description of competence to circumstances accessible to the consciousness of a competent speaker at the times when the relevant

[7] Dummett, 'The Reality of the Past', pp. 244–5, 246–7.

JOHN MCDOWELL

past-tensed sentences are *themselves* correctly assertible. He claims to
bypass those circumstances, crediting the speaker with a conception
which reaches out beyond them to the past occurrences and states of
affairs themselves. We might imagine him expressing his view of the
efficacy of the truth-value link like this: 'If I suppose that it rained
yesterday, then I am simply supposing that there obtained yesterday
just the same condition as I have so often observed.' Or perhaps, to
bring out how he purports to have made superfluous any consideration
of present warrants for past-tensed assertions: 'Rain is rain – whether
it fell yesterday or is falling now; and however I come to know
whether it fell yesterday or not.'[8]

These echoes emphasise how the debate between realist and anti-
realist about the past, as Dummett presents it, runs parallel, in certain
structural respects, with a familiar philosophical dialectic about sentience in others. If we think of ourselves as possessing a conception
of truth conditions for sentences suitable for ascribing, say, sensations
to others, we have to picture those conditions as not necessarily
accessible to our knowledge-acquiring powers, since the truth-value
of an utterance of such a sentence need not be ascertainable either
way (cf. §1). An anti-realist response to that realism would be a form
of behaviourism: competence with those sentences relates their correct
use only to circumstances guaranteed accessible if they obtain, under
which the language-learner has been taught that assertive utterances
of the sentences are in order.[9] As before, this puts the onus on a
realist to show how the relevant competence can be anything else. And
here too, a certain sort of realist will be inclined to appeal to a truth-value
link: a statement ascribing, say, pain to another person is true just in
case a self-ascription of pain by him would be true. The point of this
is, again, to bypass those behavioural warrants for other-ascriptions
of pain which the anti-realist insists are all that can figure in a description of competence with the relevant forms of words, while pur-
porting to respect the anti-realist's principle that linguistic competence
can involve a conception only of sorts of circumstance which were
available to the language-learner's consciousness in his learning of the
language. The relevant sort of circumstance is that of a person's being
in pain. According to this realist, circumstances of that sort can indeed

[8] Cf. Ludwig Wittgenstein, *Philosophical Investigations* (Oxford, 1953), §§350 and 351.
[9] 'A form of behaviourism': presumably the relevant accessible circumstances will be
broadly behavioural, and 'behaviourism' seems an appropriate name for a view which
restricts the circumstances mentioned in an account of competence with the utterances
in question to such circumstances. But I intend no suggestion that anti-realism must
be crudely reductionist: see Dummett, 'The Reality of the Past', pp. 240–3, and cf.
some remarks in §10 below.

130

have been present to the language-learner's consciousness – namely, on occasions when the person in question was himself. (We know what pain is from our own case.) The truth-value link enables the language-learner to project a conception of that same sort of circumstance – a person's being in pain – past the detectable behavioural conditions at which the anti-realist sticks, and into the inner lives of others. An other-ascription of pain is true – if it is true – in virtue of an instance of the very sort of circumstance of which the language-learner has acquired a conception, harmlessly from the standpoint of anti-realism, by having instances of it present to his awareness in his own case.

§3 A realist who thinks he needs to appeal to a truth-value link, in order to meet the anti-realist challenge, shows – unless he is confused – that he pictures the truth conditions of the problematic sorts of sentence not merely as not being always accessible but rather as being always inaccessible.

The anti-realist principle which he is attempting to respect (see §2) is that a description of linguistic competence may credit its possessor with a conception only of sorts of circumstance which he has had available to his consciousness during his training in the use of the language. He tries to respect it by pointing to the availability of circumstances which according to him belong to the required sorts, only on occasions when they constitute the truth conditions of *present*-tensed utterances, or *self*-ascriptions of sensation. If he thought circumstances of the required sorts were sometimes available to consciousness on occasions when they constitute the truth conditions of *past*-tensed utterances, or *other*-ascriptions of sensation, he could claim that the allegedly problematic conception was acquired, directly, on those occasions. There would be no need for appeal to a truth-value link, since there would be no need to regard the allegedly problematic conception as acquired by projection from the unproblematic cases of the present, or oneself. This realist, then, turns down a chance to claim that some occasions when circumstances justify assertive utterances of sentences of the problematic kinds are occasions when their *truth* conditions – which may on other occasions keep hidden from us – make themselves manifest. By appealing, instead, to truth-value links, he indicates that he agrees, rather, with the anti-realist to this extent: he regards the circumstances which actually impinge on the consciousness of a speaker, even on the prime occasions for training in the assertoric use of the sentences, as not themselves constituting cases of the obtaining of truth conditions, realistically construed – that is, construed as conditions of sorts which may, on other occasions, obtain

undetectably. The assertion-warranting circumstances which do manifest themselves, however conclusive the evidential relation between
them and the truth conditions, are distinct from the truth conditions;
and the obtaining of the truth conditions, since he thinks of it as
distinct from what is available to consciousness even when one has the
best possible justification for asserting the sentences, is pictured by him
as something which, in itself, transcends what is accessible to awareness.

All this fits comfortably into place in that familiar complex of
realistic ideas about sentience in others (§2). Another person's pain,
in that sort of view, is something essentially concealed from us, behind
a screen of facial expression and behaviour. In the case of the past,
the analogous thought would be that a past occurrence is dead and
gone, necessarily lost to our view.[10]

§4 Truth-value links are actually impotent to do what realists of this
kind want them to do.[11] According to a truth-value-link realist, the state
of affairs which consists in another person's being in pain is never itself
accessible to consciousness. An anti-realist finds it unintelligible that
a conception of such a state of affairs should be involved in linguistic
competence. The realist's purported answer is, in effect, this: 'You can
see how a person can have the idea of what it is for someone to be
in pain – when the someone in question is himself. Well, a sentence
like "He is in pain", uttered in a context which fixes a reference for
the pronoun, is understood as saying, of some appropriate other
person, that he is in that very same state.' But this, so far from solving
the problem, simply ignores it. If someone cannot see how another
person's being in pain – on an interpretation of that circumstance
which makes it inaccessible – can possibly enter into the meaning one
attaches to some form of words, one does not allay his worry by baldly
re-asserting that it does.[12]

[10] Such realism can perhaps purport to make room for the concession that there is
sometimes conclusive justification for other-ascriptions of sensation, or for past-tensed
assertions. (This would be the position of the conciliatory realist envisaged at pp. 247–8
of Dummett, 'The Reality of the Past'.) But there would be an easy slide into
scepticism. Not that *that* is the case against this sort of realism. The situation is not
that we understand well enough the propositions represented as conclusions from
the evidence of behaviour or traces, but find the inferences shaky; rather, the
purported conclusions are (purportedly) conceived in such a way as to make it
impossible to see how we can so much as understand them.

[11] Curiously enough, the temporal truth-value link figures in 'The Reality of the Past'
only as a weapon against the anti-realist, who is put to some trouble to show that he
can accommodate it. The realist's use of the link as a response to the anti-realist
challenge goes unscrutinised.

[12] 'The explanation by means of identity does not work here': Wittgenstein, *Investigations*, §350.

Similarly with the past. An anti-realist finds it unintelligible that a conception of the truth condition of a past-tensed utterance, thought of as something whose obtaining is, in itself, inaccessible, should be involved in linguistic competence. The realist's purported reply is on these lines: 'You can see how someone can know what it is for rain to be falling. Well, a sentence like "It was raining" is understood as saying that that very circumstance obtained at some past time.' Again, this does not meet the worry, but simply restates the claim which gave rise to it. The problem was precisely an inability to see how the past obtaining of that circumstance – an instance of a kind of circumstance which the realism we are considering makes inaccessible – can possibly enter into any meaning one could succeed in attaching to a sentence.

Of course I am not advocating rejection of the principles which constitute the truth-value links. In fact room must surely be found for them in any acceptable position. The point is just that they cannot serve to answer the anti-realist challenge.

It is instructive to compare the uselessness of appeals to truth-value links, in the two areas considered so far, with a role they might play in a third. Consider adverbial modifiers which yield sentences suitable for making assertions about how things are elsewhere. The truth conditions of such sentences, as uttered on given occasions, would consist in the obtaining of appropriate states of affairs elsewhere; and those circumstances – the obtaining of those states of affairs in places specified as being other than where the speaker is – might be inaccessible to the speaker's awareness. So a form of the anti-realist challenge might seem to be in place. Here, however, appeal to truth-value links yields an effective justification for continuing to use the notion of truth conditions in a theory of meaning. For the truth-value links appealed to in this case would point to ways in which – by travelling and then checking whether the truth conditions of the unmodified sentences obtain – a person could, in principle, decide whether the truth conditions ascribed to the modified sentences, by a theory which incorporates the links, obtained before the travel was undertaken. (Of course this needs qualification – for instance, to cover ruling out the possibility of change during the travel.) In this case, then, as not in the others, appeal to truth-value links might genuinely help a realist, serving to remove an initial appearance that a description of linguistic competence in terms of truth conditions is inimical to the broadly verificationist principles of the anti-realist.

§5 The attraction of truth-value links lies in their seeming to permit a realist to bypass detectable assertion-warranting circumstances. No doubt he would have to allow that such circumstances play a role in the *acquisition* of the problematic competence; but the role would be at best indirect, pointing the language-learner to the place where the required conception of a truth condition is to be found.[13] The conception itself is to be one to whose content those detectable assertion-warranting circumstances are strictly irrelevant: 'Pain is pain – whether *he* has it, or *I* have it; and however I come to know whether he has a pain or not.'[14]

When we are tempted towards a realism of this sort about other-ascriptions of sensation, we are inclined to rely on a picture of the inner world as a sort of concealed receptacle. In another person's receptacle – so we encourage ourselves by thinking – a given item, say pain, is either present or not; at any rate the receptacle's owner knows which, and so, perhaps, does God. The picture 'by itself seems to make the sense of the expressions *unmistakable*: "Now you know what is in question" – we should like to say'.[15] The parallel realism about the past draws comfort, similarly, from picturing a God's-eye view of the course of history – an extra-temporal standpoint from which events in our past can be witnessed in just the same way as events in our present. In the series of occurrences and states of affairs laid out timelessly under God's imagined gaze, a given event, say, is either present or not: God knows which, even if we do not. Here too, while we are under the spell, that seems to justify 'Now you know what is in question'.

Of course we *do* know what is in question. But these transcendently realistic positions are under attack as making it impossible to see how we could have any such knowledge; and we must not let ourselves be prevented, by our possession of an ordinary, unproblematic understanding of the sorts of sentence at issue, from seeing that insistence on instances of the law of excluded middle, with the associated pictures, constitutes no genuine rebuttal of the attack. The anti-realist's objection was that we cannot have a conception of a sort of state of affairs which is in principle inaccessible to us. To say that God, or another person who is in pain, or a participant in a historical event, knows, or knew, what is in question does nothing towards showing how it is possible that we do, given that what is in question is, as transcendent realism makes it, a state of affairs of a sort beyond our ken.[16]

---

[13] This is how, in the light of §3, we must understand the concession which Dummett envisages the realist making: 'The Reality of the Past', pp. 247–8.

[14] Wittgenstein, *Investigations*, §351.   [15] *Ibid.* §352.

[16] Cf. Dummett, 'What Is a Theory of Meaning? (II)', pp. 98–101. Note that Wittgenstein's point, at *Investigations*, §352, is not that we are not entitled to claim *truth* for the relevant instances of the law of excluded middle, but simply that insisting on them

§6 The truth-value-link realist wanted to avoid mentioning, in his description of competence with the problematic sorts of sentence, circumstances which, when they manifest themselves to awareness, warrant assertions of the sentences; and it seems that his hopes of doing so were vain (§§4, 5). If truth-value-link realism and anti-realism were the only options, as Dummett's treatment suggests, that conclusion would leave anti-realism in possession of the field. But there is another option: a realism which meets the anti-realist challenge in the way which I distinguished, in §3, from appeal to a truth-value link.

That is, there are two distinct ways of allowing, in the description of linguistic competence, mention of circumstances which, when they detectably obtain, justify the making of assertions: anti-realism, and this different variety of realism. We can bring out the difference by contrasting two answers to this question: In what sorts are we to classify the circumstances which justify assertion of the problematic sentences, on the paradigmatic occasions for training in their assertoric use? An anti-realist thinks of the circumstances as belonging to sorts which are available to awareness *whenever* they obtain. That, together with the fact that the truth values of the problematic sentences need not be ascertainable either way, blocks thinking of the circumstances as actually being truth conditions of the sentences. The realist who is distinguished in §3 from the truth-value-link realist thinks of the circumstances, by contrast, as belonging to sorts which are sometimes available to consciousness – as they are on the occasions which constitute opportunities for training – *but sometimes not*. Thus he enables himself to think of them as actually *being* truth conditions, realistically construed, for the sentences.

According to this position, what warrants the assertion that another person is in pain, on one of the relevant occasions, is the detectable obtaining of the circumstance of that person's being in pain: an instance of a kind of circumstance – another person's being in pain – which is available to awareness, in its own right and not merely through behavioural proxies, on some occasions, including this one, although, on other occasions, the obtaining of other instances can be

does nothing to justify 'Now you know what is in question'. The error is to think of 'Either he is in pain or not' as picturing logical space as it were like this:

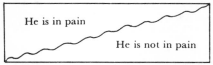

whereas if we are to think of it as a picture, it should be conceived on the pattern of the Bellman's map. None of this requires doubts about classical logic.

quite beyond detection. Similarly, what warrants the assertion, on one of the relevant occasions, that, say, some event of a specified kind occurred in the past is the obtaining of a circumstance which consists simply in such an event's having occurred: an instance of a kind of circumstance which is available to awareness, in its own right and not merely through traces going proxy for it, on some occasions, including this one, although, on other occasions, the obtaining of other instances can be quite outside our reach.

A truth-value-link realist represents the truth condition of an other-ascription of pain as something which is, in itself, inaccessible (§3); that another person is in pain can be known, if at all, only by inference from circumstances which are accessible. A realist of our different kind rejects this relegation of truth conditions to the far side of something which would in fact – as the anti-realist sees – operate as a barrier, preventing our minds from penetrating to a genuine conception of what it is for the truth conditions to obtain. In the view of this different realist, then, we should not jib at, or interpret away, the commonsense thought that, on those occasions which are paradigmatically suitable for training in the assertoric use of the relevant part of a language, one can literally perceive, in another person's facial expression or his behaviour, that he is in pain, and not just infer that he is in pain from what one perceives.[17]

The analogue, in the case of the past, would be insistence that knowledge of the past occurrence of an event of a specified kind (say) is sometimes non-inferential. Events make impacts on our senses while they occur:[18] mastery of forms of words suitable for describing

---

[17] P. F. Strawson's use, in chap. 3 of *Individuals* (London, 1959), of the notion of 'criteria of a logically adequate kind' for other-ascription has been criticised (e.g. by Hilary Putnam, 'Brains and Behaviour', in R. J. Butler (ed.), *Analytical Philosophy*, 2nd ser. (Oxford, 1965), p. 1) as involving the idea of a somehow guaranteed *inference* from purely behavioural descriptions of others to statements about their minds; but I believe Strawson intended something more like the idea expressed in the text. Note that it is *not* the point of the idea to suggest an *answer* to scepticism about other minds. On Wittgenstein's concept of a criterion, see especially the 'Postscript' to Rogers Albritton's article 'On Wittgenstein's Use of the Term "Criterion"', reprinted in George Pitcher (ed.), *Wittgenstein: The Philosophical Investigations* (London, 1968), p. 231. (The idea that there *must* be an inference, to be labelled 'tacit' if necessary, stems, I believe, from the same error as the idea that a consistent use of an expression *must* be informatively definable in terms of necessary and sufficient conditions.) Wittgenstein's best thoughts in this area constitute a subtle and characteristic refusal to take sides in the typically *philosophical* debate between transcendent (truth-value-link) realism and anti-realism; it is sad to find him widely construed as enrolling himself with the anti-realists.

[18] This is strictly false (the time-lag argument), but I believe the fact is not germane to my purpose of suggesting a way for a kind of realist to meet the anti-realist challenge.

contemporary events is acquired by training which begins by instilling propensities to respond to those impacts with appropriate verbal behaviour. The fact that training which imparts mastery of the past tense can get started at all is presumably due to the persistence sometimes, presumably in the nervous system, of some trace of the impact of a previous event on the senses, so that suitable training is able to institute a differentiation of verbal dispositions, with respect to forms of words systematically related to those with which present events are apt to be greeted, according to whether or not those presumed traces are present. Times when the persisting effects are likeliest to be present are, on this view, the best occasions for initial training in the assertoric use of the past tense. A person whose nervous system contains one of the persisting effects – a trace of the impact of an event on a knowledge-acquiring capacity – is, potentially at least, in possession of knowledge that an event of the relevant sort has occurred.[19] And the knowledge is, as required by our different kind of realist, immediate. There is nothing for it to be the product of inference from: certainly not the presumed trace, which figures in this sketch not as something available, even potentially, to the consciousness of someone who remembers – it is no such thing – but as an element in a speculative, though plausible, physiological explanation of why the training works. On this view, then, the circumstance of such an event's having occurred is, as our realist requires, sometimes itself available to awareness.

It helps to take care over how we specify the truth condition of a past-tensed utterance. If we think of the truth condition of an utterance, today, of 'It rained yesterday' as *yesterday's rain*, it is easy to slip into the idea that that is something which could be directly available only to an awareness enjoying the extra-temporal God's-eye view which a truth-value-link realist is likely to draw comfort from picturing (cf. §5). If we express the truth condition, more accurately, as *its having rained yesterday*, it becomes easier to swallow our realist's suggestion

[19] Depending on our view of knowledge, we may want to say that the potentiality is not actual until the past tense has been mastered. The point is general: on a view of knowledge which requires conceptualisation, mere confrontation with a state of affairs, however receptive one is, cannot suffice for knowledge, in the absence of an ability to conceptualise the state of affairs with which one is confronted. There is no obvious damage to the effectiveness of meeting the anti-realist challenge on the lines I am suggesting. The suggestion is not, absurdly, that confrontation with instances of the putatively problematic kinds of states of affairs would *suffice* for acquisition of the relevant linguistic competence. But truth-value-link realism made any such confrontation impossible; to the extent to which the anti-realist objection is a protest against that, the different kind of realism distinguished here can be seen to be immune to the objection, without there being any need to go into detail on the question what more might be necessary in order to teach someone the past tense.

that its obtaining can be, in memory, immediately available to consciousness.

§7 An anti-realist insists that the sorts of circumstance mentioned in a theory of meaning must be such that a language-learner can be trained to respond to them *whenever* they obtain. Our realist is differentiated from an anti-realist by his rejection of that thesis (§6). What is the justification for the thesis?

An answer emerges from a version of the anti-realist case which, rather than exploiting difficulties over the acquisition of linguistic competence, proceeds on the following lines. Linguistic competence ought to be exhaustively manifestable in behaviour; but there cannot be an exhaustive behavioural manifestation of a competence described – as competence with a language is described by a realistic theory of meaning – in terms of sorts of circumstance whose obtaining need not impinge on the consciousness of its possessor.[20] According to this version of the argument, then, realism induces an unacceptable theoretical slack between what linguistic competence essentially is – something exhaustively manifestable in behaviour – and what a realistic theory of meaning would describe it as being. Underlying the argument is the plausible principle that if a dispositional state is exhaustively manifestable in behaviour, the circumstances to which its operations are responses must belong to sorts which are always capable of eliciting those responses; that linguistic competence is such a state is exactly the thesis which distinguishes the anti-realist from our realist.

How convincing is the argument? Certainly it seems reasonable to insist that a practical capacity, such as competence with a language, should be observable in its operations. But our realist can claim that linguistic competence, as he describes it, is indeed observable in linguistic behaviour. Competence with sentences of one of the problematic sorts involves a conception of the sort of circumstance that constitutes their truth conditions: possession of the conception sometimes manifests itself in linguistic behaviour which – on our realist's view (§6) – can be observed as a response to the detectable obtaining of a truth condition.

A theory of meaning in the style of our realist ascribes to a competent speaker (among other things) dispositions to respond to the obtaining of truth conditions – circumstances of sorts which need not be detectable – when they *are* detectable. Of course nothing could be observed

---

[20] See n. 6 above. For this version of the argument, see (e.g.) Dummett, *Frege*, p. 467, and Wright, *op. cit.*

to be a response to the *undetectable* obtaining of a truth condition; but that was not the kind of response which a realistic theory credited the speaker with ability to make.

It is crucial to this realist rejection of the anti-realist argument that the conception which the realist claims the right to ascribe is a conception of a *kind* of circumstance. He claims the right to ascribe it on the basis of behaviour construable as a response to *some* instances of the kind, in spite of the admitted fact that *other* instances, on his view, are incapable of eliciting any response from the possessor of the conception. There will be an inclination to protest that the force of the word 'exhaustive', in the anti-realist argument, is being ignored. But the realist can reply, with great plausibility, that the requirement of exhaustive manifestability, if construed so as to rule out his position, is too strong. What we have to deal with, primarily, is *general* competence with other-ascriptions of pain, or with the past tense. Certainly we picture such general competence as embracing sub-competences with specific sentences or utterances; and the realist cannot claim that each such sub-competence, if described as involving a conception of a truth condition, is directly manifestable in behaviour. But the anti-realist cannot make the parallel claim either. In fact no acceptable principle can require that we be able to observe operations of *each* of the individual sub-competences ascribed, by whatever style of theory, to a competent speaker.

The fundamental articulations, within the practical capacity which constitutes mastery of a language, must relate not to individual utterances but to the repeatable semantic atoms and constructions which figure in them. Ascription of general competence with a construction, say the past tense, carries with it ascription of suitably described sub-competences with all the potential utterances in which the construction figures (conditional, of course, on possession of competence with the other materials of those utterances). Ascription of the general competence is justified if events construable as manifestations of the implied sub-competences actually present themselves to observation in the case of *some* utterances of the relevant sort: the speaker responds, with (say) an assertion, to the detectable obtaining of a truth condition (as the realist puts it), or to the obtaining of an assertibility condition (as the anti-realist might insist). In the nature of the case we shall be unable to get others of the implied sub-competences – *whichever* way they are conceived – to manifest themselves. Still, their ascription is warranted, since the general competence of which they would be applications can be observed in the operation of others of its applications.[21]

[21] See pp. 62–3 of my 'Truth Conditions, Bivalence, and Verificationism'.

§8 It will be revealing to revert now to the version of the anti-realist case which concentrates on the acquisition of linguistic competence. That version starts (see §1) from this premise: all that can be imparted, by the training which results in command of a language, is a complex correlation between sensory inputs and behavioural output. The slack between an anti-realist description of the acquired capacity and one in realistic terms is offensive, then, because it implies that the language-learner mysteriously extracts more out of the teaching to which he is subjected than there is in it. The implicit knowledge in which his acquired competence is conceived as consisting includes a gratuitous contribution from himself.[22] But if it is partly a product of free invention, or guesswork, how can it be right to count it a case of knowledge?

Against realism of our different variety, this version of the argument does no better than the other. If the premise is interpreted in the way it must be for the argument to work, the question is already begged. Our realist's claim is that the sorts of circumstances to which one learns to respond linguistically, in the relevant parts of the training, are truth conditions of sentences; thus the fact that a truth condition obtains is indeed, on the relevant occasions, an input to the senses, or available to awareness by way of a retained trace of such an input. (Of course the notion of sensory input involved here is quite different from that required if the anti-realist argument is to work.)

What the acquisition version of the anti-realist argument does effectively tell against is realism of the truth-value-link variety. According to a truth-value-link realist, circumstances accessible to the awareness of a person who is learning a language can serve, at best, as pointers in the direction of the sort of state of affairs of which he is to form a conception, in acquiring an understanding of sentences belonging to one of the problematic kinds (§5). The learner has to do the essential thing himself.[23] He has to break out of the confines of his own means of acquiring knowledge, and, in a void where he is not constrained by anything he can have been shown in learning the language, fix on some inaccessible sort of circumstance to be what he is going to express with sentences of a given kind.

Our different realist cannot be saddled with any of that. In his view, formation of the required conception needs no leap beyond the bounds of awareness: it can be drawn from actual confrontation with instances of the sort of circumstance involved.

[22] See Dummett, 'The Reality of the Past', p. 248: 'a certain latitude of choice'.
[23] Cf. Wittgenstein, *Investigations*, §210 and context, with §362 and §71.

§9 According to our realist's response to the anti-realist challenge, confrontation with particular states of affairs – themselves, of course, detectable – figures in the acquisition of conceptions of *sorts* of states of affairs which need not be detectable. An anti-realist may want to press this question: How can one derive, from confrontation with a detectable circumstance, an idea of what it would be for a circumstance of some kind to which it belongs to obtain undetectably? The puzzlement is about how the person's mind can make contact with the state of affairs in question, given that it cannot be by way of his picturing a confrontation with it.

There is no real difficulty here. Acquisition of one of the problematic conceptions is acquisition of competence with the relevant part of a language. Exercising the conception, then, is nothing but exercising the relevant linguistic competence, in speech of one's own or in understanding the speech of others. Puzzlement over how the relevant sort of circumstance can figure in a person's thoughts, if not by way of imagery, is misplaced. The possibility of its figuring in his thoughts is secured, without any need for speculation about a vehicle, by the possibility of its figuring *in his speech*. A competent speaker has words to express, if need be, what state of affairs it is about whose perhaps undetectable obtaining he is capable of, for instance, self-consciously speculating, or understanding a fellow-speaker of his language to be speculating.

'When I imagine that someone who is laughing is really in pain I don't imagine any pain-behaviour, for I see just the opposite. So *what* do I imagine?' – I have already said what.[24]

A source of dissatisfaction with this dissolution of the disquiet might be the idea that, from an account of the state in which understanding a language consists, we should be able to derive psychological accounts of how a speaker manages to exercise linguistic competence. On this view, to conceive a theory of meaning as specifying the content of implicit knowledge is to conceive it as a recipe for correct speech, the following of which is what keeps the competent speaker on the rails. When we defuse the puzzlement on the lines suggested above, we imply that if competence with, say, the sentence 'He is in pain' is conceived as implicit knowledge, the content of the knowledge can be formulated on these lines: the state of affairs expressed by the sentence, on an occasion of utterance which fixes a reference for the pronoun, is that which consists in the appropriate person's being in

[24] *Ibid.* §393.

pain. But if we want to explain a speaker's ability, in general, to cope with pain-ascribing language, in terms of his following a set of instructions, any such formulation is useless, since understanding it requires an exercise of the very ability for which an explanation is being sought.

Explanatory aspirations can make it seem that any realism must be transcendent. In suitable circumstances, I can understand an utterance of, say, 'That person is in pain'. We might suppose that what that comes to is this: I can hear the utterer to be, not merely making some sounds, but asserting (say), of some identifiable person, precisely that he is in pain. However, if it is only on such lines as those that an exercise of my linguistic competence can be correctly described, it would seem that if we picture the exercise of the competence as the bringing to bear of implicit knowledge, then the content of the knowledge involved, in so far as it relates in particular to the sentence uttered, will be specifiable only in the sort of explanatorily unsatisfactory terms considered in the last paragraph. If, then, we suppose that an account of competence must be explanatory, it will seem that, in a genuine realism, something else must lie behind those insubstantial formulations. Understanding another person's utterance, according to a view into which this makes realism tend to slide, is not, after all, simply hearing what is being said, but rather effecting a connection, in thought, between the words uttered and a state of affairs: one which enters into the thought in some way independent of the linguistic capacity in question, so that the thought can be represented as an application of a piece of knowledge which might explain this and other operations of the capacity. It must now seem urgently necessary to ask, as at the beginning of this section, how the state of affairs makes its appearance in the thought and the knowledge. As before, realism precludes its being in general by way of imagining a confrontation. What might well seem to do the trick is one of those transcendent conceptions which the truth-value-link realist purported to find intelligible.

An anti-realist theory of meaning, for its part, would be tailor-made to satisfy those explanatory aspirations. Indeed, that is arguably the deepest origin of anti-realism's attractiveness.

It is not, however, a good argument in favour of anti-realism. The best course is to deny that a theory of meaning should explain how people contrive to exercise linguistic competence. A speaker is not kept in line by inward consultation of a recipe; that idea is a myth, pernicious in its view of the mind as the locus of hypothesised mechanisms. Construction of a theory of meaning is not part of the postulation of a psychological mechanism; the aim is to say in detail what a competent speaker can do, not to explain how he does it.[25] The insubstantial formulations considered above are perfectly suitable, as they stand, to play a part in the execution of that descriptive enterprise.

§10 How, finally, does the issue between realism and anti-realism bear on the reality of the past?

There is something right about the inclination to answer like this: only realism presupposes the reality of the past; anti-realism represents the past as unreal in itself, enjoying a sort of vicarious existence in its traces. Certainly we seem to pull in our horns if we limit ourselves, in our account of the meaning of past-tensed utterances, to circumstances guaranteed to be detectable, if they obtain, at the times when the utterances are made; according to anti-realism, we mean rather less by our past-tensed utterances than, with our realistic prejudices, we had thought we did. However, such a characterisation of the difference might suggest that an anti-realist ought to disallow assertions that, say, specified past events really happened, in favour of reports of their traces – which would then, with the past dropping out of the picture altogether, cease to be viewed even as traces of it. But if an anti-realist theory of meaning can be constructed at all, it will certainly have to allow that, in approved circumstances, it is correct to assert some past-tensed sentences: that is – by way of such truisms as that someone who asserts 'It rained yesterday' thereby asserts that it rained on the day before[26] – that it is correct to assert that certain specific events or states of affairs happened or obtained (really happened or obtained, if you like). So an anti-realist should refuse to be described as denying the reality of the past. He should insist, rather, on an account of the divergence as one over how the reality of the past is to be conceived.

As long as the only realism in the field is truth-value-link realism, the best characterisation of the divergence seems to be one which the anti-realist might give, in the spirit of a diagnosis of what he sees as the realist's mistake. The realist's view of what it is, say, for something to have occurred is unintelligible. He conceals that from himself with a confused thought of a being with knowledge-acquiring powers different from ours (cf. §5). Thus the realist's view of the reality of the past can be described, with only the mildest caricature, as the idea of another place, in which past events are still occurring, watched,

[25] See Dummett, *Frege*, p. 681, and 'What Is a Theory of Meaning? (II)', p. 70.
[26] I am actually far from convinced that anti-realism can make out its entitlement to these truisms.

perhaps, by God. The anti-realist's view of the reality of the past is the thought, simply, that certain specific events and states of affairs occurred and obtained: a thought to which he is committed by past-tensed assertions which, according to his theory, present circumstances entitle him to make.

Such an account of the divergence suggests, surprisingly, that realism, whose view about how words (and thoughts) relate to the past seems intuitively obvious and straightforward, can in fact maintain itself only by appeal to a grotesque piece of philosophical mythology; whereas anti-realism, which seemed an affront to common sense, has a monopoly of sanity over what it is for something to have happened.

Once we understand, however, that realism can include not only the transcendent variety which merits that anti-realist diagnosis, but also the different variety distinguished in §3 and §6, which does not, we can see the possibility of reintegrating the inclinations of common sense. I do not believe anti-realism has any good positive reasons in its favour: its attractions lie entirely in the thought that it is compulsory if we are to avoid the sort of transcendence that is characteristic of truth-value-link realism.

Practising History and Social Science on 'Realist' Assumptions[1]

JOHN DUNN

> But yet the minds of men are the great wheels of things; thence come changes and alterations in the world; teeming freedom exerts and puts itself forth.
>
> (John Warr, *The Corruption and Deficiency of the Laws of England* (1649), quoted from Christopher Hill, *The World Turned Upside Down* (London, 1972), p. 219)

§1 This paper discusses a number of philosophical issues from the viewpoint of a practising social scientist and seeks to alert other social scientists to the significance of these issues for their conception of what they are attempting to do. Philosophers can thus afford to read the account of, for example, the indeterminacy of translation considerably more briskly than they would normally care to read a piece of philosophical writing. Moreover, 'relativism' and 'realism', as they appear here, are not proper philosophical terms of art. 'Relativism' is a name for the view that the truth is something which we make up (collectively or individually) more or less as we please. It is *ours* to make up. And if more or less, why not completely? 'Realism' names the view that whatever we make up less or more as we please is, it certainly is *not* the truth. The paper attempts to throw some light on the intuitive appeal of relativism in this context, a context in which its appeal is in some ways surprising. (Nature may be any old way. But how can *we* believe that the same is true of *us*?) It also attempts to throw some light on why any coherent version of 'realism' should be so hard to state in this context.

Do history and the social sciences possess a determinate subject matter? Do they form a cognitive field about which the truth could in principle

[1] In addition to my debts to the editors and to other participants in the Dedham conference, I am grateful to Quentin Skinner and Geoffrey Hawthorn for their helpful comments on an earlier draft and to Jonathan Lear for his patient and persistent attempts to show me why I simply could not say the first thing which came into my head on one subject after another. The result is a poor return on the investment of so much of others' intelligence and good will; but I can at least guarantee that it would have been strikingly worse without their aid.

145

JOHN DUNN

be known? If so, are there methodological principles which, correctly applied, will guarantee that we come to know some of this truth? If there are not, how can an affirmative answer to the first question be other than a bare-faced fraud or an unintended confession of intellectual confusion?

The language we use to characterise our experience reflects many presumptions as to what sorts of things 'humanly speaking' there are to describe. If these presumptions could all be made clear and if they were all valid we could conclude both that there was a determinate subject matter for the sciences of man (perhaps men as they are, acting as they act, within societies as they are, etc.) and that we knew what that subject matter was. Although we may hope that all these presumptions can be validated, it would be ludicrously optimistic to presume that this happy state of affairs must obtain. On the other hand, we plainly cannot presume that literally none of these presumptions are justifiable: to presume this would deprive us of the conceptual basis of personal identity and the instruments of rational thought. We would be unable to understand anything which we might attempt to do.

What *a priori* grounds are there for presuming the existence of a determinate subject matter for history and the social sciences? How far are these grounds in fact valid?

§2 In spite of all temptations, always and everywhere, people behave exactly as they do and not otherwise. This, at least, is not a miracle. It is indeed, we may initially presume, nothing more exciting than a tautology. Not only is it the case that this striking 'regularity' obtains; better still, we can *know* that it is true that it obtains. And, even better, we can *know* that any theory of knowledge on which this 'regularity', and our knowledge of it, comes out as a standing miracle is shown to be inadequate by this result. But from this superficially promising beginning epistemologically it is downhill all the way.

§3 Can we *know* why we ourselves or anyone else at all did, are doing, or will do anything? (In our own case, we are certainly in a different boat: you are by no means me. But is it necessarily a less leaky craft?) Can we even know *what* we ourselves or anyone else did, are doing, or will do?

Reports differ from descriptions in that competent observers in the face of identical stimuli will report them (roughly) identically, or else will misreport them, while no such starkness of choice between approved format and dereliction of duty obtains in the case of

146

descriptions.[2] Quine's thesis of the indeterminacy of translation[3] implies that even reports, the stuff of knowledge, cannot provide determinate specifications of psychological states or of intended meanings and therefore that the latter are not *objects* of knowledge. People behave exactly as they behave and not otherwise. But is it true for example that people always *act* exactly as they act and not otherwise? Is there a 'fact of the matter' as to how they act? The answer to this question presumably depends upon the type of account given of what it is for something to be a 'fact of the matter'.

§4 People behave exactly as they do and not otherwise. Part of the explanation of why they behave exactly as they do is *often* that thus, in some respects at least, is how they had it in mind to behave. Human beings (most of them) can and do act upon the world. They also describe in a language both this world on which they hope to act and the acts which they hope to perform. Hence the suspicion that the linguistic capacities of human beings stand in some constitutive relation to their capacity for agency. (It is evident enough too, from an evolutionary viewpoint, that linguistic capacities form a necessary condition for much of the present human behavioural repertoire. Among non-human animals matters are somewhat different. To know as a matter of fact just how different would be to know vastly more than we at present know about both human and non-human animals. To know in principle how to determine precisely how different would already be to have solved an impressive array of fundamental philosophical problems.)

Always and everywhere people act exactly as they do and not otherwise. This too at first sight appears nothing more exciting (or hazardous) than a tautology. But how should we picture the relation between this impressive 'regularity' in the precision of their action and the equally impressive 'regularity' in the precision of their behaviour? It is fairly widely agreed by philosophers of action that one could be perfectly informed on how someone is behaving at a particular time without knowing what he *must* be doing (since any specification of behaviour is compatible with the performance of many different actions). It is perhaps equally widely agreed that one could be correctly informed of what someone is doing on some occasion and yet be unable to determine exactly how he must be behaving on that occasion (since any action can be executed by a variety of items of behaviour). To accept that such an epistemological gap exists will appear to some an

[2] W. G. Runciman, 'Describing', *Mind*, n.s., 81 (July 1972), 372–88.
[3] See §13 below.

JOHN DUNN

ignoble capitulation to Cartesian dualism. But whether it is ignoble to
capitulate to dualism or absurd not to recognise its validity or possible,
in lieu of either option, to adopt a version of anomalous monism,[4] the
recognition of this epistemological gap cannot without much further
argument be judged to imply the falsity of 'realism'. The sentences
of history or tenseless human science are true or false in so far as they
mention truly or falsely the exact actions which people perform as
they do perform them and not otherwise or, similarly, in so far as
they mention truly or falsely the exact behaviour which people exhibit
as they do exhibit it and not otherwise. (To be true in either case, they
must assert nothing which is false and deny nothing which is true. They
need not assert everything which is true or deny everything which is
false.) The true sentences of the history or tenseless human science
of human behaviour will differ widely from the true sentences of the
history or tenseless human science of human action. But the truth of
the true sentences of the one must *ex hypothesi* be compatible with the
true sentences of the other.

§5 Where does this leave the indeterminacy argument? It all depends
what 'matter' you take the facts of seriously. If we took the 'facts of
the matter' of behaviour less seriously, why could we not read the
Quinean indeterminacy argument as a proof of the ambiguity of
behaviour? (If you cannot specify action from behaviour, so much the
worse for behaviour knowledge as a *general* cognitive vantage point.)

Always and everywhere people mean exactly what they do mean and
not something else. Now at last we have an *evident* falsehood. It is the
vagueness of meanings and the difficulty of assigning to them a clear
theoretical status which really menaces the coherence of our *a priori*
presumptions. Meanings infect intentions and thus actions with their
distinctive haziness. Does anyone *ever* know exactly what he means?
(Exactly what I mean may be a pretty inexact affair, may be much
vaguer than I hope.)[5] Do I *know* even what my present arguments
mean? Do I even know exactly what I am saying? (My ears may be
deceiving me. My tongue may slip. My grasp of my own language as
spoken by other speakers may be systematically or randomly in error.

[4] See e.g. Donald Davidson, 'Mental Events', in Lawrence Foster and J. W. Swanson
(eds.), *Experience and Theory* (London, 1970), pp. 79–101; an alternative possibility
would be to adopt Hilary Putnam's less committal defence of the autonomy of the
mental in his 'Philosophy and Our Mental Life', in *Philosophical Papers*, vol. 2: *Mind,
Language and Reality* (Cambridge, 1975), pp. 291–303.
[5] See e.g. Crispin Wright, 'Language-Mastery and the Sorites Paradox', in Gareth Evans
and John McDowell (eds.), *Truth and Meaning: Essays in Semantics* (Oxford, 1976), pp.
223–47.

148

If I did know exactly what I *was* saying, perhaps even I would scarcely have the folly to maintain it.) All these hazards seem real possibilities. If I expressed what I mean as it would be expressed by a perfect speaker of a perfect language, even *I* might be able to see that it is false. Can one ever *mean* (fully intend to assert, with a full grasp of the implications of asserting it) a proposition which is in itself false?

I assert A, not-A, and the law of non-contradiction. I intend to assert what I assert. Could I sincerely intend to assert, to hold to be true, something so *evidently* false? Either my intention must be radically incoherent or my understanding of the sentences must be spectacularly confused. Most of our brushes with the law of non-contradiction are more spaced out: the product of amnesia, inattention, congenital intellectual indolence, sheer feebleness of mind. We affirm A, forgetting a past commitment to its negation to which (if reminded of it) we would still feel deeply committed. We do not recognise quite what it is that we are saying and quite how it relates to our other assertoric inclinations. It is a permanent condition of the thought of most men that they do not and cannot think in the full light of all their best reasons. There is a full cognitive equivalent to akrasia[6] and it is at the heart of the experience of thinking. Like acting, reasoning and talking involve intentions. I can fully intend to assert a proposition which is in itself false; but only by dint of not fully understanding what I am asserting. But does not meaning X imply knowing that X and not something else is what I wish, as of now, to assert?

The intentionality of action and assertion here clashes with the meaning of speech. You may mean A (sc. intend to assert A). But what you have said means (sc. implies the assertibility of) not-A. The question is whether intentions or meanings are to be master. And yet intentions and meanings depend conceptually upon one another.

§6 If there is such a field of potential knowledge as historical, political, social etc. truth, what does it consist in? It is unnecessary to draw the boundary of such a field to establish its reality. At its core we find, in a somewhat shop-soiled but still serviceable phrase, 'real living men', past, present and future, or more broadly human acts taken under intentional descriptions,[7] past, present and future, and the causes and

---

6 Cf. Donald Davidson, 'How Is Weakness of the Will Possible?', in Joel Feinberg (ed.), *Moral Concepts* (London, 1969), pp. 93–113.
7 Why exactly? Is it simply a moral injunction: 'That's a man and you (morally) ought to conceive him in conceptually appropriate (human) terms'? ('Hath not a Jew...' Even the Nuer think. Even the British feel. Even behaviourist psychologists require and are entitled to interpretation. Etc.) Or is it a pragmatic claim: 'That's a man and

JOHN DUNN

consequences of such acts. Human agents *are* the subject matter of human history and the constituents of human society. We need to augment the ranks of human agents with other entities, if we are to provide a full specification for the field of history or social science. But human agents must remain at the centre of this field and the conditions for valid knowledge of their situation and performance are the central question for the philosophy of history or social science. In practice the conditions for acquiring knowledge about the past are very different from those for acquiring knowledge about the future; and these differences suggest the prospects for acquiring much very interesting knowledge about the human future to be poor. How can we sanely expect to be able to characterise adequately the circumstances in which men at all far in the future will have to act? Most human scientists who have supposed knowledge about the future obtainable in principle have been more or less self-consciously behavioural in approach, seeking to render human performance in an idiom in which replicability and inter-observer reliability are at a premium, in which performance can be reported and not merely described.[8] Historians, by contrast, have felt little temptation to desert the categories of action, seeing few opportunities for systematising their inquiries in purely behavioural categories. Even the stalwart advocates of a covering-law account of historical explanation have felt no obligation to eschew a data language of highly interpreted human conduct, though their opponents have sometimes used the omnipresence of such language in historical writing and the types of conceptual connection which historians use in explicating the conduct of their subjects to argue for a radical discontinuity between history and generalising social sciences.[9] More recently there have been strong defences, notably by Charles Taylor and Alasdair MacIntyre, of the central role of hermeneutic considerations throughout the human sciences.[10]

if you don't recognise it as such, you'll be making a grave mistake'? In pragmatic terms the proof of the scale of mistake should be simply the gain or loss in predictive power. There seem sound pragmatic reasons for such insistence. But there are also sound moral reasons for it. The possibility of doing the data an injustice is hardly a major epistemological hazard in most of the sciences of nature. But in the human sciences it is perhaps always the most pressing aspect of the scientist's situation.

8 Runciman, *op. cit.*
9 Carl G. Hempel, 'The Function of General Laws in History' (*Journal of Philosophy*, 1942), in Patrick Gardiner (ed.), *Theories of History* (New York, 1959), pp. 344–56. Patrick Gardiner, *The Nature of Historical Explanation* (London, 1952). Cf. William Dray, *Laws and Explanation in History* (London, 1957). W. B. Gallie, *Philosophy and the Historical Understanding* (London, 1964).
10 Charles Taylor, 'Interpretation and the Sciences of Man', *Review of Metaphysics*, 25 (September 1971), 3–51. Alasdair MacIntyre, 'Ideology, Social Science and Revolution', *Comparative Politics*, 5:3 (April 1973), 321–42.

§7 Perhaps there could be a non-human science of man of a strictly behavioural (matter and motion) kind. It would involve entry into an anti-hermeneutic circle within which intentional categories were never admitted. There do not appear to be clear principles of translation from action to behaviour categories or from behaviour to action categories. There are strong reasons for doubting the capacity of men even to *attempt* to construct such an anti-hermeneutic science (despite their amply proven capacity to believe that they are making such an attempt), and even stronger reasons for doubting their chances of succeeding in any such attempt. There are also reasons for viewing the making of any such attempt with strong moral resentment. All efforts thus far to constitute human sciences of behaviour plainly rest on the covert use of action categories. There is evident economy to such use. Furthermore, since our interest in the results of the human sciences is a human interest, it seems unlikely that the results of such an anti-hermeneutic science would remain unincorporated into human practice. If it were to be so incorporated, all the difficulties of the relation between behaviour and action categories would presumably resurface. In practice there seems little danger that humans will create or encounter such a superhuman 'human science knowledge machine'. But it appears to be an empirical question whether such a machine is or is not naturally *possible*. And it is difficult to deny at least the logical possibility that a learning machine which adopted behavioural categories of a degree of purity which no human being would be at all likely to opt for and which kept rigidly within such categories (and which kept its learning firmly to itself) could become highly prescient of the human (behavioural) future. There may be in principle no mechanical way of recording precisely what is humanly going on. But there are mechanical ways of recording non-humanly pretty precisely some of what is going on – light, heat, sound etc. – and what can or cannot be predicted on the basis of such a mechanical procedure seems as hard to foreclose on in principle as the limits of what will be successfully predicted on its basis might be easy to predict in practice.

Perhaps a *discreet* anti-hermeneutic human science could in principle even know the entire human behavioural future. But the tragedy of anti-hermeneutic human science thus far is that it has been conceived in indiscretion and nourished in some little flagrancy. And even a *true* science of human behaviour could not tell human action where it gets off. So far from being able in general simply to replace our own characterisations of our actions, an anti-hermeneutic human science can retain its epistemological respectability only by the consistent refusal to say anything about what we are *doing* and why we are doing it.

§8 Human beings speak, think, feel and act; and they do so within a frame of natural causality. Language, a social practice, enjoys a dominant role in speaking, thinking and acting, a somewhat more subservient role in feeling, and (ideally) a wholly subservient role in the analysis of natural causality. Approaches to the analysis of natural causality which prove to be sound will not necessarily transfer felicitously to a subject matter in which the status of language shifts from the instrumental to the constitutive. Keeping in mind the difficulties which these disparities may pose, we may sketch a broader specification of the field of potential knowledge of human agents. This might consist of (1) a set of texts; (2) a set of speech acts; (3) a set of actions; (4) institutional persistence and change; (5) material factors which can be seen to have some direct reflection in human consciousness;[11] (6) material factors which cannot be seen to have any direct reflection in human consciousness but which exert some causal weight on categories 1 to 5. (This last category might turn out to be coextensive with the totality of facts about nature. It is natural to present all of these categories in past or present terms; but category 6 at least could certainly be rephrased in principle to make whatever truth claims are regarded as epistemologically or ontologically respectable about the future.)

There are matters omitted from this list which might pose severe problems. What, for example, of states of consciousness which are not ever reflected in any speech act or action or which never will be so reflected? (We all have lots of beliefs which we never have asserted and which we never will.)[12] History, on any realist account, must be epistemologically confined to what can be *known* – to what took place in (in the broadest of terms) a public domain. In practice, of course,

---

[11] As is apparent from the epigraph, the present account is in some ways deeply inimical to the materialist theory of history. Much of what is claimed, politically and historically, by exponents of various versions of this theory is certainly true, and its heuristic merits are unmistakable. But if it is presented, as for example by Althusser and some of his followers, as a rigidly anti-hermeneutic theory, the empirical truth of many of its contentions could not serve to vindicate its truth. The key question is what would constitute *showing* that it was true. The position adopted here is that no theory of human social action can be shown to be true in a rigidly anti-hermeneutic fashion. Materialist theories of history of an anti-hermeneutic bent might indeed be right in what they maintained; but they must be so for the wrong reasons. They must be necessarily theoretically false, even if they were contingently empirically true.

[12] See Bernard Williams, 'Deciding to Believe', in his *Problems of the Self* (Cambridge, 1973), p. 140.

it is more restricted still – confined indeed to what has *remained* in a public domain, what has left a record. But it seems natural, again, to suppose that in this respect the future is exactly like the past except that in the case of the future we are better placed in the short run to choose what sorts of potential phenomena will achieve the status of (however evanescent) record.

§9 There is one philosophical tradition which does focus on the centrality of language in human experience, the rather disparate tradition now customarily referred to as hermeneutic, the tradition of Dilthey and Gadamer in Germany and in part, though only in part, that of Max Weber.[13] Hermeneutics in origin was an inquiry into interpretative criteria for sacred texts, texts for which truth-guaranteeing criteria of interpretation *ex hypothesi must* exist. But, God now being dead, we have no reason for supposing that truth-guaranteeing interpretative procedures for learning how to understand anything (least of all one another) are in fact naturally available. Hermeneutics is an admirable name for the good intention of attempting to understand one another. But as a name for an epistemology and its implied set of methodological precepts, it is perhaps merely a verbal placebo. If we wish to understand other people and propose to claim that we have in fact done so, it is both imprudent and rude not to attend to what they say. But whatever heuristic procedures we adopt, we have no reason to believe that they can guarantee our success.

Language is the star of a hermeneutic conception of the human sciences. Human action and human experience aspire to the perspicuousness of human speech. A full explanation of an action might be represented as an extended text, representing the pattern of attention of the agent, the set of beliefs conceived as relevant by the agent, a set of identified preferences and capabilities and the act as a rational outcome of all these. If what we wanted to explain was why an agent had performed a particular act and not some radically different act (why Caesar crossed the Rubicon rather than settling down to a life of writing bawdy poems), such a text would not be an economical statement of the explanation for which we were seeking, though it is not easy to see how it could fail to contain this explanation.

[13] See especially H. G. Gadamer, *Truth and Method* (London, 1975). Weber's views are not discussed here because of the formidable exegetic difficulties which they raise. For a helpful discussion see W. G. Runciman, *A Critique of Max Weber's Philosophy of Social Science* (Cambridge, 1972). It should be emphasised that the account offered here, even if it is properly titled hermeneutic, does not resemble that of Gadamer, particularly in its epistemological conclusions.

JOHN DUNN

And if we wanted to fit the precise action which was performed firmly and precisely into natural causality, to explain why exactly Caesar did cross the Rubicon exactly there and exactly then and not somewhere else or some other time or never, it is hard to see how we could do so, in the light of the anomaly of the mental, without conceptual access to the Telex record of such a stream of consciousness. Such a text might be improved (or impaired) by the sensitive or sardonic commentary of bystanders or psychiatric experts. If the act displayed imperfect rationality even after sustained co-operative effort and the vigorous exercise of the agent's memory, the gap between rational performance and actual performance might be explicable causally in the same way that a linguistic error or a mistake in arithmetic or even a gratuitous stumble in the street might be so explained. If we proceed in reverse, texts may be presented as composite speech acts and features of them explained accordingly.[14] What speaks to us clearly and honestly we truly can know. But is language so perspicuous, compared with nature? Do I really apprehend any other person (or even myself) more clearly and with more assurance than I do sundry features of the physical world?

§10 There are a number of different grounds for doubting the per-spicuousness of language. Human mendacity and incompetence, technical problems in the theory of translation, the sparse and somewhat randomly selected records of states of consciousness which ever enter a public domain and the far sparser set of such records which remain at all durably within one. If what persons could have said under perfect interrogation forms the perfect text of human history (at the Last Judgment) what we can rationally and justifiably believe that they *did* say is likely to be a nastily mangled palimpsest. It will certainly underdetermine drastically what we have good reason to believe them consequentially to have brought about.

There are also a number of different grounds for doubting the opacity of nature. One of these, self-evidently, is the striking progress in mechanical control engendered by the development of natural science. Another is the commonsense experience of living within a

[14] See the extended series of articles by Quentin Skinner: 'Meaning and Understanding in the History of Ideas', *History and Theory*, 8:1 (1969), 3–53; 'Conventions and the Understanding of Speech Acts', *Philosophical Quarterly*, 20:79 (April 1970), 113–38; 'On Performing and Explaining Linguistic Actions', *Philosophical Quarterly*, 21:82 (January 1971), 1–21; '"Social Meaning" and the Explanation of Social Action', in Peter Laslett, W. G. Runciman and Quentin Skinner (eds.), *Philosophy, Politics and Society*, 4th ser. (Oxford, 1972), pp. 136–57; 'Some Problems in the Analysis of Political Thought and Action', *Political Theory*, 2:3 (August 1974), 277–303; 'Hermeneutics and the Role of History', *New Literary History*, 7 (1975–6), 209–32.

naturally fairly unsurprising everyday world. Extreme scepticism about the knowability of nature seems strained and silly. And if we can know about nature at all, why not in some measure about men within the same frame of knowledge? We make many predictions about what persons will in practice do (whatever they pretend or the rules say) and a fair number of these predictions are not disappointed. To reverse Alasdair MacIntyre,[15] we are all of us unsurprised in our social life for a great deal of the time. There are worse epistemological predicaments than that of the ordinary agent.

§11 Describing is the primitive cognitive act of all sciences. The sciences of nature contain many other components besides descriptive statements. But what makes it possible for them to be sciences *of* nature is their inclusion of true descriptive statements. In the sciences of nature many such statements at particular times show the inter-observer reliability of 'reports'. Some epistemological suspicion in the philosophy of natural science has recently been focused on the social explanation of this fact. Are 'reports' a synthetic product of social complicity? Their failure in particular to show a corresponding inter-observer reliability over spans of time (unless heavily doctored to do so) raises severe technical difficulties for anyone attracted to the project of giving a realist account of the status of natural science.[16]

The sciences of man differ from the sciences of nature in at least two respects in the part played in them by descriptive statements. The first is in the relative proportions of reports to less formalised descriptive statements. Some social sciences record data largely in the form of mechanical reports, with strikingly jejune intellectual profit (except at a physiological level). Most social sciences sensibly make no attempt to do anything of the kind. The prevalence of descriptive discretion is not in itself epistemologically alarming, though it does weaken the prospects of any very crisply incremental development of the social sciences. In itself it comes no closer to imperilling the reality of human performance than variations in the taste of landscape artists come to altering the physical properties of mountains. To make it epistemologically alarming and not merely methodologically trouble-some, it would be necessary for it to extend to the assertion and negation of the same description (identically interpreted) of the same phenomena by two different competent, sincere and attentive

---

[15] MacIntyre, 'Ideology, Social Science and Revolution', 332.
[16] See Hilary Putnam, 'What is "Realism"?', *Proceedings of the Aristotelian Society*, n.s., 76 (1975–6), 177–94; and the paper by Nick Jardine in this book.

observers, Philosophers of the human sciences often write as though such encounters are frequent affairs. But in the case of a species which frequently slips below the highest standards of competence, sincerity and attention, we may take leave to doubt whether they really *are* very common, and we are on still firmer ground in insisting that their frequency is certainly not *known* by those who invoke them.[17] (Quite insufficient attention has yet been paid in the philosophy of the human sciences to the possibility that the major cause of the snail-like cognitive advance within most of these most of the time is simply the insensitivity, greatly exacerbated in professional training, of very many social scientists.) Descriptive discretion is simply not absolute.

§12   The second respect in which the status of descriptive statements within the sciences of man differs from its status within the sciences of non-human nature is more striking, and it is a formidable task to assess what its significance may be. Describing is picturing in words, verbal representation.[18] The rest of nature is a helpless victim of our representational enthusiasms: man can answer back. Describing men is picturing in words a type of creature for whom it is already a constitutive characteristic, at least in adults, that they picture themselves in words of their own choosing. Between a describer and a self-describing object there exist relations which are peculiar not merely epistemologically or even perhaps ontologically, but also morally. Confronted by interlocutors of exquisite sensitivity and awesome patience, persons possessed of formidable initial participant-observational grasp of our own culture and society and facility in our own natural language, perhaps we might be fortunate enough never to need to answer back to others' characterisation of ourselves. But if the need did arise, to be able (conceptually, not necessarily acoustically) to answer back is part of what it is to be fully a man (perhaps even the core of what it is to be *fully* a man).

The history of human beings cannot exclude the history of men as agents and as the possessors of intellects. It cannot happen 'behind

[17] It would in fact be extremely illuminating philosophically to be offered the opportunity to inspect a really full and convincing description of such a disagreement. Could it in fact be a convincingly full description without disclosing how the mishap occurred? Taylor (*op. cit.*) refers to the possibility of encountering such irreducible gaps in intuitions. But the epistemological resolution which he offers for it (esp. pp. 46–7) is suspiciously reminiscent of Mill's argument for the superior eligibility of the higher over the lower pleasures (that he had sampled both and preferred the former). On such questions, one must surely be either more of a 'realist' than Taylor here perspicuously declares himself or else be less of an (epistemological) egoist?

[18] Runciman, 'Describing'.

the backs of the consciousness of real men'.[19] To every man, then, his own truth – not a *private* truth, but a potentially public truth which truly is his. Two main difficulties follow from this centrality of the human capacity for self-description in specifying the field of the sciences of man, either or both of which may preclude the giving of a realist account of the status of these sciences. The first of these is the problem of providing clear criteria for the valid description of meanings (the problem of the determinacy of translation). The second is the related difficulty of providing a clear account of the character of human consciousness and any plausible criteria for its true or false description.

§13 The claim to know exactly what other persons mean or meant (and thus perhaps the claim to know what other persons are doing or have done) depends upon there being in principle specifiable truth conditions for correct translation. The existence of such truth conditions has been challenged and a 'realist' attitude to psychological states impugned by Quine's thesis of the indeterminacy of translation. Indeed, since radical translation, as Quine himself puts it, 'begins at home',[20] it is not only the meanings and actions of others which are rendered indeterminate on this theory, but equally our own. This challenge is certainly the most formidable threat yet identified to a realist view of the subject matter of history and the social sciences. The core of Quine's argument is the claim that

manuals for translating one language into another can be set up in divergent ways, all compatible with the totality of speech dispositions, yet incompatible with one another. In countless places they will diverge in giving, as their respective translations of a sentence of one language, sentences of the other language which stand to each other in no plausible kind of equivalence however loose.[21]

There is no question of one of these theories (translation schemas) being true and the rest false. There is no 'fact of the matter'. If we lack a pragmatist definition of synonymy, we ought not to adopt a realist attitude to the theory of meaning. Actions do not have determinate intentional descriptions, except relativised to particular theories of interpretation. (If there cannot be a pragmatist definition of synonymy, what exactly does it mean to assert that persons mean exactly what they do mean and not anything else?) These difficulties

[19] R. Hilferding, quoted in Lucio Colletti, *From Rousseau to Lenin* (London, 1972), p. 34.
[20] W. V. O. Quine, *Ontological Relativity and Other Essays* (New York, 1969). 'On deeper reflection, radical translation begins at home.'
[21] W. V. O. Quine, *Word and Object* (Cambridge, Mass., 1960), p. 27.

extend from the case of radical translation into a wholly alien language in chronologically or culturally very alien societies, through alien languages in contemporary or culturally very similar societies, or our own language in chronologically or culturally very distant societies, to our own language spoken by other persons in areas of our own society with which we are culturally familiar now and perhaps even to our own language spoken by ourselves on other occasions.

Homophonic translation theories work astonishingly well on ourselves, at least over short periods of time, and reasonably well among the speakers of our own natural language within culturally and structurally similar social niches over longer periods. If they did not work reasonably well in these circumstances we could hardly learn (be taught or teach ourselves) to get them to work so splendidly for ourselves in the short run and could scarcely formulate philosophical dilemmas, let alone decide whether we had solved them. But in the very long run for the inhabitants of very different societies speaking very different languages there simply cannot be empirically validated translation theories with unique authority in this way. Even within our own language a homophonic theory works increasingly poorly as we get further away from ourselves culturally and temporally, as historians of ideas are painfully aware.[22] When it comes to radical translation between languages, interpretation appears to presuppose the assigning of theoretically structured beliefs and the imposition of standards of rationality on the alien subjects before it can even commence.[23] There seems no way of vindicating the choice of a unique set of presuppositions.[24] A translation manual, empirically adequate in the

[22] Consider, for example, the disastrous effect on the interpretation of Locke's social and political theory of the assumption that when Locke used the word 'property' (as for example when he used it to define the content of justice and the ends of government) he meant normally what we normally mean when we today use the word 'property' outside philosophical contexts. For the most glaring example of this error see C. B. Macpherson, *The Political Theory of Possessive Individualism* (Oxford, 1962). For a conclusive demonstration of just how deeply erroneous a view it is see Mr James Tully's forthcoming Cambridge University Ph.D. thesis.

[23] Martin Hollis, 'Reason and Ritual', in Alan Ryan (ed.), *The Philosophy of Social Explanation* (London, 1973), pp. 33–49, at pp. 39–42.

[24] For a variety of attempts to show either that indeterminacy does not obtain or that its implications are no more anti-realist in the case of meaning than in the general underdetermination of theory by evidence see: Jonathan Bennett, *Linguistic Behaviour* (Cambridge, 1976), pp. 261, 263; David F. Graybeal, 'The In- and Underdeterminacy of Translation', *Dialectica*, 30:1 (1976), 9–15; Hilary Putnam, 'The Refutation of Conventionalism', *Noûs*, 8 (1974), 25–40; Michael Dummett, *Frege: Philosophy of Language* (London, 1973), pp. 589–627; Richard Rorty, 'Indeterminacy of Translation and of Truth', *Synthèse*, 23 (1972), 443–62; Donald Davidson, 'Radical Interpretation', *Dialectica*, 27 (1973), 313–28; Donald Davidson, 'Belief and the Basis of Meaning', *Synthèse*, 27 (1974), 309–23, and 'Replies to David Lewis and W. V. Quine', *ibid.*, 345–49; David Lewis, 'Radical Interpretation', *Synthèse*, 27 (1974), 331–44.

past and even in the future, could be set up to maximise the ascription of true beliefs (credal charity) or of readily intelligible desires[25] (libidinal complicity) or a number of other possibly more practical objectives, with substantial consequent divergences in the interpretation of the contents of translator/native conversations. It *might* still be correct to dispute whether this really is a natural possibility, whether more ingenious and patient testing of the empirical accuracy of the translation might not in every instance eventually offer some decisive criterion for favouring one rather than another. (This seems to be Jonathan Bennett's expectation, and in a fideist manner it seems an operating presupposition of the finer-grain hermeneutic inquiry in history or other human sciences.) But even if it is a persisting natural possibility, it could license only the most restricted form of 'relativism'. If we cannot know exactly what those noises which he made meant or exactly what he was then doing, there is a rich abundance of things which we can have strong reasons to believe that he was certainly not doing and certainly did not mean. The notion of empirical adequacy, the point at which Quine's thesis is least intuitively plausible, is also its firmest protection against serving as a shield for heuristic indolence. The day when a social scientist is forced in good faith in his interpretation of his subject's discourse or action in the *present* into a choice between one or other of several incompatible translation schemas, all empirically adequate to all practically available evidence, has yet to arrive; and we need not expect it soon.

§14

Seldom, very seldom, does complete truth belong to any human disclosure; seldom can it happen that something is not a little disguised, or a little mistaken.   (Jane Austen, *Emma*, chap. 49)

The great strength of the hermeneutic approach is that it takes consciousness and action as the core subject matter of the human sciences and treats these as essentially linguistic phenomena, the possibility of characterising which in language is constitutive of them in a sense in which it is not in the case of non-human nature. Its great – and, as perhaps we can now see more clearly, its *corresponding* – weakness is that anyone who practises it, as Schutz complained of Dilthey, 'opposes to rational science another, so-called "interpretive" science based on metaphysical presuppositions and incorrigible

---

For powerful criticism of these, on which I have depended heavily, see the paper by Hookway in this book.

[25] For a helpful brief discussion of the intelligibility of desires, see A. J. Watt, 'The Intelligibility of Wants', *Mind*, n.s., 81 (July 1972), 372–88.

"intuition"'.[26] How far it is necessary to settle for incorrigibility of intuition and what metaphysical presuppositions it is appropriate to presuppose are by no means easy questions to resolve. Here we come to the second difficulty mentioned at the end of §12.

Is it possible to understand even ourselves? – and other people? – even those with very different languages and systems of belief? Anthropological understanding of an alien community seems possible only if we make questionable assumptions about the extent and nature of their rationality. Even if one could legitimately presume that the members of another society are rational agents and had a clear conception of the necessary and sufficient conditions for being a rational agent, within what frame should such agency be located,[27] and how perfectly or imperfectly rational should such agency be presumed in practice?[28] If being a good anthropologist means successfully infiltrating an alien belief system without abandoning one's own, might not being an even better anthropologist amount simply to going native – deserting one's own belief system completely? (*Credo ut intelligam*: better anthropologists would not just translate but would try to believe.[29] Ideal anthropologists would succeed (fleetingly or permanently?) in believing.)

§15 One might claim that access to a full verbal transcript of conscious experience holds the key to understanding another person. This notion presents myriads of difficulties. We certainly do not formulate all of our experience in words – chattering incessantly to ourselves. Moreover, it is not obvious that all our experience is conscious. If available, such a transcript would be a valid description of an individual's experience: it would characterise all the relevant experiential states of which the described person was conscious for a particular auditor who could grasp all the assertions made in the description. Sentences which he customarily used in his own language would be relatively easy for him to grasp clearly. Sentences (particularly sentences reporting feelings or conceptually novel thoughts) which he had never had occasion to use would be relatively hard and in some cases probably impossible to grasp. They would need more im-

[26] Alfred Schutz, 'Problems of Interpretive Sociology', quoted from Ryan (ed.), *Philosophy of Social Explanation*, 211.

[27] Evan Fales, 'Truth, Tradition and Rationality', *Philosophy of the Social Sciences*, 6:2 (June 1976), 97–113.

[28] J. W. N. Watkins, 'Imperfect Rationality', in Robert Borger and Frank Cioffi (eds.), *Explanation in the Behavioural Sciences* (Cambridge, 1970), pp. 167–217.

[29] On trying to believe and choosing to believe, see Bernard Williams, 'Deciding to Believe', in *Problems of the Self*, pp. 136–51.

agination, and imagination has its limits. It simply *is* very difficult to understand even in outline the feelings of those with very different temperaments from oneself and, as every schoolboy knows, there are plenty of intellectually respectable conceptual structures (mathematical, logical) which cannot successfully be taught to many people.

It seems more promising to abandon the search for a total transcript, seeking, rather, a complete, accurate and fully intelligible description personalised to a particular auditor. (In one's own case this might resemble the transcript.) The idea of better or worse, even true and false, descriptions of any experience to anyone interested for some reason in understanding it at a time lacks the prima facie absurdity of the idea of a *total* transcript. It should be possible to systematise around such a conception the more obviously hermeneutic units of human history and social practice: texts, speech acts and individual or collective actions or sequences of actions. No one in practice, for reasons of economy, would attempt to grasp individual or social happening at this radically individuated and extended level. It would still be necessary to simplify enormously in order to think about society at all, let alone to live in it. But at least this can serve to set a standard, designating what there is minimally for the human sciences to understand, by which to judge the necessary deviations of more practical understanding. It would serve to specify what would count as their having understood it and hence what forms of simplification for practical purposes must be considered false because they are incompatible with it – and not merely and mercifully less interminable.

§16 The core of such a conception of 'what is or is not the case' is the idea of full true descriptions individuated to particular auditors on particular occasions. In the case of descriptions provided by agents themselves, we may employ Jane Austen's term 'disclosure'. Actual disclosures to particular auditors are seldom wholly true and perhaps never complete, though practically they often serve very adequately. Life is much too short for perfect disclosure. Nor is it any longer for practising historians or social scientists who aspire to complete their inquiries or to have their books read. All human scientists, even the most behavioural, practise in the fond hope that the deficiencies of description or the errors and gaps in the intelligibility of record will all come out in the wash. Social complicity (the taking in of one another's washing) has much to do with the maintenance of optimism among social scientists.

By this means one might characterise the set of human public acts:

texts, speech acts, actions. These stand in close, though complex, conceptual relations.[30] The primitive cognitive professional acts of the human sciences are the formation of perspicuous, true one-auditor-at-a-time individuated descriptions of such acts or patterns or sequences of action. This states (very crudely) the standards in relation to which the *truth* of professional statements in the human sciences are to be measured. Their role as standards is presumed in epistemological criticism and in professional self-justification in response to this.

§17 Simply to provide such descriptions is no easy task. But it cannot be denied that it falls in some ways drastically short of the bold cognitive ambitions of most practising social scientists and even perhaps of many historians. Even *perfect* descriptions of all individual acts would not constitute a very well explained, even perhaps an intelligible, history.[31] Such a history would omit the causal impact of all material factors not 'mentioned' in human consciousness. It would misjudge the causal force and direction of many material factors which were so 'mentioned'; and it is at best unclear how well it could be expected (even if supplemented by complete knowledge of these two types) to articulate such central aspects of the human condition as the unintended consequences of individual human actions and sets of such actions. There is plainly plenty of natural, non-intentional causality within human history and around human actions. History cannot be adequately explained at the individual level (omitting mention of social wholes, or of social wholes except as reflected in individuals' beliefs; omitting mention of material factors unrecognised by any individuals; etc.). But what counts as an adequate explanation of human history includes at the very minimum an explanation of all human acts. This specifies a necessary component of the explanandum, even if it offers little guidance on how precisely successful explanations can or might be constructed.

Social scientists certainly describe more extended objects than individual actions; but this capacity in itself could hardly militate against the view that describing human actions intelligibly and non-falsely was their main cognitive assignment. What might be thought incompatible with that view is the fact that social scientists aspire to formulate regularities (which they sometimes call laws) and that they aspire to explain social processes and outcomes. Describing plainly does not preclude the identification of past regularities (indeed the latter

---

[30] See the articles by Skinner cited in note 14 above.
[31] They might contain all the intelligibility that history can be *guaranteed* to contain.

presupposes it). The identification of correctly (non-falsely, not necessarily completely) described past regularities and the correct (non-false) description of such past regularities is the making of a historical record. Describing does not preclude in principle the formulation of true law-like generalisations of the form: If A occurs within S conditions, then B will occur. But emphasis on the epistemological primacy of description makes plainer why few, if any, candidates for true law-like generalisations of this character appear in the human sciences. If identifying regularities is to be more than accumulating a historical record (and if it is to explain occurrences in the world), the identification of these regularities must take the form of a conditional law-like generalisation: this generalisation must hold over a determinate range for a determinate class; it must at least implicitly mention some true descriptions of actions, with the truth of which it is compatible (otherwise it would be vacuous); and it must be not actually incompatible with any true descriptions of actions (otherwise it would be false). This would need drastic rewriting for probabilistic candidates; but such rewriting would not alter the point. On this account there are probably not any serious candidates for such law-like generalisations of any scope or interest in the more descriptively orientated social sciences (sociology, social anthropology, quite certainly political science), and where there are such candidates – as in economics – they can maintain the status (if they can do so at all) only within a tautologically defined, if elaborately articulated, theory and falter, alas and notoriously, if applied to the world. Plainly in fact economics (somewhat unlike sociology and hilariously unlike political science) can and perhaps even often does improve agents' judgment of what is likely to occur. It seems intuitively plausible that there must be enormously many such law-like generalisations in relation to human social and political situations which are true (some of them at least not trivial) and which could in principle be rationally believed as a result of painstaking inquiry. The trickiest part of identifying them is not specifying the conditionally related A and B but specifying the precise range within which they hold – the conditions of application. Much self-protective energy in the human sciences goes into fudging this issue: no one likes to be shown to have been a fool. Such considerations have led MacIntyre in one recent piece to argue against the possibility of a social science.[32] But it seems more sensible to read them as demanding that those who aspire to construct any such science should impose on themselves cognitive morals more austere than they have yet had either inclination or externally provided motive to adopt, and

[32] MacIntyre, 'Ideology, Social Science and Revolution'.

appreciably more austere than those which natural scientists by now have socially thrust upon them.

§18 There are two important ways in which this very individualist characterisation of the field of the human sciences is certain to be challenged. A defender of social holism might contend that propositions about social wholes can be known to be true or false irrespective of the truth or falsity of the description of any individual actions at all. I strongly doubt the possibility of this, but cannot see how to offer a general argument against it. Social holists may also complain that this characterisation presupposes falsely that all statements about social wholes can be decomposed into statements about individuals. It is unclear quite what such a claim implies and therefore difficult to tell whether such a presupposition is in fact false. But in any case the view stated here is not intended to presuppose anything of the kind, and it is not obvious why it should be thought to require any such presupposition. All it does trade on (rather heavily) is the conviction, common to most hermeneutic thinkers, that human beings are better placed to sustain cognitive claims about some individual persons than they are about any institutions, let alone societies, economies or polities.

The second challenge is more mundane. We are frequently able to explain human action and human social relations without being in a position to provide perspicuous, true auditor-individuated descriptions of any actions at all. Adopting such preposterously strong characterisations of what may justifiably be believed true of the human world simply ignores the vast amount of less fastidious cognitive exchange and complicity which clearly provides a viable foundation for practical life and might plausibly serve to do so in the fulness of time even for the human sciences. Human life is no bed of roses; but it is on the whole, on balance, livable. The conclusion urged here, by contrast, may well be thought to teeter on the verge of absurdity, to violate ordinary English usage and to offer no compensating advantages of lucidity or conclusiveness to compensate for these gross defects.

These criticisms assume that the role of true, perspicuous descriptions in this account is methodological in the sense in which the role of observation sentences or perhaps sense data might be thought methodological in some philosophical theories. But whereas the great charm of observation sentences or sense data for those who find them charming is the idea of their uniting incorrigibility with practical availability, it should be clear that perspicuous, true auditor-individuated descriptions derive such conceptual vestiges of incorrigibility as they are accorded from their extreme distance from anything directly furnished (*given*) by an observer's experience. Any incorrigibility which they can muster is a conceptual construction from the idea of a very extended range of inquiries. And their role is not to dictate a helpless passivity in the face of the unknowable to hitherto active human scientists, but to serve as an ultimate conceptual standard of whether what they believe to be true as a result of their inquiries is in fact true.

§19 How should we picture such perspicuous, true auditor-individuated descriptions of actions in the context of historical practice? How closely would they resemble Collingwood's famous specification of the historian's project in terms of rethinking the thoughts of past agents? One major difficulty which has arisen in relation to Collingwood's analysis is the obscurity of what should count as the criterion of identity for the thoughts in question. How can we distinguish rethinking the thoughts of Caesar from foisting our own thoughts on to Caesar? Caesar presumably thought in Latin. Few of us are in a position to emulate him. Even waiving the indeterminacy of translation, the purely practical difficulties of translating perspicuously from the language of a very different (and ethnographically in some respects very poorly recorded) society without anachronism or other forms of misleading implication are huge. Rethinking Caesar's thoughts has some resemblances to Winch's conception of anthropology as (at least temporarily) going native. But there is no practical possibility of actually joining (infiltrating) a *past* culture. We cannot literally become first-century-BC Romans. Furthermore, if the thoughts which we were rethinking *were* the thoughts of Caesar, they should be no less complex, involve no fewer considerations, mention no fewer terms, than Caesar's; and it seems possible that they should even take much the same time to think as they did for Caesar himself. (It would be realistic to suppose that Caesar thought about the action which we now call 'crossing the Rubicon' for some considerable time.) This is not a point simply about heuristics. A historian, unlike Caesar himself, could lavish his entire life on thinking *about* Caesar's thoughts in relation to 'crossing the Rubicon', and after so doing he might well be in a position (having had more practice than, and being perhaps smarter than, Caesar and having less at stake than the Roman Empire) to rethink Caesar's thoughts appreciably faster than their first thinker. Superior history, then, would amount to rethinking the thoughts of Caesar with our own incomparable advantages. But any such example of historical progress would risk violating the identity criterion which serves to *constitute* the subject matter of history. Caesar's thoughts, to be rethought perfectly, should be rethought as unpractisedly (as freshly) and as unsmartly as Caesar himself thought them. There seem conclusive barriers to vindicating any claim that the thoughts which we aspire to rethink can be *known* to be Caesar's thoughts, Caesar's whole thoughts and nothing but Caesar's thoughts. And even this may understate the difficulties. Can one rethink Caesar's thoughts around such a consequential issue of practical reason without troubling to refeel Caesar's feelings, a matter in which the identity criterion would clearly become an impassable barrier to emulation?

Two conclusions may be drawn from this. First, the historian's practicable project of analysing past actions is not happily represented as the execution of a deliberate metempsychosis, the success of which is guaranteed by intuitions, corrigible or incorrigible. Even those who wish to characterise historical and social inquiry in exclusively hermeneutic terms would be better advised to abandon the language of empathy and projection for a clear recognition that what can be practically attained are hermeneutic sketches, standing to full hermeneutic representations roughly as Hempel's 'explanation sketches' are intended to stand to a completed positivist explanation (full subsumption of the explanandum under the requisite set of covering laws). Secondly, the idea of description of thoughts or feelings is distinctly less mysterious than the idea of re-enacting or re-experiencing them. If there can be knowledge of other minds at all, and if this possibility can be characterised clearly in philosophical terms, there should be no insuperable difficulty in the idea of true auditor-individuated descriptions of the thoughts and feelings of others.

§20 One could not perspicuously understand anything which persons do at all without recognising that they have at a minimum both beliefs and desires. Full perspicuous descriptions would have to include full descriptions of all beliefs and desires to which an agent would have referred in candidly and carefully describing his action. This might seem too weak a requirement, because we might wish and hope to know matters about both the causation and the consequences of the action which the agent himself might omit but which it would be natural for any historian or social scientist to include within their description of the action. Persons may have some measure of privileged access to their own consciousness. But, being of limited intelligence and having other purposes besides that of understanding themselves, they do not always or perhaps ever understand themselves perfectly. Hence even if full descriptions of an action must include full descriptions of all beliefs and desires which an agent would have mentioned in describing the action himself as well as he could have described it in relation to some potential cognitive interest – and their doing so would be required for their being judged *full* descriptions at least in relation to that interest – they would not constitute a sufficient condition for being so judged. On the causal side we would need and wish to *supplement* an agent's account of what had brought him to act in a particular way with any considerations of a sociological or psychological character which we could *know* to be relevant but unmentioned, gently but firmly assisting the agent to transcend his own cognitive and moral limitations and avoid both error and deceit. We might think of this part of the inquiry as a particularly gentle and sensitive interrogation – a co-operative confessional which somehow combined charity of attitude and justice of result. (The model of psychoanalysis perhaps lurks behind this picture.)

There are two difficulties raised by this concession. The first is apparent. Can one acknowledge the possibility of *replacing* some part of the agent's description in this fashion with our observer's description? No theorist could hope to make the criterion for the validity of the supplement as strong as its compatibility with all the components of the agent's description, not all of which, because of error, are necessarily even compatible with each other. But to defend a conception of the knowledge of human action that is as strongly hermeneutic as the one advanced here, it is certainly necessary to defend the view that supplementation cannot amount simply to replacement. The most obvious way of expressing this constraint is to insist on the necessity of *mentioning* all the terms in the agent's own description (even if only in some cases to negate them). The second difficulty arises from the lack of agreement about what is at present *known* in the way of psychology or sociology. Very few, if any, laws of psychology or sociology (and none at all of political science) which might possibly relate to the motivation of action are in fact *known*, though of course many propositions of all three 'sciences' which relate to motivation are sensibly and justifiably believed by individual human scientists on occasion, as they are by the rest of us in the course of daily life. Epistemic supplementation of an agent's intentional characterisation of his action depends simply on the possibility of external observation of the particular agent in question and of other agents through time. But replacement of an agent's characterisation of his action requires a title the very possibility of which has hardly as yet been vindicated in any general way.

JOHN DUNN

On the consequential side, the possibility of supplementation raises no such problems. The consequences of an action are an externally related matter of fact. As Danto has emphasised,[33] it is a conceptually important stylistic feature of historical narratives that they contain many descriptions of actions which could not have been given by the agents themselves (for example, commencing the First World War or the Thirty Years' War or, absurdly, the Renaissance). But it would be absurd to regard these as *replacing* the intentional characterisations.

Perspicuous auditor-individuated agents' descriptions of actions and the beliefs and desires mentioned in these descriptions can thus be supplemented without weakening their ability to specify the hermeneutic component of the field of the human sciences. However psychological phenomena such as denial, self-deception and rationalisation, as well as ideology and the social determination of belief, suggest that some terms which appear in the agent's description can be discarded as redundant for explanatory and perhaps even descriptive purposes. But the claim or even the *demonstration* that some terms within an agent's description were redundant would not in any way enhance the status of theoretical claims to *replace* parts of an agent's description with other terms not mentioned (except for what he and anyone else would agree to purely for purposes of representation: economy, clarity of outline etc.). The explanatory force or status of psychological or sociological concepts of this character in relation to a particular action must be shown within an agent's own mapping of his 'problem situation' or 'set of problem situations' (action context). They must remove anomaly within, or add information to, the best description which he himself is able to offer; and it is because they must do so that it is tempting (though plainly wrong) to insist that they must provide characterisations which an agent could or even would in practice accept. When we have the best description which he is able to offer, we may well be able to illuminate him to himself, perhaps even to show him that some of his initial statements are the reverse of the truth; and our potential ability to do so will not be impugned should he not in fact wish for further illumination, wish to understand himself any better. What we cannot properly do is to claim to *know* that we understand him or his action better than he does himself without access to the best descriptions which he is able to offer. (We may, of course, believe that we have a better grasp of some aspects of it – its consequential cruelty, its extreme imprudence – than he does, even on comparatively superficial observation.) There is no doubt much redundancy and not a little error of one kind and

[33] Arthur C. Danto, *Analytical Philosophy of History* (Cambridge, 1965), esp. pp. 149–81.

168

another in agents' characterisations of their problem situations. But to know that some item is explanatorily redundant is to know the full description and to see that the part which it plays in this full description is not in any way reflected in the determination of the action. The best evidence for the redundancy of a term in an agent's description would be his truly reported true agreement (recognition) that the term was indeed redundant. If self-deception characterises a psychological process, rather than merely conveying a moral rebuke, agents ought to be *able* to know that they are or have been deceiving themselves. *Knowing* better than other people about the character of their actions must be knowing more than they do; it cannot consist in knowing less than they do but knowing it more deftly, honestly, realistically, dogmatically etc. The criterion of proof for the validity of a description or interpretation of an action is the economy and accuracy with which it handles the full text of the agent's description. The arrogance of ideological explanation of the thought of others lies in the claim to understand another's thinking more deeply than he does himself, without being in a position to provide true descriptions of almost any of it. It is a routinised claim to authority where routinised claims must be false, where all authority must be earned in detail and where the mode of its earning is by explaining persons (and their situations) more lucidly to themselves.[34]

§21 Is false consciousness, then, a literal impossibility? In so far as it involves consciousness of oneself at other times than the present or of matters external to oneself or to one's place in society or in nature, this is not entailed. Whether it can be allowed with respect to the consciousness of oneself in the present is more complicated. Not all the beliefs which we have can be second-order beliefs; but sometimes we do need to form beliefs about our beliefs in the present. For an agent A to believe at time *t* that he believes that P does not guarantee that agent A at time *t* believes that P. But (simply as a proposal about how we might recover our capacity to talk clearly, not as a conceptual claim about an agreed subject matter) we may reasonably treat it as a necessary condition for the truth of this proposition. Unless we can establish a coherent title to employ the verb 'believe' in the first person singular present indicative active, it is hard to see how we can establish any title at all to litter the past and future with firm ascriptions of beliefs to others.

Do I know what I believe? Well, I certainly have a shrewder (as well

[34] Cf. Ludwig Wittgenstein, *Lectures and Conversations on Aesthetics, Psychology and Religious Belief*, ed. Cyril Barrett (Oxford, 1966), pp. 41-52, esp. 51-2.

as more extensive) *general* set of suspicions on the subject of what I believe than you have on the subject of what I believe.

It may be a wise man that knows his own beliefs. But it cannot be only a wise man who experiences his own experiences. That privilege is open to all creatures which can experience at all. I have beliefs, experiences etc. I now believe I am in England rather than in Bulgaria. I now (conveniently) feel sick. If questioned by myself or others as to what I do believe or feel in these respects, I will, if speaking sincerely and attending to the matter, confirm that I *do* believe that not Bulgaria but England is where I am and that sick is among the things which I feel. Philosophers have emphasised many possible dimensions of mishap in such confirmatory avowals of belief or experience. I may not be as sincere or attentive to the matter as I need to be. My customary command of the English language may fail. The standard motive for attacking the status of avowals is the wish to deny that any description of experience is incorrigible. It is not necessary to establish that any avowals are incorrigible in order to claim that we certainly do experience our own experiences and that these differ from one another and differ from all the experiences which we do not have.

§22 Full descriptions of actions, then, are descriptions which characterise an agent persisting through time, the possessor of beliefs and feelings (desires, fears, hatreds, shames, aspirations, all that goes to make up a temperament), confronted by a context at a time (characterised in terms of the beliefs and desires of the agent at that time) and responding to it, for what seemed within the frame of consciously present feelings and beliefs sufficient reasons, intentionally, in a particular manner or, by naturally explicable mishap, in some other distinct manner. (It is realistic to assume that former President Ford entered few helicopters in the course of his presidency which he did not intend to enter. But it would not be realistic to assume that he struck his head on the door-frames of few of these conveyances on which he did not intend to strike his head.) Full descriptions of actions by agents may well require supplementation before they can furnish *the* explanation of the action (Why exactly *this* act? Why exactly then? etc.). Anything less than full agent descriptions cannot provide *the* explanation, though much less saturating types of record can serve very adequately to remove anomaly from and restore intelligibility to the record for most practical purposes. What to emphasise in such explanatory representations is perhaps partly a matter of philosophical taste. Some would prefer to translate all the terms into the idiom of beliefs (expected utility, subjective probability etc). Others might prefer to transpose all belief statements into some intricate form of desire.[35] Others will prefer to set the notion of sufficient reasons within the set of beliefs and feelings at the centre of their account. Provided that no material is simply omitted, the choice of format may be left to taste.

There are still no cheap ways to deep knowledge of other persons and the causes of their actions. There are no simple methods which will make the insensitive perceptive, and there are no guarantees, any more than in the sciences of nature, of making real progress at all. But if *knowing* about other persons in small or large numbers over short or lengthy periods of time is a very steep project indeed, the project of trying to understand and assess how they are likely to behave simply shades off into the living of practical life. We all hold more or less well-justified beliefs about the beliefs and sentiments and practical situations of others. We all can and indeed *must* attempt to judge methodologically how it is sound to attribute beliefs or feelings to others. Within a common physical world we are all radical interpreters of one another, assigning beliefs, desires, intentions and meanings simultaneously to one another and trying to make sense of conduct by solving the resulting simultaneous equations. A clearer understanding of the need to solve the equations for *all* of these values simultaneously would enhance observance of empirical adequacy as the criterion for valid translation manuals. A clear grasp of what principles govern our setting up of our own manual will make it easier to distinguish empirical inadequacy from variations in foci of interest. (All understanding is understanding in relation to a set of interests.) The criterion of empirical adequacy by itself establishes a domain of public co-operative and mutually corrigible endeavour which can more than absorb the efforts of all possible future human scientists. It also has the merit of licensing no cognitive claims more sweeping than could in principle be licensed, and of prescribing the most exacting and patient attention to *all* that the subjects of the human sciences do or say.

§23 This may seem superficially reassuring. But is it able to reassure merely because it *is* so superficial? What excuse could there be for using the anomaly of the mental as a flag of philosophical convenience in order to populate human history with philosophically disreputable entities and in particular determinate meanings where only indeterminacy can and should be found? May one not simply have to choose

[35] Richard E. Grandy, 'Reference, Meaning and Belief', *Journal of Philosophy*, 70:14 (16 August 1973), 439–52, at 451–2.

JOHN DUNN

between accepting the anomaly (or autonomy) of the mental and accepting the indeterminacy of translation? If you accept both the anomaly of the mental and the indeterminacy of translation, the human sciences are in danger of falling painfully between two stools. Behaviour knowledge is accessible but cannot be knowledge of humans as such. Meaning knowledge could be knowledge of humans, if it could be determinately stated. But doubts are cast on its determinate attainability even in principle. Since translational adequacy on the Quinean account is a specifically pragmatic notion, a translationally adequate science of human meanings must in principle be pragmatically accessible. But is the subject matter of which it can give us knowledge real living or dead men, as we ought to be prepared to recognise them? According to the indeterminacy of translation we can never know that X and not anything else at all is what we or anyone else mean. In our own case we readily incline to the view that we can and do sometimes know that X and not anything else at all *is* what we mean. (You may never mean anything in particular but I certainly do. You can tell my particular meaning most of the time by what I assert.)

It may be the case that intentionalist theories of meaning[36] are gravely inadequate; but could it be the case that they literally never apply? Exactly what we mean is not necessarily a very exact business. Indeterminacy of translation rationally encourages us to take the view that our meanings may be a great deal less exact than they sound to us, to regard our assertoric ventures as a good deal looser in articulation than they feel at the time. The meanings of what we say certainly have different extension from our more optimistic hopes of our locutionary abilities. They fall short and they overshoot, failing to articulate what we do intend and succeeding in committing us to what we do not at all intend. But the meanings of what we mean surely are constituted by those hopes. In a world in which it was never possible to know what we meant, much of the use of the word 'meaning' would be unintelligible. (I quite certainly did not mean *that*. Of course, I *know* that *that* is not what I meant.)

The capacity to recognise an assertion as an assertion is a presupposition of the criterion of empirical adequacy for translation manuals. To assert is to perform an action. There is no reason to suppose that indeterminacy of translation can even be *stated* coherently without the

[36] See e.g. P. F. Strawson, 'Intention and Convention in Speech Acts', and H. P. Grice, 'Utterer's Meaning, Sentence-Meaning, and Word-Meaning', both in J. R. Searle (ed.), *The Philosophy of Language* (London, 1971), pp. 23–38, 54–70; Stephen Schiffer, *Meaning* (Oxford, 1972); etc.

172

at least covert employment of the concept of agency. Correct translation is translation compatible with what speakers are asserting. (Put my meaning any way you like – use any old words – provided it catches my *meaning*: what I intend to assert.)

§24 How, then, should we picture the relation between the categories of action and the indeterminacy of translation? There appears at present to be no convincing answer to this question. John McDowell has suggested a striking relation between Quine's discussion of indeterminacy of translation and the vigorous dispute between exponents of realist and non-realist theories of meaning.[37] Neither realists[38] nor anti-realists[39] have, as he convincingly claims, succeeded as yet in showing how language and linguistic behaviour can be clearly understood. To have a coherent theory of language and linguistic behaviour would be to know how to characterise meanings. To know how to characterise meanings would be to know how to characterise the core subject matter of history and the social sciences. Until such a theory has been constructed, history and the social sciences will stand epistemologically in jeopardy. But in this predicament they will by no means stand alone.

§25 To assess the precise scope of the epistemological dilemmas raised by indeterminacy of translation and even to gauge how extreme these are likely to prove in practice is thus at present an excessive ambition for a social scientist. But the practice of the social sciences requires that we consider these issues in the context of other issues and restricts the range of options open to us by considerations which may well in themselves be (and which certainly at present appear to be) wholly extrinsic to epistemology.

Always and everywhere people act, behave, mean (intend to assert) exactly as they do and not otherwise. These are not tautologies which, in the practice of the human sciences, we can be prepared lightly to abandon. If the account which we give of what it is to know makes this come out as something which we cannot know, what this implies is that something has come adrift in our account of what in this context it *is* to know. The search for method is a search for a guarantee against error. But perhaps in most domains of knowing about humans there just are no *guarantees* against error. The fact (where it is a fact)

---

[37] John McDowell, 'Truth Conditions, Bivalence, and Verificationism', in Evans and McDowell (eds.), *Truth and Meaning*, pp. 42–66, at pp. 64–6.

[38] See especially the paper by McDowell in this book, and the article cited in note 37.

[39] See especially the work of Michael Dummett, and the articles by Dummett and Wright in Evans and McDowell (eds.), *op. cit.*, pp. 67–137 and 223–47.

that there cannot be a guaranteed method of discovering what is true about some matter does not imply that nothing *is* true about that matter.

In the theory of interpretation and translation a fine array of 'moral' principles are at present widely touted: the principle of charity,[40] the principle of humanity,[41] the principle of benefit of the doubt,[42] the principle of truthfulness (for which a more apt name might perhaps be the principle of credulity).[43] The moral tone of these principles is in one respect misleading and may render the present title of each something of misnomer. For we display these mildly supererogatory and Christian-sounding virtues in the more or less optimistic hope of doing ourselves an epistemological favour, establishing or at least bolstering a conviction that the world is indeed populated with other persons who are persons in much the same sense as we are ourselves (or suppose ourselves to be) and drawing many conclusions from this conviction. No doubt we have good reason for seeking to do ourselves whatever epistemological favours we can contrive to perform. But in the sly and instrumental espousal of these supererogatory 'virtues' we risk ignoring a duty which is absolute and in no sense supererogatory, the duty of justice. *Justitia est constans et perpetua voluntas suum cuique tribuendi.* If we claim to *know* about other men, we must try as best we can to give them what is their due, their right. This is a simple moral duty, not a guarantee of epistemological prowess. We cannot try better than we can. Even trying *very* hard will not ensure success or indeed necessarily even make it particularly likely. If the indeterminacy of translation is shown to hold, it will enforce changes upon us in how we conceive what is due epistemologically to ourselves and to other men. What it could not do is to weaken the obligation to try as best we can to render to each man, including ourselves, what *is* their due.

In the 'sciences' of man the agent, our need for clear and authoritative recipes of heuristic procedure is necessarily a less fundamental need than our need for good intentions (the intention to understand human agents exactly as they are and were and will be and not any other way). Human beings, we might say, have a right to such understanding from one another or – less vertiginously, and if 'ought' implies 'can' – they have a right to at least the effort to attain such understanding on the part of any other human being who claims to state the truth about them.

[40] See e.g. Davidson, 'Radical Interpretation'.
[41] Grandy, 'Reference, Meaning and Belief'.
[42] Putnam, 'What is "Realism"?'.
[43] Lewis, 'Radical Interpretation', 338–9.

We cannot *know* that our accounts are wholly true in the case of most human matters into which we have good reason to inquire. What we can *know* is that human matters are matters about which descriptions can be true or false (or both partly true and partly false). And as practising historians or social scientists we can reasonably believe in some cases that the descriptions which we offer, addressed to the persons to whom we offer them, convey information which is true about the human matters which they mention. Such practitioners' beliefs are optimistic in several different dimensions. The argument advanced here is that the dimension in which their optimism is best justified is in the presumption that there is something to describe. This conviction is often confused with the view that there exists some specifiable methodology which, correctly applied, would yield descriptions which would never be false or always be true. It is hard to see any grounds whatever in favour of this second view. If the arguments of this paper are correct at all, methodology *can* have no higher status than that of a counsel of prudence. ('If you want to find that out, I would not try to do so in that way, if I were you.' Counsels of prudence need not lack cogency. It is a criterion of soundness for counsels of prudence that, soundly applied, they must work for the better more often than not.) There cannot be *rules* of sociological or historical method; but there can be and are many bad historians and sociologists. And perhaps to be a bad sociologist or historian, not from genetic or cultural mishap but through the nurturing of some types of intention and the eschewing of others, may even be a category within naturalistic ethics.

Index of Names

INDEX

DATE DUE
